BKN/ ANDREWS

FOUR CENTURIES OF
Four Centuries of European Jewellery

A sapphire bodkin for the hair,
Or sparkling facet diamonds there;
Then turquoise, ruby, emrauld rings,
For Fingers: and such pretty things,
As diamond pendants for the ears,
Must needs be had, or two pearl pears,
Pearl necklace, large and oriental,
And diamond, and of amber pale.

   EVELYN. A Voyage to Maryland. 1690.

King-emeralds, male-rubies, rose-diamonds, queen-pearls, star-sapphires, they blazed on the brocaded figures till the faces seemed moon-pale amid the glow and glitter. Pendants of enamel and heavy stones, shaped into fabled beasts or ivory nymphs and satyrs, of faery ships in mother-of-pearl, lay taken in wonders of arachnean gold. Brow-jewels, breast-jewels, are the most intimate of these ornaments, bright fantastic ciphers of personality.

   R. A. TAYLOR. Leonardo the Florentine.

FOUR CENTURIES OF

European Jewellery

BY ERNLE BRADFORD

PHILOSOPHICAL LIBRARY
15 East Fortieth Street
NEW YORK 16

*Published in 1953
by the Philosophical Library, Inc.
15 East 40th Street, New York 16, N.Y.
All rights reserved
Printed in Great Britain
for Philosophical Library, Inc.
by Hazell Watson & Viney Ltd
Aylesbury and London*

Preface

THE study of antique jewellery is an absorbing one. Although few people today can afford to collect it 'in the grand manner', the facilities for the student are better than they have ever been. America itself has a number of notable collections in which can be seen many of the finest pieces of all periods. The average admirer of fine jewellery, however, is apt to be deterred from starting his own collection by the rarity and exceptional value of the pieces which he sees in museums.

It is for him that this book is written. In the chapters dealing with the historical background and growth of the craft in Europe, as well as those which concern themselves with specialized aspects of the subject, the aim has been not so much to catalogue the outstanding examples of jewellery still in existence, but to indicate the course and changes of fashion—to chart, as it were, the mainstream of European jewellery since the sixteenth century. For this reason such minor, though fascinating, aspects of the subject as European peasant jewellery, have not been touched upon. Detailed descriptions of outstanding pieces and summaries of jewellers' design catalogues have also been omitted, except in so far as they prove of relevance in tracing the outline of a period, or of a particular article of jewellery.

The processes by which jewellery is made and the changes which have occurred in techniques have been stressed. Without a knowledge of these, the student or the collector can neither judge a piece nor enjoy to the full the artifice which has created it. For the opportunity of visiting many modern craftsmen at work and of inspecting the premises of manufacturing jewellers I am indebted to many firms. In particular I would like to thank D. Shackman & Sons, Harold A. Lazarus and Mr Zoltan White. The chapter on modern jewellery has been made possible largely by the co-operation of firms such as these. For the chapter on the nineteenth century I am indebted to the Editor of the *Watchmaker, Jeweller and Silversmith* for allowing me to make use of material from nineteenth-century copies of his magazine.

For permission to illustrate pieces of jewellery, and for assistance and co-operation in many ways, I am indebted to so many private collectors and curators of public collections that it is possible for me to indicate only those without whose help this work could not have been undertaken—the authorities of the British Museum, the Victoria and Albert Museum, the Soane Museum, the Wallace Collection, the National Portrait Gallery, the National Gallery and the Worshipful Company of Goldsmiths. I am particularly indebted to the last-named for the many opportunities which they have given me of inspecting exhibitions of contemporary craftsmanship and design. Among dealers, authorities and collectors who have been of assistance to me I would like to thank especially Messrs Harvey & Gore, Gould & Palmer, Cameo Corner, Bracher & Sydenham, James Oakes, S. J. Phillips, The Goldsmiths and Silversmiths Company, Asprey & Company, Wartski, Sac Frères, Mr Henry Rushbury, R.A., and Mr R. W. Symonds.

I am indebted to Miss Judith Banister who collected many of the illustrations and who compiled the Glossary. The illustrations have been chosen not only to show as far as possible types of pieces that are still available to the collector, but also to provide students, craftsmen and others with a wide range of illustrations of pieces typical of the fashions of the four centuries under review.

1952   E. B.

Contents

Preface	5
Introduction	15
I. Jewellery of the Italian Renaissance	27
II. Sixteenth Century: Germany, Central Europe, France, Spain, England	46
III. Seventeenth Century: the Age of the Flower and the Diamond	64
IV. Eighteenth Century: the Age of the Faceted Stone	77
V. Nineteenth-century Jewellery	90
VI. The Twentieth Century	106
VII. Diamond Jewellery	120
VIII. Rings	130
IX. Enamels and Enamelling	139
X. Cameos and Intaglios	152
XI. Paste, Marcasite and Cut-steel Jewellery	161
XII. Birthstones	170
XIII. The Precious Metals	180
XIV. History and Properties of the Precious Stones	190
XV. The Craft of Gem-cutting	196

XVI. Pearls, Amber, Jet and Coral 201

Conclusion 211

Glossary 213

Selected Bibliography 219

Index 221

Illustrations

SIXTEENTH CENTURY

Portrait of Henry VIII	17
Portrait of the Duchesse d'Angoulême by François Clouet	18
Pendant design by Holbein for Henry VIII	35
Drawing by Bertoli of the cope-button made by Cellini for Pope Clement VII	35
Pendant and brooch designs by Holbein	36
An Italian pendant, *c.* 1520	36
Portrait of the young Jacqueline de Bourgogne by Mabuse	37
Gold and enamel Italian pendant, with large baroque pearl drop, *c.* 1550	38
Italian pendant jewel showing the Virgin and Child between pillars, *c.* 1550	38
Portrait of the Netherlandish School	39
Baroque pearl set in gold in the form of a mermaid	40
Rock-crystal pendant with a *verre églomisé* medallion of the Annunciation	40
The Tor Abbey jewel: a gold '*memento mori*' pendant	57
Three Spanish gold and enamelled pendants	57
Enamelled gold book-cover, probably of South German workmanship	58
Renaissance pendant in gold and enamels set with coloured precious stones and pearls	58
Portrait of a young woman of twenty-nine, dated 1582	59
The Canning jewel: a baroque pearl mounted in enamelled gold, set with rubies, pearls and diamonds	60
Venetian ship pendant of gold and enamel hung with pearls	60

The Armada jewel, c. 1588   60
Portrait of Queen Elizabeth I, attributed to Marc Gheeraedts   69

SEVENTEENTH CENTURY

Spanish jewellery: reliquary, gold cross, figure of the Virgin of the Pillar, reliquary cross, and figure of the Virgin of the Immaculate Conception   70
Italian corsage ornament in coloured enamels set with precious stones   71
Two sides of an English crucifix pendant in enamelled gold, set with seed-pearls and garnets   71
Spanish bodice brooch in gold set with emeralds and diamonds   72
Spanish bodice brooch in enamelled gold set with diamonds   72

EIGHTEENTH CENTURY

Portrait after W. Wissing of Queen Mary II   81
Drop ear-rings of silver set with diamonds   82
'Witch's heart' brooch in silver set with rubies and diamonds   82
Openwork 'bow motif' bracelet set with diamonds   82
English star brooch set with diamonds   91
Silver and brilliant-cut diamond plume brooch   91
Spray brooch of silver set with diamonds   91
Portrait of Caroline of Ansbach, from the studio of Charles Jervas   92
A pair of diamond drop ear-rings dated about 1750   93
'Ear of barley' brooch in gold and brilliant-cut diamonds   93
Marquise ring of silver set with diamonds   93
Diamond brooch in a leaf design   93
Ring set with diamonds round a large rose-cut diamond   93
Diamond and emerald suite consisting of a daisy-motif necklace and bow ear-rings with pendant flower drops   94
Diamond-enriched frame containing a miniature by John Smart   103
English rose- and brilliant-cut diamond bow-and-feather brooch   103

Illustrations

Silver star brooch and necklace set with red garnets	103
English flower-spray brooch of diamonds *pavé*-set in silver	104
Silver and diamond aigrette	104
Brooch with brilliant- and rose-cut diamonds in a setting of silver and gold	113
Watch and chatelaine of enamelled gold and pinchbeck by John Wilson of Peterborough, dated 1772	113
Georgian Maltese cross set with diamonds and a topaz	113
Gold basket-case housing a watch, made by Thomas Mudge in 1765	113

NINETEENTH CENTURY

Early Victorian brooch set with diamonds, rubies and an emerald	114
Regency watch and fob dated about 1820	114
Portrait of Queen Adelaide by W. Beechey	115
Early Victorian necklace of flower and leaf design set with rose diamonds	116
Three-row gold chain necklace set with gold filigree, and pink topaz medallions; gold and topaz brooch *en suite*	125
Early Victorian openwork scroll brooch of *pavé*- and collet-set brilliants	125
Portrait of Mme Ines Moitessier by Jean Ingres	126
Victorian ornament of amethysts and gold	143
Topaz necklace set in pinchbeck, showing the delicacy of Victorian filigree work	143
Pendant of yellow amber mounted in gold	144
Gold butterfly brooch in filigree set with opals and other gemstones	144
Pendant cross of deep purple amethysts set in gold	144
Chatelaine from a jeweller's design-book of 1886	145
Gold cairngorm brooch bordered with pearls and garnets	145
Almandine garnet brooch mounted in gold	145
Panagia by the Russian jeweller Peter Carl Fabergé	146
Elaborate late-nineteenth-century tiara	163
Pendant brooch with step-cut peridot bordered with diamonds and pendeloque peridot drop	163

TWENTIETH CENTURY

Composite diamond necklace which divides to form two bracelets, earclips and a brooch	164
Double clip of platinum set with rubies and diamonds	173
Daffodil ear-clip and cocktail ring in gold, set with diamonds and rubies	173
Asymmetrical double clip set with diamonds	173
Platinum bracelet set with sapphires and diamonds	173
Central motif of a gold necklace, of palladium wire set with diamonds and rubies	174
Spray brooch in platinum and diamonds	174
Cocktail ring of gold set with a yellow diamond surrounded by brilliants	174
Gold floral spray brooch set with rubies, sapphires and other gemstones	175
Cocktail ring with a large pearl trapped by gold wires in a gold sea-shell	175
Creole-type ear-clip in gold set with rubies	175
Asymmetrical double clip, contrasting rubies in a gold setting with diamonds in platinum	175
Necklace from a suite in palladium and diamonds made for the Festival of Britain, 1951	176
French brilliant-set diamond and palladium leaf brooch, and coiled wire ring set with a solitaire diamond	185
French leaf clip set round with graduated diamonds	185
French bracelet in palladium and diamonds	185
French diamond spray clip	185
Swiss ring, in gold and diamonds, that opens to reveal a watch	186
Swiss spray set with diamonds and freshwater pearls	186
Swiss watch case in gold	186
Swiss bird brooch of gold wire	186
Swiss covered watch in twisted gold wire and pearls	187
Swiss diamond and palladium bracelet	187
Swiss filigree gold watch-bracelet	187
Paste brooch in silver, based on an eighteenth-century design	188

Gilt brooch set with pastes and artificial pearls	188
Asymmetrical brooch and ear-clips in silver set with white and dark blue pastes	205
Necklace and ear-clips in antique-finished silver set with semi-precious stones, in the Victorian style	205
Polishing the crown facets of a coloured gemstone on a swiftly rotating copper lap	206
Amethyst, showing the modern method of brilliant cutting	206
A 'boule' of synthetic corundum made in a Verneuil furnace	206
Types of cut in common use	207
The craftsman at work, piercing a mount for a platinum and diamond necklace	207
Selecting stones before mounting	208
Inserting a diamond in a mount	208
Polishing a mount	208

Introduction

EUROPEAN jewellery of the past four centuries is dependent upon its early ancestry. It cannot be evaluated without a consideration of its historical background. Although little jewellery prior to the sixteenth century is likely to come the way of the ordinary collector, yet, for a full understanding of the period under review, its ancestry must be indicated.

The essence of all jewellery is magical. Its purpose is to heighten the wearer's personality or appearance. This definition is as true today as it was in 3000 B.C. in Ur of the Chaldees. The only essential difference lies in the fact that the modern wearers of jewellery no longer ascribe deliberately magical properties to their gems. The gems are worn, nevertheless, to effect a change in personality and in appearance.

In the advanced Chaldean civilization, revealed principally by the excavations at Ur in Mesopotamia, the importance of jewellery was well understood. The jewellers worked in gold and silver with a technical proficiency which, in some cases, is hardly equalled until Greek and Etruscan work nearly 2,000 years later. The tombs of the Chaldean kings have revealed that between 3500 and 3100 B.C. the art of the jeweller was far advanced. Elaborate head-dresses of gold, beaten thin, were of a magnificence rare in the history of head adornment. They foreshadow that fine flower of the head ornament, the silver and diamond tiara of the nineteenth century and the diamond and platinum tiara of today.

Lapis-lazuli was extensively used in Chaldean jewellery. Its popularity was to continue throughout the history of both Mediterranean and later European work. Beads were common, again principally of lapis-lazuli. That integral and basic part of the jeweller's craft, the refining and working of precious metals, had also been brought to a high degree of proficiency.

Whenever the cultural life of a continent or a state declines, it will be found that the jewellery of the period tends to become heavy, 'chunky' and coarse. Periods of richness and splendour are, in general, reflected by a lightness of touch and the use of filigree. In the 'Spanish style' combs, the large lunate ear-rings of gold, and the hair-ribbons of gold and silver fashioned by the Chaldean jewellers, this delicacy of touch is apparent. In this prosperous delta the goldsmith-jeweller created motifs that reappeared several thousands of years later in Europe.

In the Egyptian culture of the Middle Kingdom, the ninth and twelfth dynasties, the magical aspect of jewellery was particularly stressed. Amulets and ornaments of a religious nature were produced in great quantity, thus initiating the connection between jewellery and religion which ultimately became part of the European heritage. From the sacred scarab beetle carved in jasper, to the Mithraic emblem worn by the Roman soldier, the rosary of the Christian Church and the modern traveller's enamelled Saint Christopher, runs a recognizable line of ancestry.

The finest work of the Egyptian goldsmith and jeweller is found in the twelfth dynasty of the Middle Kingdom (*c.* 2200–2000 B.C.). Rings, bracelets, necklaces, ear-rings and pendants were worked in gold and silver. The extent of the jeweller's choice of materials was large. It included amethyst, onyx, chalcedony, jasper, lapis-lazuli, turquoise, rock-crystal, mother-of-pearl and garnet. Among other stones found in Egyptian work are cornelian, porphyry, hæmatite and basalt.

With his advanced technique and his wide choice of stones the Egyptian jeweller reached a very high degree of craftsmanship and design. A particular feature of some of the twelfth-dynasty work is the use of gemstones in the form of inlay. This use of stones resembles enamelling (particularly of the *cloisonné* type) in the way that the stones are held between dividing strips of metal, the whole surface forming one plane. (Later, Teutonic and Celtic pieces were also fashioned in this way.)

Gold openwork, always a test of the craftsman's ability, is found at this period. In view of the popularity of this type of work both in the nineteenth century and today, it is interesting to compare these early examples with more modern and familiar pieces. A fine example of an openwork plaque in gold is to be seen in the Egyptian rooms of the British Museum. It depicts Amenhotep IV making an offering to a deity.

Although the combined use of gold and ivory is not common in European jewellery from the Renaissance onwards, it is often found in metalwork. The Egyptians thought the combination pleasing and it was extensively used. The Greeks were later to use this same combination in their famous chryselephantine statue of Athene in the Parthenon.

A rich and elaborate period, that of the nineteenth dynasty, saw the emergence in Egypt of a baroque style in jewellery, a style which reflects its age as well as does that of the workmen to the court of Louis XIV. Gold was used lavishly and with a sense of its ostentatious quality that is found again in certain aspects of sixteenth-century Renaissance work.

Glazed earthenware beads are found in great numbers. Again, the very term now used for this work, *faience* (from the Italian town of Faenza), provides a link with

Introduction

Renaissance Italy. In a letter to Amenhotep III the King of Babylonia remarked, 'Gold is as dust in thy land, my brother'—a feeling which the jewellery of this period inspires.

The decadence which ultimately set in throughout the Egyptian arts and crafts was naturally reflected in jewellery. The trend of civilization was now westwards towards Greece and the Aegean. Later, under the Ptolemies, a backwash of this Aegean culture was for a time to revive the art of the jeweller in Egypt, but the style and the influence were predominantly Greek.

A link, as it were, between the jewellers of the East and their fellow-artificers of the new Aegean and European cultures was the use of electrum. Electrum is an alloy of gold and silver which was used in jewellery and metalwork in Egypt. As early as 2000 B.C., it was also being used by jewellers in the north of Asia Minor. Excavations at the site of Troy have revealed gold, silver and electrum ornaments of about this date. The native source of electrum is said to have been the river Pactolus in Asia Minor.

The so-called 'Treasure of Priam' found at Troy contained elaborate diadems, bracelets, ear-rings and pectorals which revealed a high standard of civilization and craftsmanship. Geometrical designs as well as naturalistic motifs were used by these jewellers. Openwork flowers set with lapis-lazuli and rock-crystal are the ancestors of that Greek fifth-century work which was ultimately to have so great an influence on Renaissance designs.

It has been said that 'the art of Europe is foreshadowed by its armouries', and in the Bronze Age this metal of war was also used for jewellery. Bronze ornaments are found inlaid with gold, silver, electrum and also *niello* (see page 41). This last form of decoration was to undergo a great popular revival in the sixteenth century and Cellini devotes a section of his *Trattati* to the methods of working in it.

The Heroic or Homeric Age, as are all ages of transition, was unfavourable to the art of the jeweller. Important, however, among Aegean influences was the work of the Minoan craftsmen. In their hands the native Mediterranean instinct for decoration produced—almost for the first time—that unique blend of East and West which is one of the most stimulating features of European jewellery. An elegance and also a use of colour—which reach sixteenth-century Italy *via* Greece and Rome and the rediscovery of their arts—is revealed.

Granulated goldwork is found not only in some of the Trojan pieces, such as ear-rings, but elsewhere throughout the Aegean. In its simplest form granulated gold is made by pouring molten gold into water. The metal, as it falls through the air, is separated into liquid drop form and takes on its shape as a small sphere, being cooled by the water. This, no doubt, was the method employed by these early craftsmen. (The use of granulation was later to become a popular feature of much Victorian jewellery.)

Archaic Italian and Greek jewellery (700–500 B.C.) was very largely influenced by Eastern designs. In Etruria, however, the Etruscan workmen brought granulation to a pitch of almost incredible fineness. The delicacy of their work in this particular sphere has, perhaps, never been surpassed.

Much of the technique in the jeweller's workshop at this period has its counterpart today. Indeed, it can safely be said that the making of jewellery has changed less than any of the other handcrafts. The precious metals were stamped into shape with punches, somewhat similar to the dies used in certain modern work. Thin sheets of gold were fashioned into jewellery by passing them into and over a countersunk design. The metal was then hammered into the 'die' so that it took on the required shape. In the case of an ear-ring, for instance, two similar halves would be produced in this manner and then soldered together, back to back.

In both Greek and Etruscan work the stylized figures and the geometric patterns which had succeeded them were both in their turn to give way to a naturalistic treatment. The importance of Greek fifth-century work, in particular, is that it produced a style which was *twice* to be revived in European jewellery. These gold figures of sphinxes, syrens and satyrs, together with pomegranates and lotus and palmette pendants, were destined to have a major influence on Italian Renaissance work. Later, in the eighteenth century, under the added stimulus of the discovery of Pompeii and Herculaneum, they became the dominant motifs of much gold and pinchbeck work.

The early history of enamelling is difficult to trace. Enamelwork is found in Egyptian pieces and again among some examples of jewellery of the Minoan period. It reappears in the fifth century B.C. in Athens and is widely used. As late as the second century A.D., however, the Greek writer Philostratus commented: 'It is said that the barbarians who live in the ocean . . . pour these colours [enamel] into bronze moulds and that . . . the colours become hard as stone, thus preserving the design.' This sounds like a slightly inaccurate description of *champlevé* enamelling. (see Chapter 9). However, the inference is that at this time enamelling was not generally or widely known. The phrase 'the barbarians who live in the ocean' has usually been understood to refer to the Celts in the British Isles.

As Greek art pursued its course from the archaic to the naturalistic—culminating in a degenerate sentimentality—jewellery followed the same course. From pendant flowers of gold, enriched with enamelwork, the style alters to embrace naturalistic figure work. Figures of Victories, Cupids and doves repeat in their miniature world the triumphs of Pheidias and the sculptors of the golden age of Pericles. Garnets cut *en cabochon* become a popular feature of designs. Cameos and intaglios follow from the time of Alexander the Great, and then comes the full flower of Greek glyptic art. The Romans, who imitated the Greeks in cameo and intaglio work, never reached the same degree of craftsmanship and elegance. It was the rediscovery of their two contributions to the art of gemstone-cutting, however, which had so important an influence on the Renaissance craftsmen.

In the main, Roman jewellery derives from three sources. The early work has, of course, its origin in Etruria. Later, the dominance of Greece as a cultural influence inspired the Romans not only to copy Greek techniques, but also to bring over to Italy Greek gem-cutters and jewellers. Thirdly, as the Roman Empire expanded, the citizen was brought more and more into contact with the barbarians to the north on one hand, and the civilizations of the East on the other. The Eastern influence was by this time diluted by Greek culture. The Celtic and Germanic influence, however, was pure and undiluted. This resulted in a fashion for heavy gold work, lavishly set with garnets and coloured stones. At this point, for the first time perhaps, Britain may be said to contribute to the history of jewellery in Europe through the skill of her Celtic craftsmen.

Under the Roman Empire, gems as distinct from jewellery began to occupy a position of importance, a position they subsequently maintained. The Eastern Empire which brought Rome into contact with the fabled wealth of the Orient created among the wealthy classes a passion for cut gemstones. Apart from their use in jewellery, gems were collected for their individual interest and quality. Emeralds and sapphires were particularly esteemed.

Amber and amethyst were among the less valuable gemstones which had a wide vogue. The Romans' skill in glass-blowing produced one of their major original contributions to the art of jewellery. Paste beads of every colour were manufactured and seem to have resulted in the creation of a popular jewellery, somewhat similar to the 'costume' jewellery of the twentieth century.

Rings were an important feature of Roman life. Under the Emperor Tiberius they were considered a sign of rank and only men descended from three generations of freemen were entitled to wear them. With the growth of a rich freedmen class, however—such men as the Trimalchio described in Petronius' *Satyricon*—it was inevitable that this rule should be relaxed. (It was still decreed, however, that only a freeborn Roman might wear a *gold* ring.) The increased demand which ensued necessarily widened the jeweller's scope and gave rein to his powers of invention.

'Originally,' to quote the elder Pliny's *Natural History*, 'it was the custom to wear rings on one finger only . . . later it became an accepted thing to put rings on the finger next to the thumb [as well as the one next to the little finger] . . . among the people of Gaul and Britain, they say, that the middle finger is used for this purpose.'

In the days of the Empire pearls assumed their place as an important item in jewellery, a position which they have held ever since. Most of these pearls came from the fisheries of the Red Sea. Some of them were also of the type known as freshwater pearls. They were used both in necklaces and in pendant ear-rings. It was not until the Renaissance, however, that the curiously shaped, or baroque, pearls were exploited and their eccentricities made to form parts of naturalistic designs.

With the establishment of Byzantium as the capital of the Christian Church and as the inheritor of the crafts of civilization, metalwork and jewellery were profoundly changed. The influence of the East was more marked and classical feeling tended to become subordinated to it. This tension between Eastern and Western influences (observable in Byzantine work) is, as has been indicated previously, one of the recurring factors in the history of European jewellery.

The splendour of Byzantine enamelling is too well known to need description here. Its influence, however, was to be far-reaching. Much of this tradition of craftsmanship became the heritage of the Russian Orthodox Church and was preserved in such pieces as icons. More than a thousand years later something of this Byzantine perfection of workmanship, though strangely transmuted into fashionable Edwardian extravagance, was to return to western Europe through the productions of the House of Fabergé.

Niello work was much used by the Byzantine craftsmen. It is of an extreme delicacy of execution—not to be rivalled until the work of fifteenth- and sixteenth-century Florence. Equally delicate was the enamelling, which was mainly of the *cloisonné* type as opposed to the *champlevé* that had become familiar to the Roman world *via* Gaul and Britain.

Much Byzantine jeweller's work was destroyed during the period of ferocious iconoclasm under Basil in the ninth century: as J. A. Symonds says in his introduction to the *Life of Benvenuto Cellini*, 'The artist who aspires to immortality must shun the precious metals'. History substantiates these words, unhappily only too often. Apart from such deliberate iconoclasm there are always three devils which beset the jeweller's craft—War, Poverty and Fashion. All three result in the breaking up and destruction of precious pieces, and the last of them is by no means the least offender.

The jewellery of the early Middle Ages has often, and incorrectly, been described as 'barbarian work'. This description perpetuates an error latent in the term 'barbarian', a term which has today a different connotation from that which it had for the Greeks who coined it and for the Romans who adopted it. Barbarian, in the sense of being primitive and unskilled, the metalwork of the Middle Ages certainly is not. Two main contributory streams feed the central river of the crafts during this period. One of these is the Teutonic, the influence of that Germanic invasion which swept over Europe and Italy and contributed largely to the destruction of her empire. The Teutonic style of jewellery was the product of excellent craftsmen, working, certainly, to a less developed aesthetic standard than the Greeks and Romans of the great periods. Implicit in it, however, is the great technical skill of the German race—a skill which later made Nuremberg the centre of jewellery fashions.

Characteristic of this jewellery is the employment of gemstones in the same manner as enamel. This 'inlaid' jewellery of gold and silver is constructed with the technique employed in the craft of *cloisonné* enamel. Compartments or *cloisons* of metal are set with gemstones, the latter being ground flat and level with the height of the metal.

The second major influence is that of the Celt. Here the Celtic element in British history plays a large part. A magnificent example of the skill of the British craftsman, a piece of jewellery which, in a sense, disproves the term 'Dark' as popularly applied to the age, is the Kingston brooch now in the British Museum. Found at Kingston in Kent in 1771, the brooch is approximately a thousand years old. Made in yellow gold, it combines the type of 'inlaid' work, which was a characteristic of the Teutonic style, with granulated gold and wire work. Garnets and blue paste are used, while sections of the design are filled in with lapis-lazuli ground down to fit into the gold cells. An integral part of the design are the repeated zoomorphic patterns which are traced in granulated gold.

These zoomorphic patterns—fantastic and conventionalized themes of men, horses, monsters and animals—are a regular feature of Anglo-Saxon and Merovingian work. The Kentish school of jewellery, some fine pieces of which can be seen in the British Museum, contains much work of this type. It can be said that the skill of the native Celtic craftsman and his successors in Great Britain has left us with a permanent legacy and tradition—one which is as evident today as it was when Philostratus first referred to the 'barbarians who live in the ocean'.

Among the gemstones used by the craftsmen of this period are turquoise, mother-of-pearl and garnets. The lapidary work of these early British craftsmen was of an extremely high order. Garnets were cut in much the same manner as today, the stone being pressed against a rapidly revolving wheel charged with emery-dust paste.

A marine gem also found in work of this period is amber. As the principal source of amber is the Baltic, it is found largely in Teutonic and Frankish jewellery and reached England through the medium of Continental trade.

One of the most fruitful and most fascinating sources for the collector or student who desires to gain a detailed picture of the goldsmith-jeweller in the later Middle Ages is the work of the monk, Theophilus. His book of Various Arts, *Schedula Diversarium Artium*, contains a unique picture not only of the techniques employed in gold and silver work, but also of the mental climate inhabited by the craftsman. Coupled with invaluable technical information goes a strange mixture of legend and folklore concerning the properties of the various stones and the methods of treating them.

The later Middle Ages throughout Europe witnessed in jewellery, as in most arts, a gradual blending of influences. Working in the peaceful atmosphere of the monasteries the jeweller-monk was enabled to perfect his technical skill. The ecclesiastical tradition of non-representational figure work, however, still held back the craftsman of the time from the full exploitation of his material. Apart from the rediscovery of classical art, it was largely the freedom from this convention which gave such an impetus to the work of the Italian Renaissance.

As the communities of Europe became more prosperous so, inevitably, the taste for jewellery increased. (Conversely it is always to be remarked that, during periods of war and unrest such as we have witnessed in the twentieth century, the jeweller's craft tends to decline.) The growth of the Guild system with its insistence on rigorous apprenticeship brought the craft to a high degree of technical efficiency. Meanwhile the new demand for jewellery not only of an ecclesiastical type, but also—and primarily—for fashionable display, led to the gradual divorcement of the craft from the over-riding influence of the Church.

By 1238 in England the 'Mystery', as it was termed, of goldsmithing was given an added impetus towards stabilization and recognition by a decree in council of Henry III. This consisted of an order to the Mayor and Aldermen of London instructing them to choose six reputable members of the craft to test the quality of the silver used. By 1300 these *gardiens*, the first Wardens of the Goldsmiths Company, were entrusted with the duty of marking with the leopard's head—a device taken from the Royal coat of arms—all pieces of silver that reached the required standard.

Throughout Europe conditions of prosperity and the spread of the 'new learning' were now re-activating the Continent's arts and crafts. The long road leading from the workshops of Ur and Egypt through Crete, Greece, Italy, France and the British Isles, takes a fresh turning. With the Renaissance, the birth of the modern world, we meet those forms of jewellery which deploy to the full all the resources of the craft—jewellery which, although it is in itself only a microcosm, reflects the many advances and achievements, both scientific and aesthetic, of the past four centuries.

CHAPTER ONE

Jewellery of the Italian Renaissance

THE Italian Renaissance has well been called the mother of our own civilization. In this sense it may also be called 'the mother' of modern European jewellery. Too often described as a revolt against tradition, the Renaissance was in fact a return to an older one. The rediscovery of Greek and Roman art which played so large a part in the pure arts such as painting and sculpture was also reflected in the crafts of the jeweller and the goldsmith.

In the jewellery of the Italian Renaissance—and this is true of almost all Renaissance work in Europe—it is the originality and diversity of design that is outstanding. While the standards of craftsmanship and execution in medieval work are as fine as those of almost any other period in history, yet the design is usually bounded by a rigid ecclesiastical convention that gives little or no scope for naturalistic figure work. By the middle of the fifteenth century, however, naturalism and fantasy, human and animal figures, and creatures from classical mythology are constantly found. The importance of jewellery in social life was once again emphasized. In the revival of the pagan learning was implicit the importance of the individual in the *pagan* sense. The importance of the individual in the Christian sense, with its connotation of humility and lack of display, was overwhelmed by the idea of 'every man an emperor'. Each princeling or rich merchant, liberated to some extent from his mental subservience to the Church, felt the desire to give expression to his own personality. Jewellery, which is magical in essence and whose part it is to heighten the personality, was therefore much in demand.

An almost naïve delight in the use of colour marks the age. This use of colour was reinforced by the employment of naturalistic motifs, technical improvements in enamelling, and by the greater variety of gemstones made available. The jeweller in Italy was not, as he is today, a worker in a minor backwater of the arts. Indeed, a list of those painters and artists who at one time or another were employed in, or designed for, the jeweller's workshop would include many of the most famous names of the Renaissance. Lorenzo Ghiberti, Donatello, Pippo di Ser Brunellesco, Lorenzo Dalla Golpaia (a famous clockmaker), Andrea del Verocchio and Andrea Mantegna, all at one time or another practised the jeweller's craft.

Another famous artist who worked at one time as a goldsmith was Antonio Pollaiuolo.

As in the other arts, it was the revival of the Antique which gave the main stimulus to Italian jewellery of the late fifteenth and sixteenth centuries. The enthusiasm for the great past of Italy set every Italian digging, as it were, at the ground beneath his feet in order to discover those treasures which had been forgotten for nearly four centuries. Almost every enterprising jeweller dealt in antiques as well as in contemporary pieces. Apart from re-setting many of the gems, he used them also as prototypes and designs from which to make copies. During the sixteenth century in Italy the traffic in antiques and, therefore, not unnaturally, in fakes was as great as it was in China during the days when the British were engaged in the discovery of Chinese art.

Above all, the antique cameos and intaglios excited the interest of the Renaissance jeweller. Their fineness of execution was unrivalled; indeed, the technique used in cutting them seemed to many almost magical. Vasari states that 'cameos, the sardonyx and other fine intaglios were found daily among the ruins of Rome'. He also refers to '. . . the art of carving hard stones and gems, which was lost after the fall of Greece and Rome'. Like a number of Vasari's statements this latter is open to suspicion, since some cameos are found in medieval work which clearly are not of classical origin. However, it would certainly be just to say that the peak of excellence attained by the classical craftsman was never reached by any medieval jeweller. These classical cameos and intaglios remained also a constant challenge to the skill of even the finest Renaissance lapidaries in Italy. It is certainly true that little progress was made in the art until the time of Popes Martin V and Paul III.

The art of cutting precious stones was spurred on in Florence by the fondness of Lorenzo de Medici for intaglios. His son Piero was also a great collector of cut gemstones, particularly of grey chalcedony and cornelian. In this connection we may quote from Cellini's *Trattati*: 'The age of a good prince whose delight is in the encouragement of all beautiful things is the age for men of talent.'

The main types of jewellery, fashionable during the sixteenth century, and examples of which are still in existence today, were necklaces and pendants, rings, ear-rings and *enseignes*. In general, the jewellery is fashioned in gold, the metal being enriched with enamel which is applied as a coating over sections of the work. The outstanding feature of this Italian work is the careful way in which the enamel is used to pick out details and to point contrasts with the gold. White enamel is most commonly found, the white being of a particularly rich texture. Also widely used was a red enamel, *smalto roggio*. This is an attractive rich colour and easily distinguishable from most modern red enamels. The goldwork found in necklaces and pendants is almost invariably well modelled. For certain applied details, castings were used. The metal is both engraved and chased, and in many pieces a mixture of both *repoussé* work and flat chased work is found. Granulated gold was also used, though hardly, if ever, is the standard of granulated work as fine as that of the Greeks or Etruscans. Both necklaces and pendants were set with precious stones. In the middle of the fifteenth century these are usually cabochon-cut but, as the craft of the lapidary was improved, faceted gems became more common.

The four stones which were considered of precious as opposed to semi-precious quality were the same as those which still hold pride of place today, namely, the ruby, the emerald, the diamond and the sapphire. It is interesting to note that in the middle of the sixteenth century their relative value was in the order given. (Today, in order of value, the list would read: diamond, emerald, ruby and sapphire.) The rarity of the ruby in Europe at this time, when trade with the Orient was not very extensive, most probably accounts for its position at the head of the list. That the diamond is placed third in order of value may be accounted for by the fact that the lapidary's craft was not sufficiently developed for him to be able to bring out the best in the stone.

Although many gems were still cut *en cabochon*, table-cut or faceted stones tended to replace the cabochon gems as the sixteenth century advanced. Apart from the four precious stones already mentioned, the Italian jeweller made use of a number of the semi-precious or lesser-known gemstones. In necklaces and pendants, however, the accent of the design was placed not so much upon the jewels as upon the gold and enamelled work. It will be observed that later in the history of European jewellery, as the lapidary became more proficient, the accent of jewellery design tends to be centred more upon the gems than upon their settings.

In cheaper work, not only for pendants and necklaces but also for rings, much use was made of Milanese paste. The art of making good paste substitutes for real gems had been highly developed in Roman days, and in fifteenth- and sixteenth-century Italy it was the jewellers of Milan who inherited this legacy and specialized in pastework. In view of the inexact methods which then prevailed for gem identification it is not surprising to find that there was much deliberate falsification. An interesting sidelight on history is afforded by Cellini in his *Trattati* when he describes the Milanese imitations. Referring to the emerald and the sapphire, he says that these are 'stones which are often falsified by the jewellers in Milan'. It is reasonable to assume it was with a somewhat superior chuckle that he then dictated to his amanuensis a brief note that 'the King of England was so tricked by a

Milanese jeweller'. The King of England to whom he refers was most probably Henry VIII.

As might be expected, the adornment of the hand with rings was of primary importance to individuals who desired to express their wealth and their position. Throughout the fifteenth and sixteenth centuries the thumbs were quite commonly adorned with rings, many of which were extremely elaborate. The second and third fingers, the index fingers and the middle and the upper joints of the fingers also carried rings. Clearly, since rings were worn in such profusion, there must still remain a great many examples of them in existence, and both national and private collections throughout the world are well endowed with examples of fifteenth- and sixteenth-century Italian rings.

Gold was chiefly used in their construction and is often decorated with enamelling. The stone is usually held in a plain box-like collet and, as with other items of jewellery, tends to be cabochon-cut up to the middle of the fifteenth century, gradually giving place to a table-cut gem. In the sixteenth century the shoulders of the ring acquired a great importance and were often lavishly decorated. A typical sixteenth-century Italian ring may have a large single stone table-cut and set in a rectangular bezel. The shoulders may be enamelled in white or red. Chasing is often used on the shoulders and they are sometimes supported by small gold figures.

Signet rings of very fine workmanship are also common. The intaglio work of these, from the sixteenth century onwards, is of very high quality, as the art of gem-engraving became a specialized profession. One of the early masters of this art was Giovanni del Cornioli (of the Cornelians). Another notable gem-engraver and a rival to Giovanni was the Milanese Domenico de' Cammei. Vasari records a famous piece of his, a portrait of Lodovico il Moro cut in a ruby.

During the papacy of Leo X the craft was further advanced, two notable practitioners being Piermaria da Pescia and a certain Michelino. A famous intaglio worker, who was employed by Alfonso Duke of Ferrara, was Giovanni da Castel Bolognese. This Giovanni was later employed by Pope Clement VII (for whom Cellini did much work). Among other things he carved for the Pope figures of the four apostles in crystal. It is recorded that when he died in 1555 he possessed an income of more than 400 crowns. Vasari, who devotes considerable space to a discussion of the cameo and intaglio workers with whom he was familiar, remarks in conclusion, 'I could tell of many more who have done medals, heads and reverses, surpassing the ancients. . . .'

In view of the importance of the signet ring in Italian life it is natural to find a very wide diversity of methods and designs. Designs range from copies of classical Roman work to inscriptions, monograms and portrait heads of the wearer. Although rings are dealt with at greater length in a later chapter, one type should be mentioned here—the silver *niello*ed ring. These rings are commonly of the *fede* variety or the well-known *gimmel* ring. A typical fifteenth-century example is in the Waddesdon Bequest collection at the British Museum. It is described in the catalogue as follows: 'Silver. Flat circular bezel engraved and formerly *niello*ed with a woman's head to left within an octagon; the shoulders with roundels filled with rosettes; the hoop formed by clasped hands with sleeves. . . .'

Ear-rings were almost invariably of the pendant type. Although they rarely, if ever, attained the delicacy of the Greek pendant ear-rings yet the Italian ear-rings of this period have an attraction of their own. Gold is the usual metal employed for setting, and enamelwork is common. A fountain-like delicacy, however, is given to many of the examples by the use of small seed-pearls suspended on gold wire. These seed-pearls are an important feature of Italian dress-decoration, but are nowhere more charmingly used than in the pendant ear-ring. One style which may often be found is a bell or flower-like piece of gold from which are suspended lines of 'drop' seed-pearls. The attractive irregularities of baroque pearls are also employed in the same manner. Ears, of course, were pierced and the rings held in place by curved pieces of gold wire. The screw or 'snap' ear-ring is a comparatively modern development and appears to have been unknown during the Renaissance. Cellini does, however, mention what may be the first clip ear-rings in history. He is describing how he dressed up a young friend of his to impersonate a woman at a party given by Michelangelo: 'In his ears I placed two little rings, set with two large and fair pearls; the rings were broken; they only clipped his ears, which looked as though they had been pierced.'

An important feature of Renaissance dress and fashion during the sixteenth century was the *enseigne*. This was a hat ornament worn by nearly all men of any wealth or distinction. It bore some motif, monogram or inscription applicable to the owner and was usually disc-shaped and made of gold. A typical example can be seen in the Waddesdon Bequest collection. This is possibly Italian and belonged, as an inscription on the back shows, to Don John of Austria (1545–78). The *enseigne* is of gold, enamelled and set with diamonds and rubies. The conversion of Saul in relief forms the central design and there is an inscription round the edge in gold on black—Durum Est Contra Stimulum Calcitrare. A number of these *enseignes* are still in existence and have sometimes been erroneously described as brooches, However, there is plenty of contemporary evidence, quite apart from portraits, to show how they were worn. (A portrait of Lodovico il Moro by Boltraffio in the Trivulzio collection, Milan, shows a good example of an *enseigne*. It is an initial device—M—from which hangs a pendant jewel.) Cellini has the following comment: 'It was the custom at that epoch to wear little golden medals, upon which every nobleman or man of quality had some device of fantasy of his own engraved; and these were worn in the cap.'

Before turning to a consideration of prevailing styles and themes to be found in Italian jewellery of the sixteenth century, it may be as well to give some examples taken from Cellini's autobiography of the jewellery which he himself made. Although there is no jewellery in existence which can confidently be ascribed to Cellini, his own descriptions give a fair idea of certain pieces then in demand and of the style in which they were worked. It has been well said that 'he is a typical example of the fact that the most famous men in history are not always the greatest'.[1] Nevertheless, he has left us one of the most vivid of autobiographies and one that is invaluable to the student of Renaissance work and methods. The dates given for the fabrication of the pieces detailed below are approximate.

1518 Man's silver belt buckle ('. . . as big as a little child's hand'). Carved with cluster of leaves, cherubs' heads and other masks—all in the 'antique' style. Made in the workshop of Francesco Salimbene.

1529 Silver belt (three fingers broad) to be worn by a bride. Worked in half relief with small figures in the round. Fashioned for Raffaello Lappaccini. Workshop of Salimbene, Florence.

1523 Reset and redesigned 'lily motif' jewel, enamelled with masks, cherubs and animals and set with diamonds. For Sulpicia, the wife of Gismondo Chigi, a Sienese living in Rome.

1524 Large gold medal or *enseigne*, engraved with Leda and the Swan. For Gabriele Ceserini, Gonfalonier of Rome—retained by Cellini. Made in Cellini's own workshop which was opened in this year.

1524 Several steel finger-rings chased and inlaid with gold. Clearly part of his normal stock in trade at this time ('. . . for making one of them I sometimes get more than forty crowns'). Cellini's workshop.

1524 A gold *enseigne* designed with four figures on it. (Undertaken in rivalry with Ambrogio Foppa, a noted goldsmith of the time.) Cellini's workshop.

1527 Gold *enseigne* depicting Hercules and the Nemean lion. Made for a Sienese, Girolamo Maretti. Cellini's workshop in the Mercato Nuovo, Florence.

[1] W. R. Valentine in *The Detroit Art Quarterly*.

1527 Gold *enseigne*. Atlas bearing the world upon his shoulders. The figure was engraved on a thin plate of gold, the heaven on his back being a crystal ball 'upon which was cut the zodiac on a field of lapis-lazuli'. Engraved beneath the motto, SUMMA TULISSE JUVAT. Made for Federigo Ginori, a friend of the poet Luigi Alammanni. (Later given by Alammanni to François I of France.) Cellini's workshop in Florence.

1529 Pope Clement VII's cope-button. In gold, set with a large diamond in the centre. God the Father is seated on a diamond, His right hand raised in benediction, the diamond itself being supported by three cherubs with uplifted arms. The middle cherub in high relief, the other two in half relief. Other cherubs are surrounding the main composition. Workshop of Rafaello il Moro in Rome.

1536 Papal ring set with a tinted diamond. For Pope Paul III.

1538 Gold ornaments and jewellery. For Francesca Sforza, wife of Girolamo Orsini, Lord of Bracciamo. Cellini's workshop in Rome.

1545 A gold belt, richly worked and set with gems. For the Duchess Eleonora of Toledo. Made in Florence.

1545 An elaborate pendant set with a large diamond. For the Duchess. (Later, according to Cellini, reset in a simpler form by a foreign workman.) Florence.

Motifs used by the Italian Renaissance jeweller are, as have been indicated, largely derived from classical and mythological themes. Favourites were those offsprings of Neptune, the merman, the mermaid and the hippocamp. All of these figures lent themselves to attractive designs, in many of which the baroque pearl figured largely. The ingenuity of the Renaissance jeweller in incorporating the eccentricities and irregularities of baroque pearls into his design is a frequent feature of the work of this period. A sharp contrast between the attitude of the modern jeweller and his Renaissance predecessor is well illustrated by this question of choice. In sixteenth-century Italy it was often the irregularity, the individuality and—one might almost say—the eccentricity of a pearl or gemstone which gave it first place in a design. Today, on the contrary, the whole basis of gem-set jewellery is that the stones should all be as regular and uniform as possible. (Witness, for instance, the carefully selected and graduated modern pearl necklace as opposed to the use of pearls in Renaissance work.) It may be permissible to see in the comparison between modern and Renaissance work a striking difference between two attitudes of mind. Sixteenth-century humanism, which granted so much importance to individual singularities, was naturally prone to select the unusual for its gems. Perhaps today's mass uniformity, the age of the Common Man, is matched by a similar uniformity in jewellery?

Baroque pearls were also frequently used in pendants. They are usually suspended below the main theme in a triangular grouping with two small pearls, one to either side, and a large baroque pearl in the centre. To the Renaissance jeweller the baroque pearl provided a source of inspiration similar to the old and mildewed walls described by Leonardo da Vinci in his *Treatise on Painting*. 'If you look at some old wall covered with dirt, or the odd appearance of some streaked stones, you may discover several things like landskips, battles, clouds, uncommon attitudes, humorous faces, draperies, etc. Out of this confused mass of objects, the mind will be furnished with abundance of designs and subjects, perfectly new.'[1]

Flowers and fruit and grape-clusters and foliage are all employed either as motifs or as integral parts of the design in necklaces, pendants and even rings. Cherubs or *amorini* were also popular, executed 'in the round', i.e. in relief, as described by Cellini in the case of Pope Clement's cope-button. Female figures, such as figures based on classical caryatids, are quite commonly found. They are used as supporters to the shoulders of finger-rings, their hands holding up, as it were, the collet and bezel. In intaglio work the 'Emperor' style was popular, in which a portrait or idealistic portrayal of the owner was executed in the same manner as Roman work, often with the familiar laurel wreath round the brow.

It is important to realize that, with the wide diffusion of the new learning throughout Europe, the craft of the goldsmith and jeweller became again, as during the Roman Empire, international and cosmopolitan. Books containing jewellery designs were fairly widespread. These had, indeed, been in use throughout the Middle Ages, but the development of the printing trade naturally increased their influence. The result was that many jewellers in Europe were working from similar designs, and—apart from certain differences of craftsmanship and motif—it is this similarity which renders difficult the certain ascription of any one piece to any one country. From the sixteenth century onwards this cosmopolitan aspect of jewellery becomes more and more marked. Articles of jewellery were made then, as today, for specific foreign buyers and markets in the style requested. Anyone familiar with modern Parisian, London or American work will agree that there are sometimes certain differences between them that are discernible to the expert. However, with French jewellers working in London and Continental jewellers working in America it can readily be seen how difficult it is to make this distinction. This difficulty is even greater in dealing with antique jewellery. Too often one sees the confident

[1] *A Treatise on Painting*. Leonardo da Vinci. Trans., London, 1796.

Right: *pendant design by Holbein for Henry VIII. It has three drops, and embodies the King's monogram, Enricus Rex. (In the British Museum.)* Below: *drawing by Bertoli of the gold cope-button made by Benvenuto Cellini for Pope Clement VII. A pointed diamond is set in the centre, and surrounded by four large emeralds. The four smaller, table-cut stones are rubies and sapphires.*

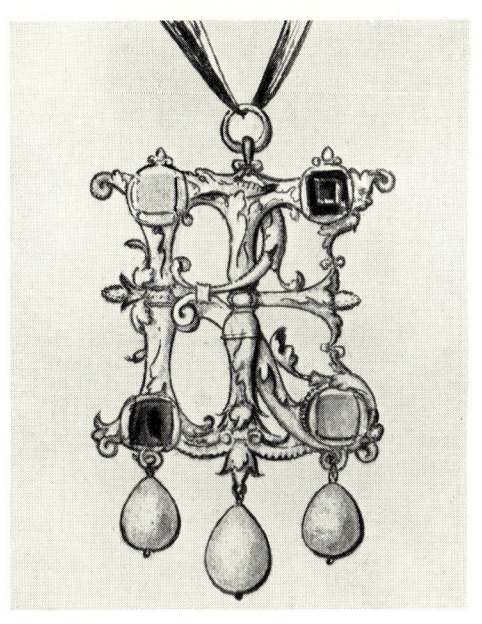

The pendant, worn on a chain or pinned to the bodice, was fashionable throughout sixteenth-century Europe. Many had pendant pearl or coloured-stone drops attached to them. Above: *two more jewellery designs by Henry VIII's court painter, Hans Holbein the Younger. The pendant has a drop pearl, and is set with five gemstones. The design above (right) is probably for a brooch to be made in gold and enamels. (In the British Museum.)*

Left: *an Italian pendant, c. 1520, in gold and enamel, set with emeralds and rubies. The large drop is a faceted ruby.*

Portrait of the young Jacqueline de Bourgogne by Mabuse (1472–1535), showing a pendant with a drop pearl and a jewelled necklet. (In the National Gallery, London.)

Left: *gold and enamel pendant with large baroque pearl drop, containing a representation of the Crucifixion. The front is of rock crystal. Italian, c. 1550.* Right: *another Italian pendant jewel, c. 1550, showing the Virgin and Child between pillars. In gold and enamel, with drops of emerald, ruby and pearl.*

Opposite: *portrait of the Magdalen (?) of the Netherlandish School. She is shown wearing a magnificent suite of gold jewellery set with pearls and square-cut stones. (In the National Gallery.)*

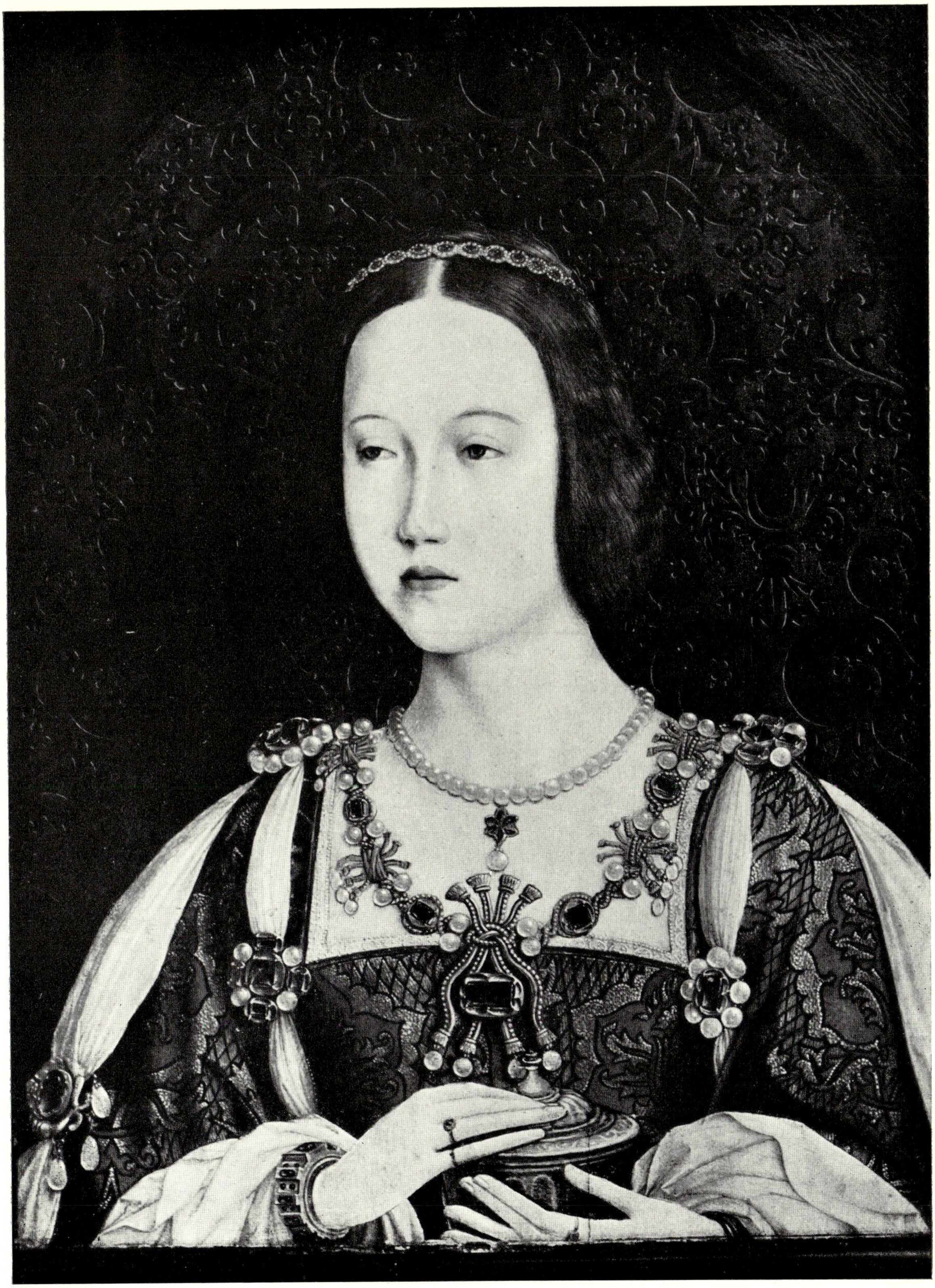

Left: *a superb example of the use of the baroque pearl in sixteenth-century jewellery. The pearl, with two pendant pearls, is set in the form of a mermaid in enamelled gold.* Right: *a rock-crystal pendant with a verre églomisé medallion of the Annunciation. Italian, late sixteenth century.* (Both in the Wernher Collection, Luton Hoo, Beds.)

ascription of a piece to some particular country, where no such confidence is justified.

As we have seen, the irregularity of a stone was not considered a misfortune by the Italian jeweller. Where the stones were set *en cabochon* the closed setting was often used. This setting is in the nature of a small box of gold (or other metal), the upper edge of which is rubbed over the stone to hold it in place. Renaissance work in gold was often filed up from the solid metal and used, by our standards, somewhat lavishly. In order to give it workable properties, gold is alloyed with varying quantities of copper and silver, the two together giving a soft gold colour—a higher proportion of copper a reddish tinge, and a higher proportion of silver a greenish tinge. Open settings for stones were also used. These may be either a rim, as in the closed setting—but with the bottom cut away—or a circlet of claws. The two are also used together, but this is more common in German work. *Pavé* settings, which are sometimes still used, were scooped out of the solid metal, the stone then lowered into place and the edges of the metal rubbed over the stone.

'*Granaglia*'—granulated metal—was made from gold or silver cuttings which were heated in a crucible. The cuttings were put into the crucible together with charcoal and, as they melted and the crucible was rotated, took on the form of perfect spheres. Once melted, the charcoal was washed away and the metal granules sorted for size. This would appear to have been the standard method of making granulated gold and silver, although there would seem little doubt that for certain types of work the device outlined by Theophilus in his *Schedula Diversarium Artium* was still employed. This was a 'beading tool' which Theophilus describes as a block cut in two, with slots in the lower and upper half designed to form various patterns of beads or granulations. Into these slots the gold or silver wire was placed, the top then being hammered down so that the wire took on the impression of the grooves.

Niello work was much employed in sixteenth-century Italian jewellery. This method can be used to enrich either gold or silver, but is most commonly found in the latter. The metal was first engraved with the required design, after which a black alloy of silver, lead, copper and sulphur was spread over the surface. (First found in Egyptian jewellery, *niello* work has been popular throughout the centuries in Europe and has been described by Pliny, Theophilus and Cellini.) After the alloy had been applied to the surface the piece was heated until the *niello* melted. The alloy then set into the engraved portions. Finally, when the whole piece cooled, the surface was polished until only the engraved section, where the *niello* lay, was left black. This technique is found in much Renaissance work and was very popular for silver rings, helmets, sword hilts, etc.

The following formulas are taken from *Niello*, by Herr Mark Rosenberg.

Pliny, *Natural History* XXXIII. 46	Silver Sulphur Copper	3 parts 2 parts 1 part
Cellini, *Trattati*	Silver Sulphur Copper Lead	1 part half a handful 2 parts 3 parts
Augsburg Recipe 1	Silver Copper Lead	1 part 1 part 2 parts
Augsburg Recipe 2	Sulphur Lead Quicksilver	1 part 1 part 1 part

In the technique of the jeweller's craft the use of foils to improve the colour of stones was a major feature. Today, with modern methods of stone-cutting and greater knowledge of gemmology, stones are selected or rejected for their quality and colour. The Italian jeweller, however, had to take his stones much as he found them and was therefore compelled to use special methods for heightening their brilliance or enhancing their colour. For instance, if a ring is set with a ruby in a box setting it may well be found that, beneath the stone, foils have been placed to aid the ruby's colour.

Foils or reflectors were of especial importance in the case of the diamond. The full brilliance of this stone was never revealed to the Renaissance jeweller and, although Cellini refers to 'those lovely shapes so familiar to us, the table, the faceted and the point' (*in tavola, a facetta, e in punta*), any student of antique jewellery will realize that the diamond in its full glory is seen only in the rose cut or the modern brilliant cut. For 'tinting the diamond' a paste-like composition, reflective and of a suitable colour, was used to 'back' the stone. The following formulas for the foils used as a backing for diamonds are taken from the *Trattati*. There seems little doubt that, although each jeweller undoubtedly had his own ideas on the subject, the compositions were in general much the same.

Yellow foil
9 carats—fine gold
18 carats—fine silver
72 carats—fine copper

Blue foil
16 carats—fine copper
4 carats—fine gold
2 carats—fine silver

Red foil
20 carats—fine gold
16 carats—fine silver
18 carats—fine copper

Green foil
10 carats—fine copper
6 carats—fine silver
1 carat—fine gold

Diamonds were cut and faceted in much the same manner as today, upon a steel wheel charged with diamond dust. The diamond was held in a small pewter cup which was pressed against the manually operated wheel. Because of its simplicity the most common type of diamond cut in the sixteenth century was the 'point'. This was a pyramidal shape, the four facets of the diamond leading 'starwise to the point'. Where the diamond was cut in this fashion and set in a ring, it was usually high-mounted. This is the so-called 'writing' diamond, since it is known that it was sometimes used for writing inscriptions on glass. The principle reason, however, for so setting a diamond was merely one of display.

Another device of the sixteenth-century jeweller was the 'reflector'. This was used where the diamond was 'too delicate' (i.e. a pure white colour) to be best offset by a tint. The reflector's purpose was the same as that of a mirror—to catch the light falling through the diamond and reflect it back again. It was set in the bottom of the setting below the stone, the bezel itself being suitably tinted.

Diamonds were set both in closed and open settings, although the claw setting became popular from the middle of the sixteenth century onwards. The famous diamond which was set in Pope Clement VII's cope-button was backed by a foil, was cut 'starwise to a point', and held between four claws. This diamond thus serves as a good illustration of three important aspects of diamond setting during the period.

Minuterie work, which has been described as 'all that class of work done with the punch, such as rings and pendants and bracelets', serves as a reminder that not all sixteenth-century pieces were entirely raised by hand. Punches, the ends of which were countersunk with the required designs, were used in much the same manner as the modern mechanically operated die. Stamps or presses—similar to that described by Theophilus for beading work—were used for cutting out other designs. Where, for instance, a simple shape such as a circle or oval of gold might be constantly required for medallions, etc., the metal would be placed over a stamp sunk with the design in question. This was then hammered down in the manner of a press.

Small castings, such as reliefs to set in rings, details of foliage and flower sprays, were most probably made in cuttle-fish bone. This is a simple method still used by some jewellery craftsmen today. A perfectly clean and uniform cuttle-fish is cut in half and each face rubbed flat. The pattern from which it is desired to take copies is laid between the two faces of the cuttle-fish, which are then pressed together. When the impression has been taken, a small funnel or groove for the metal is cut from the top of the two halves down to the impression. The mould is then closed and finally tied up ready for casting.

Other processes used by jewellers were sand-casting and piece-moulding. The *cire-perdue* (waste-wax) process was likewise known to the sixteenth-century Italian jeweller. (A form of waste-wax moulding was used by Cellini for his bronze Perseus and the methods are graphically recorded by him.)

The jeweller's art is almost invariably an anonymous one. Although we know the names of certain great Italian craftsmen such as Marso Finiguerra (famous for his *niello* work) and Piero di Nino (a worker in filigree), it is impossible to point with certainty to any work executed by them. Even in the case of Cellini, who has left us his detailed and vainglorious personal record, there is no piece of jewellery in existence which can confidently be ascribed to him. Apart from individual items of jewellery which have remained in the same family or collection for centuries, and whose history is well documented, even the expert will tread warily when ascribing a piece to some particular country. However, as has been shown, there are certain styles and methods of working which apply particularly to one era or century and, in some cases, particularly to one country or even town. Working from these principal sources of information and, above all, with a sense of style and period, it is possible to make a reasonable approximation. Any judgment made must be assisted principally by a knowledge of lapidary work, since it is the lapidary's craft which has been the subject of the major changes in the last four centuries. In Italy, for instance, between the middle of the fifteenth and the late sixteenth centuries, the principal changes affecting jewellery lie in the style of gem-cutting. Mid-fifteenth-century stones are mainly *en cabochon*, but by the late fifteenth and early sixteenth century, important stones are table-cut, cut to a point in the case of diamonds or haphazardly faceted. This haphazard faceting is found particularly in the diamond, since this was the only way of disguising natural blemishes. As a general rule, the more faceting, the more were the flaws.

Towards the close of the sixteenth century, in rings, necklaces and jewellery in general, the single, prominent stone tends to give way to groups of smaller gems. The diamond is also found used in conjunction with coloured gemstones, instead of being set separately. These developments, again, were the result of improvements in the lapidary's craft.

CHAPTER TWO

Sixteenth Century: Germany, Central Europe, France, Spain, England

OUTSTANDING among the great trading centres of sixteenth-century Europe were two Bavarian cities whose names have become almost synonymous with the craft of the jeweller and goldsmith. These were Augsburg and Nuremberg.

They owed their importance primarily to their situations at the junction of the main trade routes of the time. Augsburg, which was part of the Dukedom of Bavaria, was the centre of the trade between Italy and Northern Europe, while Nuremberg was the intermediary between Italy and the Orient on the one hand, and Italy and Northern Europe on the other. Although both of these towns were adversely affected by the discovery of the sea route to India towards the close of the fifteenth century, they retained their importance right up to the time of the Thirty Years War. This war, which was to leave Germany devastated and its people with a permanent persecution complex, also contrived the ruin of these two great homes of the arts and crafts.

Nuremberg will always be remembered as the fountain-head of German art. Among its sculptors were Adam Kraft, Peter Vischer and Veit Stoss, while its painters included Dürer and Wohlgemuth. Nuremberg was the birthplace of modern horology, for it was here that the watch was invented. Another invention of importance to the jeweller was the discovery of wire-drawing, while other contemporary inventions numbered objects as remote from each other as the air-gun and the celestial globe. Not unnaturally, in a centre at once so wealthy and so fertile with ideas, the craft of the jeweller reached new heights. A large majority of Renaissance pieces which still survive are probably the products of Nuremberg or Augsburg.

The latter city, although second in commercial importance to Nuremberg, was the home of those merchant princes, the Fuggers and the Welsers, a fact which gives Augsburg a place of especial importance in history. Describing the Fuggers, the late Gordon Selfridge wrote, 'of all the merchant princes of those times, the Fuggers of Augsburg took first rank in wealth, as standing as bankers to Kings and

Emperors, and in feudal grandeur'. To the student of history they are of major importance since their correspondents throughout the world kept their principal office, the Golden House at Augsburg, informed of all local events—particularly as they affected trade. These News-Letters, as they have been termed, are also invaluable to anyone interested in antique jewellery for, in view of the prominent part played by jewellery at the time, no description of a wedding, a pageant or a festival was complete without some reference to the jewels worn by the participants.

It was under Anton Fugger (1493-1560) that the House attained its peak of prosperity and magnificence. Both Anton and his brother, Raimond, were great patrons of the arts, a patronage that was inevitably reflected in the jeweller's workshop. A further stimulus to the craft of the goldsmith and jeweller was the Fugger interest in the Tyrolese silver mines. This helped to make the metal a fairly common one in the households of the day. The proximity of Augsburg to Italy, quite apart from its commercial importance, meant that there was a constant stream of craftsmen moving between the great centres of the Italian Renaissance and the Bavarian town. This interchange of ideas and techniques was naturally stimulating to the German jeweller, who showed himself a master of the delicacy essential to this craft.

The profusion of jewellery in German dress is well proved by many existing portraits by such famous painters as Altdorfer, Wohlgemuth, Hans Baldung Grien, Lucas Cranach and Dürer. The German nobleman or rich merchant excelled himself in this type of display and bedecked himself with a quantity of gem-set and enamelled pieces to a far greater extent even than his Italian counterpart.

Dürer was himself the son of a jeweller, and the extreme fineness and delicacy of many of his drawings may perhaps be traced to this initial influence. Examples of Dürer's work as a designer for jewellery still exist and help to give us some idea of his own conceptions in this sphere and also of the working designs with which the jeweller of the day was confronted. Three sketches of Dürer's for pendant whistles—a favourite toy of the time—were to be seen before the war in the Kunsthalle, Bremen. These whistles were used for calling domestics. (A number of seventeenth- and eighteenth-century English tankards had a similar purpose, for they have a whistle fitted into the handle for calling the potman or landlord.) A design for a whistle by Dürer is in the British Museum; it is lion-shaped, the ball of the whistle being held in the lion's mouth.

The Italian Renaissance gave a new impetus to the craft of the German jeweller, until then enslaved by the Gothic conventions of design. The Germans have always been—and remain—masters of precise, detailed, small work, and this innate craftsmanship was now allied to the invigorating creative impulses of the Renaissance.

There are several points which in the main distinguish the German style from the Italian—always allowing for the international quality of jewellery and for those pieces which were made to a specific commission. There tends to be, for one thing, a greater emphasis upon elaboration in German gem-set jewellery. The Germans' technical skill, coupled with the new aspects of design, seems to have intoxicated them much as earlier painters—Ucello comes to mind—were intoxicated with the possibilities of perspective. Another feature of their work is a greater use of what may be called 'architectural design'. Where, for instance, in an Italian pendant of similar period a figure—mythological, human or animal—will form the central motif, in the German piece it is likely that the figure will be set in a small alcove or shrine where it becomes of secondary importance to the conception as a whole. A third aspect in which German work sometimes differs—and one to which little attention appears to have been given in the past—is the Teutonic love of the macabre. In the artistic history of no other country does the idea of mortality, the skeleton at the feast, appear so often as in that of Germany. Even the Spanish saint with his skull seems a mild figure compared with these Germanic reminders of *'vita est brevis'*. The 'Dance of Death' is a dark thread which runs throughout the whole of German art and is consequently to be found reflected even in jewellery, articles which should be, above all, symbols of life, colour and human pleasure. This aspect of jewellery design is one which will be encountered again in eighteenth-century England's mourning rings and in the jet and onyx gems of the Victorian period.

Fifty years ago, the tendency in classifying antique jewellery was to ascribe most of the pieces to Italy and, if the article in question was particularly ornate, to add 'possibly by Cellini'. In recent years, however, the more precise methods of modern scholarship have been applied to jewellery—as to most other branches of the arts. The outcome has been to concede more and more to the German jeweller, thus paying to his craftsmanship a tribute long overdue. The time has now been reached, however, when it is right to take stock and to wonder whether the pendulum has not swung too far in the other direction. Museum catalogues and catalogues of private collections tend, nowadays, whenever the ancestry of some particular piece is doubtful, to label it 'South German (?)'. This is, of course, a step in the right direction, since it is known that so great a quantity of gem-set articles were made in this area. However, the character of jewellery has been an international one for so many centuries that over-confident ascriptions should be avoided.

One reason for the ascription of so many fifteenth- and sixteenth-century items to the South German jeweller is that there exist numerous engraved designs from German sources for articles of jewellery. Pieces, moreover, are still in existence which can definitely be said to bear all the marks of having been conceived from these designs. For example, the Waddesdon Bequest collection at the British Museum has several items which resemble designs by Erasmus Hornick (c. 1560). It is not enough, however, for a piece of jewellery to resemble a known design for a definite decision on the piece's country of origin to be given. (There is in my possession a volume of jewellery designs issued from Paris within the last few years which has been circulated not only to jewellers in London but also to New York and the British Dominions.)

A notable designer who worked in Germany during the sixteenth century, and examples of whose work still exist, was Hans Muelich (1515–73) who was goldsmith at the court of Duke Albrecht V. Some of these designs were to be seen before the second World War in the Royal Library at Munich. They are of particular interest in that Muelich was a miniature painter who was commissioned by the Duke to paint an exact inventory of the pieces belonging to his wife, Anne of Austria. Another outstanding figure was Virgil Solis (1514–62) whose reputation rests principally upon his designs for pendants, a magnificent series that shows the Renaissance in full flower, the details of the pieces being executed with an airy delicacy. Two other late-sixteenth-century designers who have certain aspects of their work in common were Theodore de Bry (1528–98) and Hans Collaert (1540–1622). The former was a Frenchman born at Liège who migrated to Frankfurt with his two sons, Johann Theodore and Johann Israel, some time after the middle of the sixteenth century. The work of this family is notable for the fact that so many of their designs are based upon the use of white enamel upon a black ground—a very distinctive feature and one not to be found in Italian jewellery of the same period. Arabesques, grotesques and Renaissance swags of fruit and flowers are typical of their work and it is in this connection that they are akin to Hans Collaert. The latter worked mainly, as far as is known, at Antwerp and was responsible for the most important known jewellery publication of the late sixteenth and early seventeenth centuries, the *Monilium bullarum inauriumque artificiosissimae icones* (1581). His work is, indeed, more typical of the seventeenth century, for he moved away from—or was never influenced by—the Renaissance figure idiom, and concentrated mainly on designs which have a strong geometrical feeling. The appearance of this publication tended to encourage a colder and more abstract style of jewellery design than is typical of the sixteenth century as a whole.

Another source of information, particularly about German designs, is provided by the lead castings which jewellers took to preserve the features of their designs. This procedure was advocated by Cellini in his *Trattati*. Its value to the craftsman was that it not only enabled him easily to reproduce an article, but also, at a time when patent rights did not exist, constituted a perpetual proof of his own handiwork should disputes arise. At both Basle and Munich a number of these lead castings exist, those at Munich being of particular value in that they show the productions of one family of Augsburg craftsmen over a period of 250 years.

Items of this nature, coupled with contemporary designs, assist in the cataloguing of antique jewellery. It should, however, once again be stressed that they are more of use in determining the century of manufacture than the exact locality.

All of the types of articles which were made in Italy will also be found in German work. There is also another important department in which German examples abound—although these are by no means confined to Germany. These are the *miscellanea* of the jeweller, the *minuterie* which were attached to the girdle of the woman of the house. Among them are the small jewelled whistles whose function has already been described. Other items are pomanders, scissors, looking-glasses and ornamental covers for household notebooks. Books of devotion were also considered a fit subject for the jeweller's art; a magnificent example of one of these is to be seen in the Victoria and Albert Museum.

Two central European countries which produced fine jewellery during the sixteenth century were Hungary and what is now Czechoslovakia. (The latter has, indeed, remained a centre of the jewellery industry up to the present day and is one of the principal manufacturers of marcasite, paste and imitation pearls.) Prague in the sixteenth century was famous for its enamelled jewellery, and the city's craftsmen benefited from the lavish patronage of the Emperor Rudolph II (1552–1612) who was King of Hungary and Bohemia. Specimens of goldsmiths' work executed to his order exist today in the Viennese art collections, some of which were on exhibition in London during 1949. In his palace on the Hradshin in Prague Rudolph II formed the largest art collection of his time. Apart from his patronage of such artists as Dürer and Pieter Bruegel the elder, Rudolph was a great lover of precious stones. The Milanese craftsmen, the Miseroni, were appointed 'Stonecutters to the Court' and there is little doubt that some of the elaborate examples of this work still to be seen in the collections were the products of this same family. One notable feature of this Hungarian work was the use of the so-called 'filigree enamel'. This does not appear to have been used elsewhere in Europe except, as will be seen, in some Hispano-Moresque work. The feature of this enamel is that although the technique is similar to that of ordinary *cloisonné*, the cells (*cloisons*) are made of twisted gold or silver wire and the enamels are opaque in colour. Hungarian jewellery has a lavish, opulent quality, which is later reflected in much middle-European peasant jewellery.

The influence of the Italian Renaissance, in its westwards surge through Europe, was naturally felt in France some time before it affected the art and craftsmanship of the British Isles. This is a fact which is amply proved by examples of silverware still in existence. The British pieces preserve a plain, English, Tudor form long after the rest of Europe, dominated by the Italian style, became obsessed with figure work, fruit and foliage motifs, and the like.

François I, who came to the throne of France in 1515, might well stand as a typical figure of the Renaissance. He was, indeed, pre-eminently the Renaissance monarch, endowed with vitality and quick wit, a love of art and life and a flair—something which is essential to the great patron—not only for recognizing genius when he saw it, but also for securing the affections of the great men who worked for him. For the last two and a half years of his life Leonardo da Vinci worked under his patronage, thus bringing into France the fine, sophisticated quality of his unique art. Other artists who were employed by François I included Francesco Primaticcio and Rosso del Rosso.

Outstanding among the Italian goldsmiths and jewellers who were employed by François I was, of course, Benvenuto Cellini. The story of his stay in France is admirably recounted in his *Memoirs* and presents, as vividly as Cellini always does, the atmosphere of wealth and enthusiasm for the arts which reigned in the Court. Curiously enough there is no mention in the *Memoirs* of any specific items of jewellery made in Cellini's workshop during this period. Undoubtedly there must have been numerous pieces, but Cellini is too busy describing his more important commissions to catalogue any of the smaller pieces. He does, indeed, say of his first meeting with the King at Fontainebleau that 'The Cardinal of Ferrara saw that the King had been vastly pleased by my arrival; he also judged that the trifles which I showed him of my handicraft had encouraged him to hope for the execution of some considerable things he had in mind'. The 'trifles', apart from a silver ewer and basin which are described, most probably included items of jewellery such as any jeweller would have as his stock-in-trade for showing to important clients.

François I's passion for jewellery is well known, and his admiration for the Italian artists and craftsmen inevitably meant that their influence predominated in France. The rare examples of French Renaissance gems which remain in existence confirm this Italian influence. Unfortunately, the subsequent vicissitudes through which France passed have left very few pieces on which to base any judgment.

Many references in Rabelais confirm the important place held by jewellery in the France of that time. 'But had you seen the fair embroidery of the small needlework pearl, and the curiously interlaced knots, by the Goldsmith's art set out and trimmed with rich diamonds, precious rubies, fine turquoises, costly emeralds and Persian pearls . . .' 'For the jewel or broach which in his cap he carried, he had in a cake of gold, weighing three score and eight marks, a fair piece enamelled, wherein was portrayed a man's body . . .' 'To wear about his neck he had a golden chain, weighing twenty-five thousand and sixty-three marks of gold, the links whereof being made after the manner of great berries, amongst which were set in work green jaspers, engraven and cut dragon-like . . .' 'As for the rings which his father would have him to wear, to renew the ancient mark of nobility, he had on the forefinger of his left hand a carbuncle as big as an ostrich's egg, enchased very daintily in gold of the fineness of a Turkey seraph. Upon the middle finger of the same hand he had a ring made of four metals together, of the strangest fashion that was ever seen; so that the steel did not crush against the gold, nor the silver crush the copper. . . . On the medical finger of his right hand, he had a ring made spireways, wherein was set a perfect baleu [*Balas*] ruby, a pointed diamond, and a Physon emerald, of an inestimable value.' These four extracts are all from the chapter on 'The Apparelling of Gargantua', but, in fact, hardly a chapter of Rabelais passes by without some reference to the goldsmith's and the jeweller's art. His whole book, being a paean in praise of life, is inevitably coloured by those jewels without which the fortunate people of the Renaissance would have considered life drab and colourless. It is noticeable that in Rabelais' ideal 'Abbey of Theleme' there is detailed description of the dress and the jewellery worn by the Abbey's inhabitants.

Even if there are few remaining pieces of jewellery which can be certified as belonging to the sixteenth century in France, there remain a number of designs from the hands of outstanding contemporary jewellers, which show prevailing styles. As has been said, the Italian influence is predominant but, as with other countries, there are local divergencies which serve to differentiate the French work. Designs by Jean Duvet (1485–*c.* 1560), who was goldsmith to François I and also Henry II, show a delicate use of scroll-work and enamel. The French genius is essentially fond of the delicate and 'precise' in gems and objects of art, and already we can see the first stirrings of a style which later dominated European jewellery. Also working in the latter half of the sixteenth century was the French designer, Etienne Delaune. Reputed to have been employed in Cellini's workshop, Delaune moved at a later date to Strasbourg where he continued to carry on his trade. His designs show something of the same elegance and delicacy as those of Jean Duvet. His influence would appear to have been considerable, for we find a series of pen-

Sixteenth Century: Germany, Central Europe, France, Spain, England

dant designs by a Dutchman, Abraham de Bruyn (late sixteenth century), which echo Delaune's style.

Two other designers of note were René Boyvin (1530–98) who worked at Angers, and Pierre Woeiriot, of Lorraine (1532–c. 1590). The former employs a style which is reminiscent of Italian work, with much use of pearls, figure work and carving 'in the round'.

Charles IX (1550–74), the patron of Ronsard, was another King of France who combined a love of the major arts with a fondness for gems and precious metals. One of the most interesting of the Fugger News-Letters records the presents which he gave to his bride on the occasion of his marriage in 1570. The document is of particular value in that it records three objects which are now in the Vienna collections, one of which is the famous gold salt-cellar made by Cellini for François I.

'The King of France caused to be given to his Bride, the said Princess Elizabeth, the daughter of His Imperial Majesty:

1. A necklace, that is valued in all at 50,000 *scudi*, consisting of three diamonds in clusters, the least of which is valued at 10,000 *scudi*, four large rubies, sixteen large pearls, each one of which is valued at 100 *scudi*.

2. A ring with a diamond hanging, set in four golden bands so that it can be seen on all sides. It is valued at 12,000 *scudi*.

To the Archduke Ferdinand:

1. A small chest in the form of a ship, viz. a salt-cellar of pure gold, fashioned with great art, with Neptune, holding his trident in his hands and gazing upon his goddess, Thetis by name.

2. To lave the hands, a pitcher or can for water, made of agate, set with pearls and a handle with an emerald to lift the lid thereof.

3. A drinking-cup of crystal beautifully ornamented with pearls, rubies and diamonds.

4. A golden drinking-cup embellished with various precious stones.

These four pieces are altogether worth 16,000 *scudi*. The old Queen, Mother of the King of France, has presented:

A chain all of rubies, diamonds and emeralds from which is suspended a large diamond. At the top there is a large ruby, and thereunder hangs a large pearl, like a pear. This is all valued at 20,000 *scudi*.

The Duke of Anjou, the brother of the King of France, has presented:

A necklace of diamonds, rubies and pearls. It is valued at 12,000 *scudi*.

The Duke of Alençon, the King's brother, has given:

A necklace of diamonds and large and small pearls. This is valued at 5,000 scudi.'

It is sad to note that the only items which can certainly be stated to be in existence today are Nos. 1, 2 and 4 of the gifts made to the Archduke Ferdinand. The pieces of jewellery have all disappeared in the course of centuries, although some of the stones may still, perhaps, remain, disguised in other settings. The list, however, does furnish yet another proof of the importance attached to articles of jewellery in this century.

The new wealth from the Americas pouring into Spain during these years made her the richest country in the world. As always, these riches were reflected in the craft of the jeweller, who is, more than any other artist or craftsman, governed by the trading situation of the country in which he works. 'This is a pretty penny which will give new life to commerce,' writes a Fugger correspondent in 1583, on viewing the arrival of the gold fleet from Spanish India into Madrid. It is a remark which was doubtless echoed in the hundreds of goldsmiths' and jewellers' workshops throughout the Peninsula. Gold, silver, precious stones, all these made for a luxuriant development of Spanish jewellery. Foremost among the stones which were set in Spanish jewellery of the time, and which distinguishes it from that of other European countries, was the emerald. The great emerald mines of Peru provided a rich source, so it was natural that these stones should be used more by the Spanish craftsman than by any others. (The emerald, indeed, remains the predominant stone in Spanish work right up to the present day.)

Distinctively Spanish are the long pendant ear-rings whose popularity with the Spanish woman has also remained an unchanged feature of the nation's jewellery. These tend to make more use of enamelling, and the attractive effect of the ear-ring is achieved by the suspension of two or three faceted stones: again the emerald is the most popular. A treatment of these stones used in ear-rings which is particularly Spanish is the engraving of designs on their backs. The face of the stone which lies towards the back of the wearer's head is ground flat and upon this side of the stone the engraver cuts delicate scrolls, foliage motifs, etc. Gold pendant ear-rings are also treated in the same manner—sometimes both front and back of the metal being engraved.

Large brooches, worn on the breast at the point of the dress neckline, were fashionable. These were usually of gold, enamelled and set with table-cut stones. A favourite design is in the shape of a bow or fan. As in Italian work, a lavish use of white enamel is found in these pieces. Gold openwork is another feature of these breast ornaments, the reason for this use of openwork being, clearly, to reduce the 'drag' of the brooch upon the dress material. (Today, fashionable large dress-clips will be found pierced and cut away for the same reason.)

More religious jewellery was produced in Spain than in any other European country. The delicate figure work found in the crucifixes and reliquaries is similar to the Italian style but, where the majority of Italian pieces tend to have a pagan or mythological subject for their central motif, in the Spanish article the central figure will probably be the Virgin or the figure of Christ. Reliquaries, which, by virtue of their nature and, often, their size, give the jeweller great scope for detailed work, are exquisitely wrought. The use of *verres églomisés* (panels of tinted glass) is common in reliquaries. This technique was known in the Middle Ages, but the Spanish jeweller brought it to its finest peak. The technique is comparatively simple but produces most attractive effects. The under-side of a piece of glass—or, in some cases, rock-crystal—is covered with gold leaf. On this surface is traced the outline of the design which it is intended to preserve in gold. This design is then protected and the remainder of the gold removed. The design is then completed with paints. As in ordinary enamelling, the process is a lengthy one since different colours and tints must be applied in a careful order. Colour tones are finally perfected by the application of different thicknesses of varnishes, these latter also serving to preserve the paint and the gold leaf. In some cases minute shreds of silver leaf were then affixed wherever the design called for a highlight. The whole glass sheet was then backed with a reflecting foil of metal.

A number of drawings exist by Spanish jewellers of this period which confirm the main trends of Spanish design. Differing slightly from pure Spanish jewellery are those pieces usually catalogued as Hispano-Moresque. These tend to be more opulent and colourful, employing the style of filigree enamelwork as was used by the Hungarians. Here again the link is established with the main trends of European peasant jewellery.

Although the Elizabethan age is rightly recognized as one of the most important in English history, it must be remembered that England had not yet 'arrived' as a major power or trading nation. The whole of the sixteenth century was, in fact, the period during which England was establishing, or winning, a new position for herself. During most of it she was not, however, recognized as a 'civilized' nation among the councils of Europe in the same sense that Spain and France were. As the movement of the Renaissance was from east to west, it was natural that its influences should reach England last, having previously traversed Southern Germany, Spain and France. Any comparison of English metalwork with that of the Continent will always show this time-lag.

An examination of the Fugger News-Letters shows that London during this period was not considered one of the major trading centres. The most important of these were Rome and Paris, Hamburg, Frankfurt, Cologne, Venice, Antwerp, Middelburg, Nuremberg and Augsburg. England was also disturbed by the Reformation, which inevitably set her apart in certain respects from the Continental countries. The Reformation was directly responsible for the destruction of much fine religious jewellery. The severance of the craft of the jeweller from Church influence was thus effected in such a way as to give him an outlook completely different from that of a country such as Spain, which was still dominated by the Catholic Church.

The clothing and appearance of King Henry VIII is vividly sketched in a letter written by the Venetian ambassador, Giustinian: 'He wore a cap of crimson velvet in the French fashion, and the brim was looped up all round with lacets and gold enamelled tags . . . very close round his neck he had a gold collar, from which there hung a rough-cut diamond, the size of the largest walnut I ever saw, and to this was suspended a most beautiful and very large round pearl . . . over [his] mantle was a very handsome gold collar, with a pendant St. George entirely of diamonds . . . his fingers were one mass of jewelled rings.'

Henry VIII was, like François I, very much the 'man of the Renaissance', and his delight in articles of luxury is well attested. From contemporary records we learn that in 1511 he paid to his jeweller £199 (a considerable sum at the time) for a chain weighing 98 oz. Many Italian craftsmen were employed by Henry VIII, who thus emulated his fellow monarch in France. The greatest of the foreign artists who benefited by his patronage, however, was undoubtedly Holbein the Younger. He entered the King's service in 1536, and until his death in 1543, apart from his many other more important commissions, designed jewellery for the King. We are fortunate in that a number of these same designs are still preserved in the British Museum. Throughout, they show that same Germanic instinct for precise detail which is found in similar work by Dürer. An interesting example is a pendant incorporating the King's monogram E.R. (*Enricus Rex*). In style it is typical of much Renaissance work and can be compared with the *enseigne* worn by Lodovico il Moro in the painting by Boltraffio. A number of *enseignes* are recorded in an inventory made of Henry VIII's jewels in 1526. This monogram type of *enseigne* was particularly favoured in England, as were brooches and other jewels incorporating the owner's initials.

Right: *a gold 'memento mori' pendant known as the Tor Abbey jewel. English, late sixteenth century.*

Below: *three sixteenth-century Spanish gold and enamelled pendants. The dog is set with emeralds, spinel and rock crystal; the parrot with a garnet and pearls; the pelican-in-her-piety (a favourite motif in Renaissance jewellery) with pearls and a cabochon garnet.* (All in the Victoria and Albert Museum.)

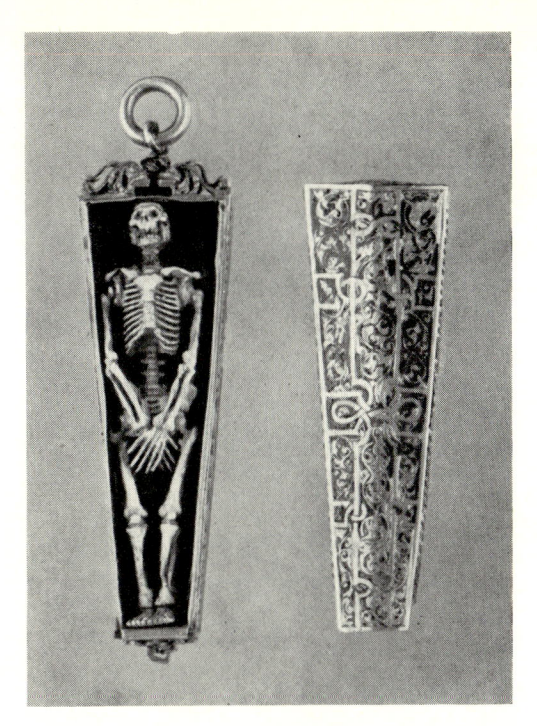

Above: *an enamelled gold book-cover reputed to have belonged to Henrietta Maria, queen of Charles I; probably South German, c. 1600. The two scenes depict the Fountain of Youth and the creation of Eve.*

Left: *a favourite type of Renaissance pendant in gold and enamels set with coloured precious stones and pearls. The subject is the Annunciation.*

Opposite: *portrait of a young woman of twenty-nine, dated 1582. She wears a jewelled pendant, similar to that shown left, attached to an elaborate necklace, and head-dress, gold chain and medallion, girdle, bracelets and rings. (In the Victoria and Albert Museum.)*

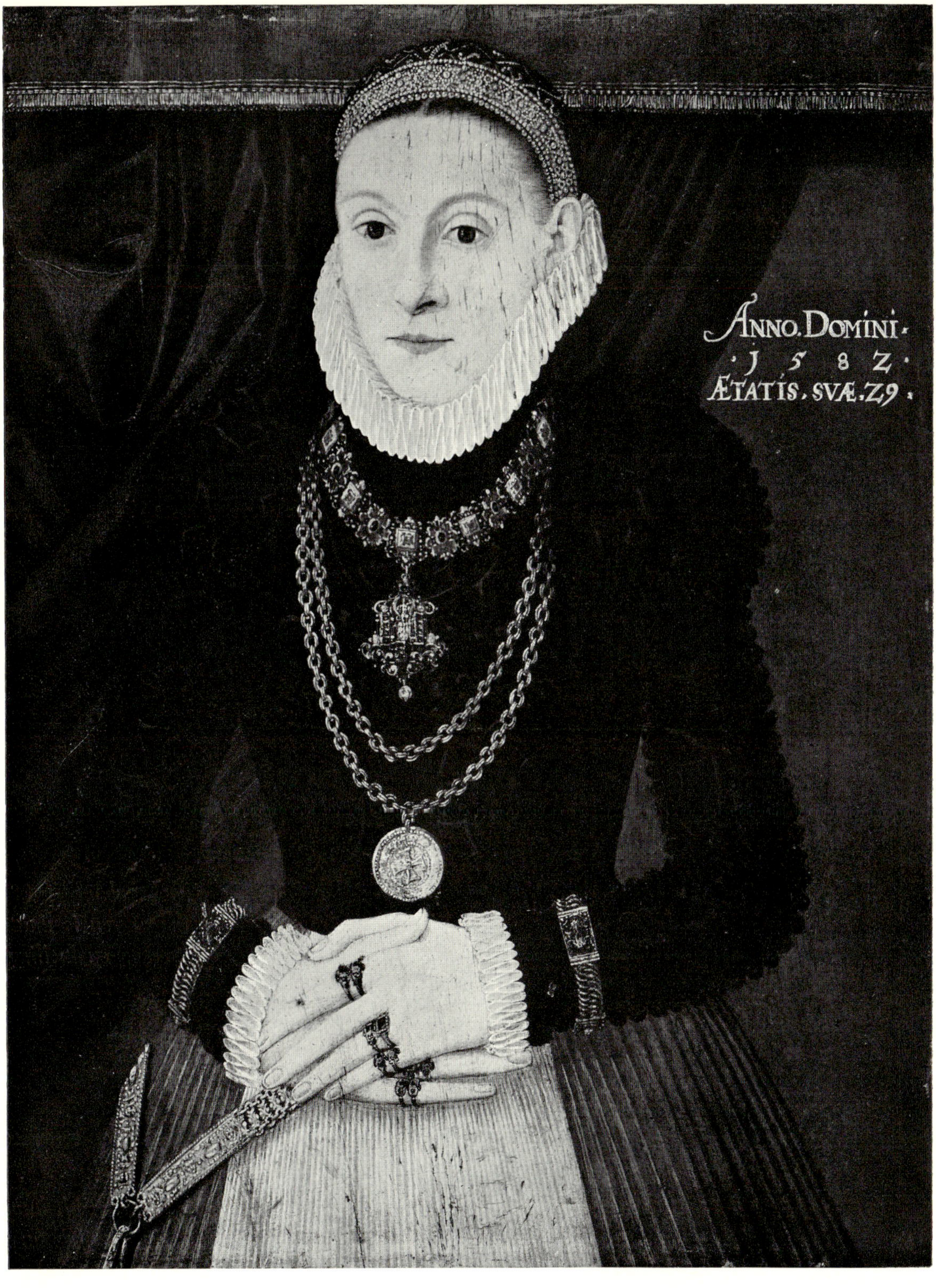
ANNO. DOMINI.
·1 5 8 2·
ÆTATIS. SVÆ. 29.

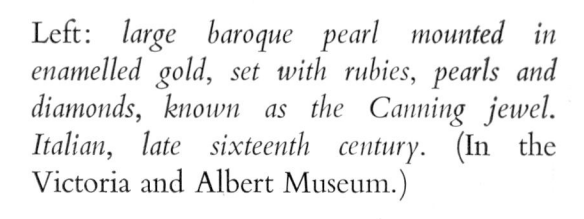

Left: *large baroque pearl mounted in enamelled gold, set with rubies, pearls and diamonds, known as the Canning jewel. Italian, late sixteenth century. (In the Victoria and Albert Museum.)*

Above: *the Armada jewel, about 1588. Though the miniature of the Queen is uninspired, the piece exhibits excellent enamelling.*

Left: *Ship pendant of gold and enamel, hung with pearls. Venetian, late sixteenth century. (In the Victoria and Albert Museum.)*

A portrait of Anne Boleyn in the National Portrait Gallery shows her wearing a gold brooch with three pendant pearls. This arrangement of pearls was one which, as has been seen, was fashionable throughout Italy and was later adopted in England. Some of the designs by Holbein in the British Museum show the same arrangement of pearls, a symmetry which seemed to appeal to Renaissance jewellery designers, perhaps in some sense as a compensation for the lack of symmetry in the stones themselves. Enamel jewellery was popular in Henry's Court and a number of examples showing a delicate use of the *champlevé* variety are still in existence.

Hall's *Chronicles*, describing a festival at the Court, seem to echo Rabelais in the delight at the precious gems which were worn: '. . . every garment full of poysees, made of letters of fine gold in bullion as thicke as they might be, and every person had his name in like letters of massy gold.'

Many other articles, such as the appendages for the girdle, were an important province of the jeweller's art in England, as in Germany. Dr Joan Evans in her book *English Jewellery* remarks of certain of these: 'A fashion which gives the modern world an idea of the somewhat barbaric splendour of this time is that for jewelled tooth and ear picks of gold.' There is a fine example of one of these 'picks' in the Victoria and Albert Museum in the shape of a miniature pistol, the barrel of which releases the various items. (That 'barbaric splendour' is not entirely confined to this period of history is proved by the fact that I have myself within recent years seen examples of jewelled toothpicks made by contemporary British craftsmen. On this occasion, however, they were not designed for use in these islands but for export to South America.)

Pomanders were, in England as elsewhere, a favourite item for the exercise of the jeweller's talent. Inside these delicate cages of gold and gems were held the scents, cloves and ambergris which helped to render contemporary life supportable.

Ear-rings were also a prominent feature of Renaissance jewellery in England. In this country, however, they would appear to have been more favoured by men than by women, for there are several contemporary references which confirm this. Women's hairstyles in England were, in fact, unsuited to the wearing of the pendant ear-rings so popular in Spain. It is recorded in Holinshed's *Chronicles* that 'some lusty courtiers also, and gentlemen of courage, do wear either rings of gold, stones or pearls in their ears, whereby they imagine the workmanship of God to be no little amended'.

By the reign of Queen Elizabeth the full tide of the Renaissance had set in. No longer does one find the exceptional influence of some foreign craftsman predominant for, by now, the English metal-worker had absorbed and taken to himself the current idiom. Elizabeth herself, like Henry VIII, was so devoted to jewellery that it might almost be said that she was obsessed with it. The numerous portraits of her almost all show us a woman who can hardly be seen beneath fountains of gems. Paul Hentzner, a visitor to England in 1598, describes her thus: 'The Queen had in her ears two pearls with very rich drops; she wore false hair and that red; upon her head she had a small crown; her bosom was uncovered, and she had on a necklace of exceeding fine jewels. She was dressed in white silk, bordered with pearls of the size of beans, and over it a mantle of black silk shot with silver threads.' The lavish use of jewels, particularly of pearls, which were stitched into the clothes, resulted in constant losses of these stones.

In an age which loved above all an extravagance of sentiment, the passion for jewellery which infected the English Court is easily understood. Not only were these gems symbolic of the new learning that the country was absorbing, but also of the position which England was winning for herself in the world. Every exploit of men like 'this pirate Drake'—as the Fugger News-Letters term him—brought new wealth into the city of London and into the hands of those private adventurers who financed Drake's adventures. The exploits of these former ancestors were later revered and it is for this reason, perhaps, that we owe the preservation of a number of Elizabethan pieces.

An age so notable for elaboration—as Spenser's *Faerie Queene* and Lyly's *Euphues* bear witness—inevitably displayed the same elaboration in its dress and articles of adornment. Elizabethan jewellery displays an extravagance of gesture which is Italian, and combines with it a technical complexity that owes much to the craftsmen of Nuremberg and Augsburg. The Lennox, or Darnley, jewel, which belongs to the Royal Family, contains no fewer than twenty-eight emblems worked into its design and, in addition, six mottoes. It is an achievement of which even Lyly would have been proud.

Prominent among the motifs popular with Elizabethan jewellers was, as might be expected, the ship. At a time when every month brought in further news of England's mastery of the seas the ship became more than an attractive device; it became almost a national emblem. As might also be expected, after the defeat of the Spanish Armada, the output of these ship emblems in the form of brooches, pendants and *enseignes* was almost as great as was that of portraits of that other great Queen, Victoria, during the later years of her reign. The gems used in these and similar pieces were usually table-cut, while in England, as elsewhere, the most common form of diamond cut was the four-sided pyramid shape.

Pearls were the passion of the Elizabethans and few portraits of the Queen exist in which she is not 'star-scattered' with these gems. The vast quantity of pearls which appear to have been used in Elizabethan dress prompt the suspicion that some of these may have been imitation. A method of fabricating imitation pearls had already been discovered on the Continent and, though these imitations would not have passed as the genuine article—and indeed were probably never intended so to do—they may well have been considered adequate for use on dresses. A type of imitation pearl probably akin to these earlier ones was still manufactured in France up to the end of the nineteenth century. The 'pearl' in this case, was formed by a glass bubble into which wax was poured, the resulting smoky colour giving it some similarity to the real pearl.

Rings were worn in considerable numbers, as they were in France. One fashion which appears to have been peculiar to England was the attachment of rings by silken threads to the garment. Bracelets were still rare, for the long-sleeved fashions of the day kept the wrist covered. Exceptions to this are known and in some cases it seems that the sleeves were slashed to allow bracelets to show through. This was a practice also adopted with gloves both in England, Italy and France. Contemporary portraits exist which show the gloves slashed on each finger to allow the glitter of the gem-set rings to be seen.

It is perhaps difficult for us today, at a time when Europe is in danger of declining into something akin to that lethargy from which she was awakened by the Renaissance, to visualize the richness and splendour of the sixteenth-century scene. The stirring of new life, the revived vitality, the sense of wonder at man's potentialities, all these were reflected in the jewellery of the times. We may well feel some sympathy for those Spanish soldiers, of whom it was written by the Fugger correspondent that, during a procession in Lisbon, '[their] mouths watered much for the jewels and they wished for nothing better than that there should some day come an opportunity for plunder'.

CHAPTER THREE

Seventeenth Century
The Age of the Flower and the Diamond

IF the sixteenth century may be described as the 'Age of Mythology and the Baroque Pearl', the century which followed may well be termed the 'Age of the Flower and the Diamond'. The marked feature of seventeenth-century jewellery is its use of floral motifs, while the diamond assumes its place as the first of precious stones.

The main features of the jeweller's craft in Europe during the preceding two centuries were the imaginative freedom imparted by the Renaissance spirit, the use of colourful enamels, and the rediscovery—or revival—of the gem-cutter's art, particularly as this applied to cameos and intaglio work. During these years the lapidary was, in fact, laying the foundations of his craft. But he still had far to go in the matter of revealing the latent beauty of gemstones. It is for this reason that the main emphasis in the earlier work of the jeweller rests on the contrast between enamels and gold. The jewellery of the seventeenth century, however, establishes what has since become the main European tradition—the display of the dazzling line of faceted gemstones.

Principal and most beautiful of these stones is the diamond. Until the fifteenth century the diamond had been reckoned uncuttable and this, while giving the stone an almost mystical value, naturally prevented its general use by the jeweller. Despite the widely accepted story that Louis de Berquem of Bruges discovered the properties of diamond dust, charging a metal wheel, for cutting the diamond, it is more probable that this discovery originated—as did so much of the lapidary's craft—in India. Throughout the fifteenth and sixteenth centuries, as has been seen, the chief forms of diamond cut used in Europe were the pyramid or diamond point and the table cut. The former consisted of the natural faces of the diamond ground regularly and leading, as its name suggests, up into a point. This was the so-called 'writing' diamond. The table cut was an improvement on this, although even here none of the stone's real brilliance was revealed. The regular octahedron of a more or less perfectly shaped diamond (colour was not taken into account) was ground down at one corner until it was approximately half the stone's width, the sides being ground until they were at right angles to one another.

It was in the seventeenth century that the rose cut was discovered. This discovery has been attributed to Cardinal Mazarin (1602–61). A more likely suggestion is that the Cardinal was the first European known to possess diamonds cut to this shape. Again, it is probable that the rose cut originated in India and that diamonds cut in this manner, were imported into Europe by traders. Whatever its origin, the rose cut transformed the jeweller's craft in Europe. From now on the diamond became the queen of gemstones, a position which it has retained up to the present day.

The most usual and symmetrical rose form contains twenty-four triangular facets and a flat base. Several variants of the rose are known, most of them having names such as the Antwerp rose, the half Dutch rose, since one of the great lapidary centres was, and still is, in Holland.

The soft and—if such an expression may be used—'dark brilliance' of the rose cut immediately became accepted as the height of fashion. It is, perhaps, suggestive that the rose cut was attributed to Cardinal Mazarin of France, since it was France, rather than Italy, which set the fashions in jewellery throughout this century. As France assumed the position of *arbiter elegantiarum* to Europe, so it is possible to detect a distinctly feminine elegance and grace in the jewellery of the period. While the more robust and florid element which exists in Renaissance work may, perhaps, be largely attributed to Italian influence, so equally to France may go the credit for the prevailing styles of the seventeenth century.

The improvements in the lapidary's craft did not end with the discovery of the rose cut. The faceting of all gems became vastly more skilled. From now on the emphasis in jewellery was on the stone rather than on the metal, and from this time also dates the severance of the craft of the jeweller from that of the goldsmith. During the sixteenth century a goldsmith was both jeweller and a worker in silver and gold, as was Cellini. He was expected to be able not only to fashion a ring or pendant for his patron, but also to hammer up a silver ewer or a gold cup. He was also his own designer. Now the gold- and silversmith took over the creation of domestic and ceremonial plate, leaving the jeweller more and more to the task of designing and executing personal ornaments. Even his designs could now be purchased or copied from elsewhere, without any stigma attaching to the craftsman who executed the piece. Here was the birth of the modern conception of the crafts—where the manufacturing jeweller is quite divorced from the silver- and goldsmith. Enamelling, too, became a separate craft, and the lapidary, again working separately, polished and faceted his gemstones, which were then sold to the jeweller who made the mount and set them.

Unfortunately, less precious jewellery in its original form remains from the seventeenth century than from its predecessor. The reason for this is not difficult to discover. The fact that the emphasis of design was now on gemstones meant that, at a later date, these same stones could be removed, reset, and even recut. But enamelled Renaissance pendants and brooches, if broken up, would yield little but their gold and a few stones—and these most probably of second-rate quality and cut *en cabochon*. The temptation, therefore, to break up jewellery of the fifteenth and sixteenth centuries was never so great.

In England, the disturbances of the Civil War inevitably resulted in the destruction of much personal jewellery. How this affected even the great City Companies of London can be gauged from the records of the Worshipful Company of Goldsmiths. In the first quarter of the seventeenth century the Company's collection of plate and jewels was in a most prosperous condition. By the beginning of the eighteenth century, however, it was reduced, relatively, to a few pieces. The toll which was exacted upon the Company's possessions was initiated by a loan levied upon the City of London in 1627 by King Charles I. The loan amounted to £120,000, a very considerable sum in those days. To meet its share of this loan the Company was forced to sell many of its pieces.

This was but the first of many plate sales. In 1641 the King ordered all plate to be sent to the Mint and melted down, while in the years between 1640 and 1643 the Company was forced to find £14,000 for the King and the Parliament party. If such was the position of a large and important City company, it can well be imagined what toll was exacted upon the personal possessions of the King's supporters. It must further be remembered that many of these supporters were of the rich nobility, the class upon whom the jeweller has traditionally depended and the class most likely to possess many items of jewellery.

Despite the relative scarcity of seventeenth-century English work there remains one notable collection—the so-called Cheapside Hoard, now in the possession of the British and London Museums. This collection, which represents most probably the stock-in-trade of an ordinary, working jeweller of the period, was discovered in 1912 when a house in the City of London was demolished. None of the pieces is of a very extravagant or costly nature, and it is because they are ordinary, 'everyday' articles that they are so important in showing the main trends of design and craftsmanship.

The collection consists largely of bracelets, necklaces and ear-clips. All of these pieces possess one attribute in common—they are fashioned in a light, elegant style, a style quite remote from the heavy, baroque richness of the Renaissance period. Gemstones used include amethysts and emeralds; most of the stones are faceted, being either table- or rose-cut. Some of them are of the 'flat' rose cut and the half Dutch rose, while the briolette, a modified double rose of pear shape, is also found. Where enamel is used—as, to take one instance, in an amethyst-set bracelet—it is employed sparingly, thus allowing the faceted stones to predominate. Particularly attractive are drop ear-rings, the 'drop' of which consists of carved gemstones, amethysts and emeralds, the carving representing bunches of grapes. These are reminiscent of the earlier Italian use of seed-pearls, but they have a delicacy and grace which is quite individual and strikes a new note in jewellery.

The motifs which predominate are floral. Gone are the masks and *amorini*, the rich swags of fruit and sea monsters. Tudor roses and other flowers are delicately executed in enamel, the prevailing colour of which is white. A favourite jeweller's device, and one which remained popular for many centuries, is the chain bracelet or necklace, in which the flower-heads, forming the chain, are set at the heart with gemstones. Bow and scroll motifs are repeated widely throughout the designs, a style which remained fashionable until its peak was reached in the eighteenth-century diamond bracelet, composed of openwork bows.

Apart from the technical improvements in the lapidary's craft which played so great a part in determining the form the new jewellery was to take, the change of fashion in clothes affected the jeweller's designs. As the opulence of Elizabethan dress, with its jewels sewn to the robes themselves, yielded place to a fashion for damask, silks and lace, so the jewels were altered to accord with the lighter stuffs and the more delicate styles.

A book of designs by Arnold Lulls, a Dutch jeweller at the Court of King James I, is preserved in the Victoria and Albert Museum. These show the change in style from what may be called 'typically Renaissance' to the lighter, more airy mood of the middle and late seventeenth century. Comparing them with the designs left by Holbein, it is possible to find a number of points in common. The three drop pearls, hanging below a brooch or pendant, are still there, while the general conception remains somewhat similar. It is in the details, however, that the difference really lies, for Lulls's designs show a more delicate quality with a far greater emphasis on the stones than on the goldwork. Several show a single stone dominating the design. This, in itself, is a relic of earlier work, for the seventeenth century tended to use more and more groups or lines of faceted gems. The detail of the drawings, however, reveals that the cabochon cut has largely disappeared and the gems are drawn as faceted or table-cut.

King James I had a great love of jewellery and his influence naturally set the fashion for a wide use of personal adornment in the Court circle. One of the most outstanding pieces which is directly associated with the King is the famous Lyte jewel, now in the British Museum. This is an oval pendant made in gold and finely enamelled. The pendant is set with twenty-five table-cut and four rose-cut diamonds and contains a portrait of James I that has been attributed to Nicholas Hilliard. In its delicacy of execution, its lavish use of the diamond and its delicate enamelling it is a wonderful example of the work of the period, showing, as it does, the contemporary use of the diamond and delicate enamel and metalwork. The cover is in exquisite openwork. The jewel was given by James I to Thomas Lyte of Somerset (d. 1638).

Another pendant containing a portrait of James I, also in the British Museum, is of interest for its unusual enamel technique. The surface is rendered in translucent enamel on to which the parts of the design are engraved, the spaces between being filled with gold or silver foils. These foils have been impressed with yet further designs and the whole covered with another layer of translucent enamel.

Advances in the technique of enamelling were among the many achievements of jewellers in this century. *Champlevé* enamelling, two distinct methods of which appear to have been used, was the most popular. One of these is reminiscent of *niello* work in that the metal surface is first incised or engraved and the enamel then applied. Finally the whole surface is scraped and polished so that only the engraved design remains, containing the enamel within its fine lines. The application of this method to pendant-backs and watch-cases produces a delicate and charming effect. The second *champlevé* variant is somewhat similar to *cloisonné*. The metal is cut away in such a manner that the design itself is formed by the thin, upstanding lines where the metal is left. Into these cells the enamel is then poured. The difference between this technique and true *cloisonné* is that, in the latter, the cells containing the enamel are formed of applied metal strips. Although these styles are found in some pieces which *may* be of English origin, they would appear to have originated, or been most widely used, on the Continent, and particularly in France.

Another enamel technique which is first found in this century is known as *émail en resille sur verre*. Here, a surface of glass is used as the base. Into this cells are cut in much the same manner as described above. These cells are then lined with foil, after which they are filled with enamel, designed to fuse at a lower temperature than the original glass base.

Italian corsage ornament in coloured enamels, set with sapphires, emeralds, rubies, diamonds and pearls; c. 1650.

The two sides of a seventeenth-century English crucifix pendant in enamelled gold, set with seed pearls on one side, garnets on the other.

Opposite: *seventeenth-century Spanish jewellery.* Top: *reliquary of rock crystal and enamelled gold set with precious stones.* Far left: *enamelled gold cross with table-cut topazes.* Centre: *Virgin of the Pillar in enamelled gold.* Right: *reliquary cross in enamelled gold and diamonds.*
Below: *Virgin of the Immaculate Conception in enamelled gold set with emeralds and a foiled paste.* (In the Victoria and Albert Museum.)

Bodice brooch in gold set with table-cut emeralds and diamonds. Spanish, mid-seventeenth century. (In the Victoria and Albert Museum.)

Bodice brooch in enamelled gold set with table-cut diamonds. Spanish, mid-seventeenth century. (In the Victoria and Albert Museum.)

The enameller of the period who is best known to us was Jean Toutin of Châteaudun, some of whose designs were published *circa* 1619. They are chiefly for lockets or watch-cases, and show the characteristic delicacy of the period. Notable for their use of scroll and leaf patterns and arabesques, they are intended for execution on a black ground, the sections forming the design itself being enamelled in white. This somewhat austere elegance is typical of much seventeenth-century work and forms a marked contrast to the earlier, more opulent styles.

Also ascribed to Jean Toutin is another enamelling technique which became extremely fashionable. The metal surface is first covered with an opaque, monochrome background—much as a painter may tone down his canvas with a low-tone monochrome wash. On top of this background the design itself is painted in opaque colours, fusible at a lower temperature than the background. This is, incidentally, much akin to the method that is still used today for articles such as enamelled brush sets.

Among the individual items of jewellery which enjoyed a great popularity was the *aigrette*. This was a plume or feather, fashioned usually in silver, although examples in gold are known. The simple, decorative shape—sometimes given an added delicacy by the use of saw-piercing to outline and differentiate the edges—provided an admirable opportunity for the jeweller to achieve the maximum effect with his cut diamonds. These were usually held in carved settings, the silver or gold being 'carved' away to make a receptacle for the stone, the edges of the metal then being burred over to grip it in place.

Another article of jewellery which assumed greater importance was the chatelaine. More lavish than before and comprising a greater variety of objects, the chatelaine was made in both gold and silver. From it were suspended scissors, thimbles and their cases, household notebooks in metal cases, books of devotion, watches, and so on. It was to the housewife of the day what the handbag is to her successor.

The watch-case provided an important subject for the exercise of the jeweller's talents. As the watch became more and more a feature of everyday life, and as the improvements effected by horologists enabled its size to be reduced, so the case itself was considered suitable for ornamentation. A number of gem-set and enamelled cases dating from the seventeenth century are still in existence, although their intrinsic and historical value puts them beyond the reach of most collectors.

The jeweller must undoubtedly have worked in close collaboration with his fellow-craftsman, the watchmaker. In the early days it is just possible that they were sometimes one and the same person. As the century advanced, however, the two crafts became completely separate. But the link between them still remained, and during the eighteenth century—that age of great clock- and watchmakers—a steady part of the enamellers' and jewellers' income came from decorative work on watch-cases.

Cameos, intaglios and seals remained an important part of the jeweller's work. Although it cannot be said that any great advances upon the standard of excellence established by the previous century were made, the quality of the work was uniformly high.

Of the gemstones favoured during the age, the diamond, of course, comes first. Amethysts and emeralds were also widely used, and, among less precious gemstones, the garnet enjoyed much favour. Pearls were less lavishly used than before, as attention was given chiefly to the newly discovered possibilities of faceted gemstones. However, that favourite device of the Renaissance—the three pendant pearls—remained in fashion for brooches and pendants. One notable feature of the seventeenth century was the popularity of jewellery incorporating symbols of mortality. The Dance of Death, which had captivated Germany in the previous century and which, in a more literal and terrifying sense, was indeed reducing her to ruin during the Thirty Years War, invaded the jewellers' workshops of Europe and England. A notable example of this class of work is the seventeenth-century Tor Abbey jewel now in the Victoria and Albert Museum. This consists of a coffin pendant, made of gold and enamelled. In this rests a very perfectly modelled human skeleton. An inscription reads: 'Through the resurrection of Christe we be all sanctified'.

Many other similar pieces exist, the best known of which are the mourning rings that recorded the death of a wife or husband. Inscriptions on these include phrases such as *'Memento Mori'* and 'As I am so must you be'. These rings are often found with the bezel in the shape of a skull, or with skulls 'in the round' or enamelled on the shoulders of the ring. The refrain of the Roman legionaries, *'hodie mihi, cras tibi'*, was another popular inscription. A further stimulus to the production of rings and brooches of this type was furnished by the execution of Charles I. Many memorial jewels were made which, apart from commemorating the King's martyrdom, reminded the owner of his own mortality.

The rings of this century show other departures in style from those of earlier periods. *Niello* work was still largely used to enrich the shoulders, but enamelling, not only on the shoulders but on the whole haft, was very popular. Flowers painted on a white enamel surface enrich many examples. Inscriptions and mottoes, such as reminders of constancy, were engraved on the inside of the haft. A further elaboration of the floral theme was the *giardinetti* ring, the bezel of which formed a floral nosegay set with stones. This style has continued in popularity up to the present day.

In England the century was notable for the great influence exerted by foreign workmen upon the crafts of the goldsmith and jeweller. Charles I, that great Royal connoisseur and patron of the arts, employed many foreign artists and craftsmen at his Court. He also established the connection between England and Holland which Charles II was quick to revive after the Restoration. This influx of foreign craftsmen was beneficial in many ways and helped to lay the foundation upon which the superb English craftsmanship of the eighteenth century was based. That jewellers were men of standing and importance during this century is readily shown. George Heriot of Edinburgh, who was appointed jeweller to James I, was a man of great position and wealth. So too was that 'Prince of Jewellers', Sir Robert Vyner. During the latter part of the century an outstanding figure was Sir Francis Child, who was appointed jeweller to William III and was one of the founders of a great banking house.

The Arbiter of Elegance, however, was France, and it was in France that much of the inspiration and most of the new trends in design originated, as Germany, ravaged by the Thirty Years War, lost her predominance in the crafts of metalwork and jewellery. The main heart-beats of trade were no longer felt in Augsburg and Nuremberg. The greatest days of the House of Fugger were over. It was to Paris and to the French Court that men chiefly looked for guidance as to what was elegant and fashionable.

In addition to Jean Toutin, a number of French jewellers of first rank have left us designs by which to judge their styles and the degree of their influence. Daniel Mignot, who was working during the early years of the century, was one of the first to stress the display of cut gemstones rather than that of goldwork. Strapwork and cartouches play a large part in his designs. Similar use of strapwork is also found in English jewellery at a slightly later date, while the cartouche remains a favourite device throughout the century.

Another innovation, almost certainly French, was the 'peapod' style, the *genre casse de pois*. This is most clearly seen in *aigrettes*, although it is also used in forming the surrounds to lockets, pendants and miniatures. Curved strips of metal, often resembling not so much a peapod as a curved leaf, are set with stones. They are also used, particularly in lockets and miniatures, to frame the individual gemstones, thus calling attention to the stone's beauty and faceting.

Other French jewellers of note are Gedeon Légaré (1615–76), Giles Légaré, who was Court jeweller to Louis XIV, and Balthazar Moncornet. The two latter are known to us by publications of designs, *Livres des ouvrages d'orfèvrerie*, which summarize many of the trends of fashion. Floral motifs, lovers' knots and bows, symbols of mortality and careful display of rose-cut diamonds are predominant. Interlaced strapwork and Moresque patterns characterize much of this French work, and these motifs were later found in similar articles by English jewellers.

Throughout the century the flower, however, is the principal motif in jewellery. Its decorative possibilities once so well established, the flower remained a permanent favourite of the European jeweller. The Renaissance interest in natural forms undoubtedly contributed largely towards the new naturalism which is found in the jeweller's treatment of flowers, fruits and grasses. (Leonardo da Vinci's notebooks and Dürer's drawings reveal with what meticulous thoroughness these great masters recorded the everyday flowers of their countries.) A further incitement to the use of floral themes was the passion for tulips which arose in Holland shortly before the middle of the century and which has been well named 'Tulipomania'. It was natural therefore that the small mirror which the jeweller holds up to the world of his day should have reflected this enthusiasm. Tulips abound in Continental work, while another flower which received much attention was the tiger-lily. The influence of the Dutch painters is undoubtedly to be felt in much of the realistic interpretation of flowers in jewellery. Those perfect and naturalistic set-pieces, in which Jan Brueghel excelled, immediately come to mind.

Two other fashions, both of which were Continental in origin, were the *Sévigné* and the pendant suspended round the neck on a velvet bow. The latter fashion persisted throughout the eighteenth century, was revived in the Victorian era and again in our own times. The *Sévigné*, which owes its name to the famous French letter-writer, was a bodice ornament that resembled the Spanish type described in the previous chapter. The design was usually a bow or fan shape of gold or silver openwork. This allowed for a lavish display of diamonds.

The closing years of the seventeenth century were notable for the discovery, by a Venetian lapidary, Vincenti Peruzzi, of the brilliant form of diamond cutting. As the new century dawned the bright, unique fire of this stone burst forth for the first time in history. It was appropriate that the age which had witnessed the diamond's ascendancy in jewellery should close on this true note of 'brilliance'.

CHAPTER FOUR

Eighteenth Century
The Age of the Faceted Stone

In the seventeenth century the diamond was established as the premier stone in European jewellery, but it was the eighteenth century which finally confirmed it in this position. The advent of the brilliant cut for diamonds elevated the stone to a degree of popularity that no single gemstone had ever held before. Throughout the eighteenth century we find that the cut or faceted stone plays more and more of a part in jewellery design, while that aspect of the craft which may be called goldsmith-jeweller's work declines.

References to diamonds and to their importance in the fashionable world abound. Few books or collections of essays or letters do not mention them in one respect or another—and always with the assumption that the reader will be familiar both with their value and their importance. Dean Swift's *Polite Conversations* (written in 1731) contains the following passage:

Neverout. Miss, I want that diamond ring of yours.
Miss. Why then, want's like to be your master.
            Neverout looking at the ring.
Neverout. Ay, marry, this is not only, but also: where did you get it?
Miss. Why, where 'twas to be had; where the devil got the friar.
Neverout. Well; if I had such a fine diamond ring, I wouldn't stay a day in England: but you know, far fetched and dear bought is fit for ladies. I warrant, this cost your father two-pence halfpenny.

There is certainly something reminiscent of our present times in the remark of *Neverout*: '... if I had such a fine diamond ring, I wouldn't stay a day in England.' Then, as now, diamonds were an international currency.

The eighteenth century, from the point of view of the jeweller, was the age of the faceted stone. While it is true that the previous century had concentrated upon this aspect of jewellery, many of its major triumphs had been achieved in the sphere of enamelwork. In this century, however, the importance of the lapidary was more firmly established than before—so much so that, towards the closing years of the century, most jewellery became little more than a display of gemstones, the craft of the enameller and goldsmith being relegated to a very minor position.

Whereas, during the seventeenth century, most of the jewellery in which enamel played any part was enamelled both on the back and front, it is a sign of eighteenth-century work that, even if the front is so enamelled, the back is usually left plain. Where a brooch or pendant was constructed in gold, the back was often engraved, but was rarely enamelled. Even in many pieces of quality, where the gem-setting and design are unexceptionable, the gold back may not only *not* be enamelled but may also be left quite plain. Eighteenth-century jewellers saw little point in decorating that area of an article which would not be immediately visible. The semi-mystical quality which had previously been attributed to gemstones and jewellery was superseded by the modern conception of utility.

The classical revival played a great part in determining the designs of the jeweller as it did that of his fellow-workers in the other domestic arts and crafts.

A book of designs published in London in 1710 by J. B. Herbst exemplifies the work of the first quarter of the century. In these designs are revealed most of the major trends in fashion—the accent on faceted gemstones, the use of engraved goldwork and the influence of France. Despite the fact that the eighteenth century is generally regarded as being the age in which Great Britain evolved for herself a unique and personal style—whether in furniture, architecture, pottery, clocks and watches or goldsmiths' and jewellers' wares—it remains true, at least as far as jewellery is concerned, that French influence was predominant during the first twenty-five years.

The rococo style in silverware, which reached England from France, and which reached its peak of excellence in the masterpieces of Paul de Lamerie, is also found in the jewellery of the period. This *rocaille* style, as it is known, was similar to that prevailing in other branches of metalwork in that it placed great emphasis on the asymmetrical arrangement of forms. In the sixteenth century, for example, despite the use of the baroque pearl, the jeweller's designs were usually symmetrical—as was that most common feature, the arrangement of three pendant pearls, one large pearl placed centrally with two graded pearls on either side. But the *rocaille* style, in much the same manner as rococo architecture, deliberately procured an asymmetrical effect. Like all such forms of art, it must be considered a decadent one since its appeal resided not in the perfection of balanced form and design, but mainly in the artificial stimulus of novelty.

The 'Chinoiserie' style, which plays so large a part in the furniture, ceramics and silverware of the period, is little found in jewellery. This is not to say that it never existed, but the lack of surviving pieces tends to suggest that, if it did exist, it was uncommon. The 'Chinoiserie' style of decoration is, in fact, more suitable to the other branches of the crafts since it is predominantly a form in which the area of engraved or decorated surface must be fairly large. The small size of a piece of jewellery offered little scope to the engraver, while typical Oriental pictorial designs could not be employed with any success on small articles of metalwork.

Despite the fact that the achievements of British craftsmen during the eighteenth century tend to give the impression that it was a period during which the country evolved its own strong and masculine style—a style which one is tempted to think is entirely of native origin—it is true to say that throughout this century British jewellery remained largely influenced by foreign fashions. The distinction, however, between this century and others was that the increased power and prosperity of the country induced many foreign craftsmen to migrate to Britain, a country which they respected and to which they paid tribute by conforming or by moderating their ideas so as to meet the overwhelming influence of British classicism. There was thus born a school of craftsmanship which had its roots in the Continent, but which possessed a certain almost austere elegance, remote from the extravagances of the Continental rococo. Even in the silverware of a craftsman such as Paul de Lamerie—silverware which must certainly be reckoned among the most extravagant of any ever fashioned in Britain—there is some restraint and discipline imposed upon the riotous detail. It is a discipline which is not found in contemporary examples of Continental rococo.

The number of foreign craftsmen and artisans working in London during this century was often a cause of bad feeling among their English fellow-workers. The bulk of these foreign immigrants consisted of Jews, Germans, Frenchmen and Dutchmen. Writing in 1777, Lacombe, in his *Tableau de Londres*, makes the following observation: '*Depuis douze années la quantité d'ouvriers étrangers établis à Londres a produit une efflorescence utile au commerce, malgré le peu d'encouragement qu'ils reçoivent de la nation et des riches entrepreneurs, mais la misère et la despotisme Allemand et Français peuplera toujours cette Babilone, le seul refuge des infortunés.*'

This injection of foreign blood and of Latin taste and vitality undoubtedly contributed in no small measure to the excellence of the jewellery produced in the London workshops.

An outstanding feature of the eighteenth century was the emergence of a definitely popular type of jewellery, a cheap and non-precious style somewhat akin to the costume jewellery of our own century. Social changes, such as the growth of a prosperous bourgeoisie, led to a widespread demand for jewellery which imitated the precious article worn by the rich and the aristocracy. Glass pastes, marcasite, cut steel and various types of imitation goldware were the principal forms which emerged to satisfy these new customers.

Alloys of copper and zinc, such as that evolved by the watchmaker, Christopher Pinchbeck, were widely used to counterfeit gold jewellery. Many of the articles fashioned in these alloys are worthy of being considered true items of jewellery, since their design and the degree of craftsmanship involved in their production was not less than that employed in pieces made of gold and set with precious stones. Christopher Pinchbeck's discovery led to a widespread demand for work of this nature. Other jewellers, notably on the Continent, evolved their own formulae for pseudo-gold wares, but the fact that several French references to such work describe them as 'Pinsebeck' or 'Pinchbeck' would seem to suggest that the English watchmaker was recognized as the inventor. Many lesser articles of jewellery were fashioned in pinchbeck, among them chatelaines, buckles and other types of *minuterie*.

Cut steel, paste and marcasite are dealt with at greater length elsewhere in this volume, but their place in the history of eighteenth-century jewellery must be recorded, since so many pieces of both French and English work still survive. The best paste was set in exactly the same manner as diamonds. All the prevailing styles of diamond jewellery were copied, and the types of prevailing setting, such as claw and *pavé*, were also used. The English pre-eminence in the manufacture of flint glass gave the paste-makers of this country an advantage over their Continental rivals, although then, as now, some of the finest paste came from France and Italy. Very fashionable were the opal pastes which were used in bracelets and necklaces.

The manufacture of paste in Britain was on a large scale, much of the best work being done in the Derby area. Uttoxeter was one of the centres of the paste-makers and much opal paste was made in this area. Most of the paste-makers were not themselves concerned with the final article of jewellery. The products of their craftsmanship were dispatched to London and Birmingham, where the manufacturing jewellers set the pastes into their silver, gold or pinchbeck settings.

The growth of Birmingham as a great manufacturing city occupied with the trades of metalwork and jewellery was another feature of the age. As early as 1726 Birmingham's potentialities had led to the appointment of a Parliamentary committee to enquire into the condition of the road communications to the city. Since

Birmingham was at this time still dependent upon London merchants for its orders and for the export of its manufactured goods, the question of transportation between the two centres of industry and commerce became a matter of the greatest moment.

Among the men who played a prominent part in the establishment of the Birmingham jewellery trade was Matthew Boulton, who helped to form the Birmingham Metal Company, upon which the city's later prosperity was largely based. Boulton's factories produced, among other wares, a great quantity of cut-steel jewellery which was very fashionable during the later years of the century, particularly for items such as shoe-buckles and buttons. Belt-buckles and chatelaines were also manufactured in cut steel. On April 11, 1771, the articles of the Birmingham Metal Company were signed. In these it was declared that the shareholders should be 'Joint traders in the Trade, Art and Mystery of making and selling Brass, spelter and other metals'. So great was the consumption of these metals that by 1790 Birmingham was taking more than one-third of the total output of the Cornish mines. Thus was established Birmingham's connection with the manufacture of popular and inexpensive jewellery—a connection which has led to the city being recognized today as the headquarters of the silver and metalwork industries.

Cheap articles of jewellery were in demand not only because of the increasing prosperity of the English middle classes; their production was also stimulated by the unsafe conditions of the roads, which made travellers wary of taking their valuables with them on expeditions of any length. The prevalence of bandits, cutpurses and highwaymen—who abounded on British roads—made a journey between the towns and the outlying country a somewhat hazardous affair. The diamond necklaces and bracelets were accordingly exchanged for necklaces of marcasite, diamond paste or coloured paste, and the traveller had the satisfaction of knowing that, if she were robbed, the loss would be comparatively small. Diamond pendant ear-rings were copied exactly in silver and diamond paste, shoe-buckles and other articles, which in London might be diamond set, were similarly imitated in paste or marcasite. Chatelaines of enamelled gold were copied in the formula of the 'ingenious Mr Pinchbeck'. By means such as these the traveller insured himself against loss.

Men's dress fashions also gave the jeweller scope for the application of his art. Much use was made of imitation materials. A shoe-buckle set with diamonds was something which few could afford, while a similar buckle set with good paste would serve the purposes equally well. Most of these buckles were made of silver, although cheaper types made of steel, with cut-steel facets, came in during the last quarter of the century. Buttons were equally decorative and were made in a wide range of materials from silver, gold and pinchbeck to Wedgwood cameos and Sheffield plate.

Fobs were elaborate, and the fashion for suspended charms and seals assisted in that revival of the gem-cutter's art which is a distinguishing feature of the second half of the century in England. Again, as in the days of the Renaissance, it was the importance attached to classical learning—together with the stimulus of the discovery of Herculaneum and Pompeii—which gave rise to the demand for intaglio seals. Some of the eighteenth-century gem-cutters' work is extremely fine and delicate, but it can rarely be confused with the true classical or even with the Renaissance classical revival. As always, the conception of what was classical in spirit was a conception peculiar to the century itself, and the intaglio cut 'after the antique' usually betrays its origin.

The mention of Sheffield plate in connection with the manufacture of buttons leads to a consideration of the part played by this discovery in the history of jewellery. Although the term 'Sheffield plate' is chiefly associated with the larger articles of plated ware, the process was used first of all by its inventor, Thomas Bolsover, for the manufacture of small articles such as buttons and snuff-boxes. (Sheffield plate must not be confused with the modern products of the city which are electroplated. True Sheffield plate is made by covering copper with silver by a process of fusion.)

Thomas Bolsover was originally a maker of knives and scissors; his great discovery was, like so many others, the result of an accident. Engaged in undertaking repairs to a knife, Bolsover discovered that the application of heat had caused the silver and the copper, to which it adhered, to become fused. Further experiment led him to the discovery that if the two metals, combined, were pressed through rollers, the copper and silver still retained their relative proportions. Thus was born the great Sheffield plate industry of which the major productions were articles of flat-ware and hollow-ware, but among which must also be reckoned many of the items of everyday jewellery, trinkets and accessories. As early as 1760 Horace Walpole observed: 'I have passed through Sheffield . . . one of the foulest towns in England in the most charming situation, where there are 22,000 inhabitants making knives and scissors. One man there has discovered the art of plating copper with silver. I bought a pair of candlesticks for two guineas that are quite pretty.'

In addition to buttons and buckles, Sheffield-plate mounts for cameos and similar articles are quite common. A number of Wedgwood cameos were mounted in this way. In his Birmingham factory Matthew Boulton specialized in articles of plated ware, among them being mounts for jewellery, chatelaines and their equipment. The numerous accoutrements belonging to the lavish chatelaines of the period included scissors, thimbles and their cases, notebook covers and key-holders. Some of the Sheffield-plated scissors are charming articles, embodying very often the vine and cluster motifs which are found on the larger plated articles.

Among those subsidiary articles of jewellery, which are exclusively an English contribution to the century, must be counted the products of the enamelling factories of Battersea and Bilston. These 'toys', which might be anything from scent-bottles to chatelaines and snuff-boxes, were being manufactured at Bilston in Staffordshire from the middle of the century onwards. Similarly at Battersea, from 1753 'toys and trinkets' were being produced under the guidance of a city merchant, Theodore Janssen. Laid on a copper base, the enamels of Battersea are notable for their warm, soft colours. Although the description 'Battersea enamels' is commonly associated with the small items of boxware which bear the name, the range of articles produced by the Battersea factory during its short life was very great, as is shown by the following excerpt from a sale advertisement in a copy of the *Morning Advertiser* of 1756: '. . . a quantity of beautiful enamels, colour'd and uncolour'd of the new manufactury carried on at York House at Battersea, and never yet exhibited to public view, consisting of Snuff-boxes of all sizes, of a great variety of patterns; of square and oval pictures of the Royal Family, History and other pleasing subjects; very popular ornaments for the Cabinets of the Curious; Bottle Tickets with Chains for all sorts of Liquors and of different subjects; Watch-cases, Tooth-pick cases, Coat and Sleeve buttons, Crosses and other curiosities, mostly mounted in metal, double gilt.'

Enamelwork of a very delicate nature was a feature of much Continental jewellery during the first half of the century. The Parisian enamellers, particularly, excelled in this branch of the jeweller's craft, and a number of pieces dating from this period are still in existence. Enamelling was applied to the shoulders and the hafts of rings. Inscriptions were popular and phrases such as '*Gage de mon amitié*' are quite often found on items such as miniature pomanders, as well as on finger-rings. These small pomanders, which supplanted the larger types formerly in use and which were held in the hand, were often no larger than one to two inches in depth and could be worn suspended on a chain round the neck in the manner of a locket. Alternatively they were attached to the chatelaine. Although this fashion would appear to have been French in origin, it was adopted in Britain and a number of these small scent-bottles or pomanders can still be acquired. Some of the English specimens were made at Battersea and Bilston. Many of the French pieces were constructed in onyx or quartz, the hinge and other applied sections of the decoration being fashioned in gold or a gold substitute.

Prominent among the English enamellers, specimens of whose work are still known to us, was the Swiss, George Michael Moser, who was one of the founder-members of the Royal Academy and who distinguished himself by his enamelled figure work executed after the classical tradition of the day. Among the important jewellers of the first quarter of the century was the Parisian, Jean Bourguet, who was working between 1700 and 1723. A book of designs from his hand, the *Livre de Taille d'Epargne*, is extant and contains within its pages an apt summary, as it were, of the principal motifs and trends of design fashionable at the time.

Items of precious jewellery which belong particularly to the eighteenth century are the *aigrette*, the *girandole* ear-ring and the *parure*. The *aigrette* was a hair ornament which, in its most extravagant form, was entirely diamond-set. It thus enabled the lapidary to demonstrate his mastery over the cutting of the faceted stone, the rose-cut or the brilliant-cut diamond. When set with diamonds, the *aigrette* is invariably mounted in silver, since this intensified the stone's brilliance. *Aigrettes* are usually designed somewhat after the 'ear of wheat' motif, having a number of upstanding stalks of silver in which the stones are set. These stalks are banded at the centre, or just below it, by another silver and diamond mount containing the slide or pin for fastening the *aigrette* to the hair. In many examples these fine stalks are mounted so that they vibrate at the slightest touch. The resilience and flexibility of silver make it the perfect metal for this purpose, the effect of which, as can be imagined, is delightful, as the trembling settings cause the diamonds to flash and scintillate. These vibrating settings were very popular during the eighteenth century. They are found not only in *aigrettes* but also in brooches. Two fashionable motifs were birds and butterflies. These again were usually diamond-set and were mounted on small spirals of silver wire. The slightest touch set them in motion.

The *girandole* ear-ring was an elaboration of the simple pendant ear-ring. The *girandole* form has a large stone (usually circular) set at the top where the ear-ring is attached to the ear lobe. Below it are suspended three pear-shaped pendant stones. Again, the *girandole* was designed principally for the display of diamonds, although *girandoles* are also found set with lesser gemstones such as amethysts. A popular variant of the *girandole* was the pendant ear-ring with one large brilliant at the top from which was suspended a silver, oval-shaped hoop, also diamond-set. In the centre of this hoop was a second large diamond which could swing backwards and forwards independently of the rest of the ear-ring.

The *parure*, the suite of matching jewellery, was popular in France, where an almost vulgar display of cut gemstones was fashionable. The *parure* might contain a necklace, bracelet and ear-rings to match, or might also have a matching *aigrette* and *Sévigné*. More than a hint of *nouveau riche* ostentation is to be observed in the contemporary descriptions and the extant designs of much of the jewellery worn in France. The story of Marie Antoinette's famous extravagance, a gem-set necklace worth £90,000, is well known. The necklace would appear to have been little loss to artistic history in the sense that so vast a display of faceted stones could only be inartistic and ostentatious. Delicacy and refinement are the hallmarks of good jewellery, and these are qualities which can be found just as easily in an inexpensive article as in a sumptuous one.

The *Sévigné* bow brooches, mentioned in the previous chapter, continued in favour throughout the century. As the century advanced, however, they tended to be supplanted by an elaboration of the *Sévigné*, a type of gem-set stomacher. These were often massive openwork brooches, somewhat similar to the Spanish style. They provided an opportunity for a lavish display of faceted precious and semi-precious stones.

Finger-rings were worn by almost all classes in England and the importance of the ring set with faceted stones is part of the taste of the period. Diamonds and other precious stones were set in silver or gold settings very much like those used today. The *marquise* ring enjoyed a great vogue and a number of these, set either with gemstones and pastes, are still to be had. A *marquise* ring should have an oblong bezel set with one large stone or paste, the surround to this stone being small diamonds or brilliant-cut pastes. The shoulders are often pierced. The setting may be either silver or gold. The *marquise* was in keeping with the display of cut stones in the *parures*. Claw, rub-over and *pavé* settings were commonly used.

During the last quarter of the eighteenth century the vogue for mourning jewellery reached its height. Rings enamelled with the name and date of decease of the husband or wife or child, and lockets and brooches decorated with enamelled funerary scenes, were common. The Grecian female figure bending over an urn or resting one hand upon a tombstone will be familiar to all collectors. So much of this memorial jewellery was produced that it is impossible to catalogue all of it in detail. Much of it is commonplace, but here again, in common with many other styles of popular jewellery, only individual taste and judgment can decide. It is certainly true to say that most of the memorial rings are not only attractive but also good examples of contemporary enamel craftsmanship.

Sometimes of a memorial nature, but more commonly objects presented during betrothal or marriage, are the eighteenth-century lockets containing miniatures. These naturally depend upon the skill of the miniaturist for their attraction and cannot therefore be judged solely in terms of jewellery. The settings are often very delicate borders of small pearls or cut stones. The goldwork of the locket cases is commonly engraved. The miniatures themselves may be painted on ivory or vellum or chicken skin. In common with other types of pendants, these were often suspended round the neck on a velvet band. Bracelets too were often formed of a velvet band on which was pinned an oval locket or other item of jewellery. Miniatures were often worn in this manner, as were enamels.

During the last twenty-five years of the century, particularly in Great Britain, the overwhelming influence of classical art produced a more austere and dignified type of jewellery—often seen at its best in openwork bracelets set with diamonds. Links of silver, set with cut gemstones, were fashioned so that each link repeated the overall design. Bow and scroll motifs were popular for these diamond bracelets. Enamelwork is sometimes found on the clasps, but the enamelled bracelet formed of repeating links—so typical of the seventeenth century—is uncommon.

The enameller's craft was saved from decadence by the wide demand for its application to chatelaines and watch-cases. In London, watchmaking was at the peak of its excellence and prosperity during the century. Quite apart from the home demand for watches, England was also conducting a large-scale export trade not only with the Continent but also with the Near East and countries such as Turkey. The volume of work transacted by the watchmaking industry can be gauged from the fact that Clerkenwell, the home of the trade, possessed 7,000 artisans in 1798. Some of the prosperity enjoyed by the watchmakers was undoubtedly shared by the enamellers, for the demand for enamelled watch-cases was considerable. Similarly, chatelaines were a constant source of income as enamelwork on these articles remained consistently fashionable.

The position of the artisan and craftsman in the London jewellery industry during the century is proof of the importance attached to the products of his craftsmanship. Working on piecework, a jeweller's assistant could earn as much as £3 or £4 a week, a considerable sum at the time. The apprenticeship system was rigorous and did much to ensure that the standards of the craft were not allowed to decline. Some indication of the value attached to the training received by apprentices can be gauged by a record from the Middlesex Sessions of a certain Samuel Wood who was discharged from James Heley, Goldsmith. The record gives as the reason for his free discharge the fact that he 'had not been instructed in the art of a goldsmith or in the business of a buckle maker, which Heley mostly followed, but was wholly employed in drawing potts of drink and carrying the same out to his customers'.

That the general condition of the country was comparatively prosperous is proved by the fact that it was not only the upper classes—or even the bourgeoisie—who patronized the jeweller. Watches and shoe-buckles of silver were not beyond the means of many of the labouring class. *The Working Man's Way in the World*, the autobiography of a journeyman printer published in the nineteenth century, refers to conditions obtaining during the writer's youth and informs us that 'he considers himself fully provided against every emergency by the possession of a capital silver watch upon which he could raise £2 whenever he wanted it'. No doubt to many of the working class the possession of some silver article was equivalent to a bank account. In the same manner today, in many parts of the East, the women of the household wear upon their persons the family's entire fortune in the shape of gold and silver jewellery.

In the closing years of the century the pearl emerged from its semi-obscurity and became foremost in fashion. Imitation pearls, made in France, enjoyed a great vogue among those unable to afford the real article. The manufacture of imitation pearls does not seem to have been practised in Britain at this time.

The influence of classical art which had dominated the century was reinforced by the excavations that were carried out on the site of Pompeii. Imitation mosaic-work and enamelled classical scenes were the forerunners of the new era in jewellery, an era in which a deliberate austerity and a paucity of jewellery-display took the place of the rich elegance that had characterized the best work of the eighteenth century.

CHAPTER FIVE

Nineteenth-century Jewellery

THE term 'nineteenth century' is apt to depress the collector. This is usually true whether it be applied to furniture, porcelain, portrait painting, silver or jewellery. The denigration of the achievements of the nineteenth century is something which has been with us since the decade immediately following the first World War. In recent years, particularly in politics and literature, there has been a reversal of this judgment. The natural tendency of the disillusioned generation who fought in, or grew up during, the first World War was to place all the blame—whether for political or cultural failure—upon their predecessors. In our day this has been superseded largely by a certain nostalgia for the security which our Victorian ancestors enjoyed.

In the three-fold sphere of goldsmith's, silversmith's and jeweller's work it is, perhaps, difficult to find much that is good to say about the first two. The extravagant elaboration of design, coupled with the new-found mechanical processes which enabled the same tea-set to be present in a thousand and one Victorian drawing-rooms, reduced with fatal swiftness the high standards that had been set by the eighteenth century. But in the field of jewellery, although there is much that can easily be disparaged, it would only be blind ignorance or obtuse snobbishness that could condemn out-of-hand the products of the century. There are far too many pieces of real excellence in existence for the wise collector to ignore them.

The amateur of jewellery, particularly if his purse is not large, would be wise, when dealing with nineteenth-century work, to consider two important aspects of jewellery collecting. Firstly, if one may presume that he buys because he likes a piece, i.e. is guided by his aesthetic instincts and not by the attraction of great names, he has every chance not only of exercising his own discrimination but also of 'backing his fancy'. Secondly, if he considers his collection in some sense an investment—and few collectors can afford not to do so—then he is in a position to speculate in a market which has not yet received its due attention and which, providing always that his judgment is sound, is bound to appreciate in value.

The definition of an antique given by the British Antique Dealers' Association is

The star was a very popular eighteenth-century motif. This English star brooch is set with rose-cut and haphazardly faceted diamonds.

Left: *silver and brilliant-cut diamond plume brooch. English or French, eighteenth century.*

Floral designs abounded in eighteenth-century jewellery. This typical spray brooch, dating from the latter half of the century, is of silver set with rose- and brilliant-cut diamonds.

A Queen's jewellery: Caroline of Ansbach (1683–1737); studio of Charles Jervas. (In the National Portrait Gallery, London.)

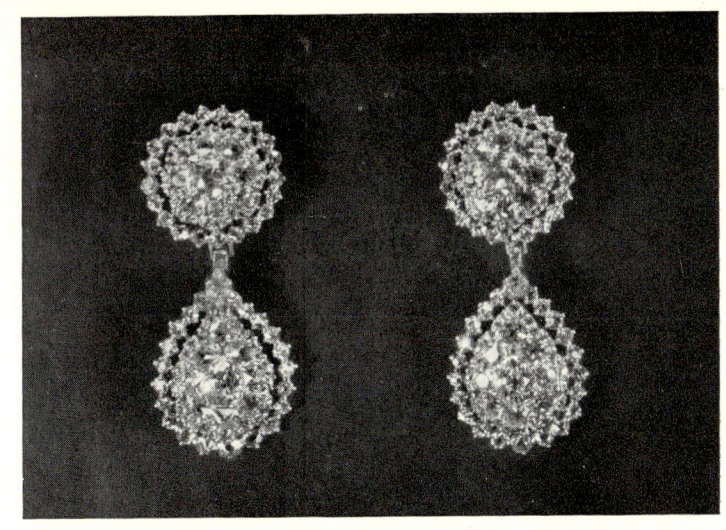

Eighteenth-century jewellery designs were largely dominated by the diamond. Above: a pair of diamond drop ear-rings dated about 1750. Below: 'ear of barley' brooch in gold and brilliant-cut diamonds.

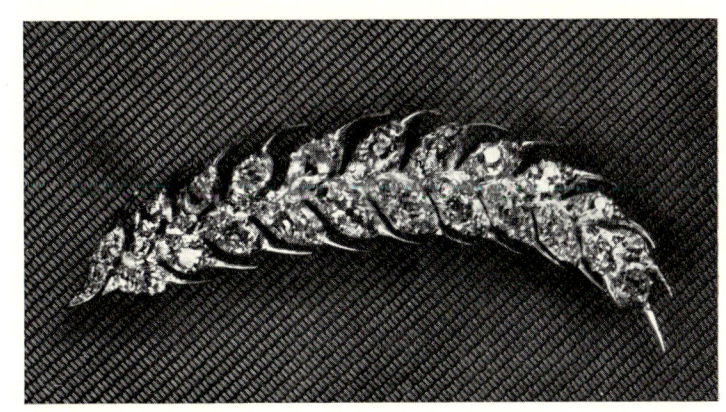

Diamond-cut brooch and rings of the eighteenth century. Top: marquise, or cluster, ring of silver set with diamonds. Centre: diamond brooch in a leaf design typifying the jeweller's use of natural motifs. Below: ring set with diamonds round a large rose-cut diamond. Either English or French.

Late eighteenth-century diamond and emerald suite consisting of daisy-motif necklace and bow ear-rings with pendant flower drops. The bow is typical of pieces made about 1770.

'one hundred years old or more', taking 1830 as the dividing line between modern and antique. This definition was framed some years ago, before the second World War, and is almost certain to be altered, in due course, to take in a further decade or two. Those articles which have, until quite recently, been despised as mid-Victorian will thus enjoy the cachet of being legitimate antiques. Although one may regret the snobbery which sets a high price upon something because it can be termed antique, yet it must be conceded that it exists. If the collector, bearing this in mind, buys jewellery of the Victorian era, he can build up a collection which is most likely to appreciate in value. He can also, by using his own judgment, save from destruction pieces which are worthy of preservation.

The opening years of the nineteenth century—in jewellery as in the other crafts—saw no great change in styles. It is, in fact, only the artificial division of history into periods of centuries that leads one in any way to expect that there should have been. The influence of France remained predominant—despite the Napoleonic wars. One has only to read any of the diaries of the period—or, to take a well-known instance, the letters and essays of Hazlitt—to see how, immediately after the cessation of hostilities, the fashionable world of England flocked to France and particularly, of course, to Paris, in order to put themselves once more *au fait* with the dictates of fashion.

The Directoire style is a term familiar to most people through the furniture made in this period (1795–99). Less well-known is the Directoire style in jewellery, despite the fact that a reasonable amount still survives. Made to accord with the classical simplicity of dress which was then the mode, it is natural that the jewellery is equally simple and, from a craftsman's point of view, somewhat uninteresting. The long, pseudo-Greek dresses—often worn damped to reveal the figure better—did not call for any great elaboration of jewellery. The comparative poverty of the settings was also due to the change in conditions and personal fortunes brought about by the Revolution. While there was still a considerable amount of money in the possession of many of the *citoyennes*, large numbers of the wealthy nobility had fled overseas, taking their possessions with them. Apart from this, it was considered incorrect for the new France to ape the lavish display of wealth associated with the old Court.

Gold substitutes such as pinchbeck were much used for settings. Paste, both plain and coloured, was widely manufactured and employed in every type of article where previously diamonds or precious stones would have been set. The lesser, semi-precious stones, such as moss-agate, enjoyed a vogue quite out of proportion to their intrinsic value. Even colourful pebbles, polished smooth and set *en cabochon*, were accepted as part of the jewellery of the day. As always, the arts of luxury were the first to suffer at the hands of Equality.

There is certainly some connection between the paucity of good jewellery of this period in France and the destruction of the apprenticeship system which took place towards the close of the eighteenth century. The previous system, which was very much like that which existed in England and, indeed, throughout most of Europe, had undoubtedly led to certain abuses. (We are familiar with the 'closed shop' principle in England today.) On the other hand, it had also led to a very high standard of craftsmanship in the jewellery and metalwork trades. Almost overnight this sound basis for excellence was swept away. 'Jobbing' jewellers opened their workshops all over Paris. No longer had they to deal with clients who were cultured and critical but, as always after revolutionary changes, with a new semi-educated class and with the new rich.

Among the products of this decade were many cameo brooches and ear-rings. The standard of the work was not very high and, though some of the cameos are passable imitations of the antique style, they are often carved in coarse or flawed stones.

Although in England conditions were much better for the jeweller than on the Continent, there is not a great deal which can be said to differentiate the work from that of the previous thirty years. The craft did, however, receive an undoubted stimulus from the arrival of numerous French jewellers who set up their workshops in London. The enamelwork on English watch-cases at this time is often very fine. Where these enamels are signed it is not at all unusual to find that a French enameller was responsible for the work. In the sphere of *minuterie* work, such as snuff-boxes, the French jeweller and engraver had the tradition of several centuries behind him and did much to set the very high standard of the smallwork of the period.

The establishment by Napoleon of a full Court contributed largely to a revival of the art of the jeweller in France. Its influence upon English styles was equally marked. The *parure*, which, as has been seen, was a characteristic form of jewellery *en suite* during the eighteenth century, was revived by the Napoleonic Court and, although little of this jewellery has survived, the form it took is well known. The *parure* still consisted of ear-rings, necklace and brooch, sometimes with other buckles or clips to match. It was usually diamond-set. Other stones employed with the diamond were rubies, sapphires and emeralds. Mounted usually in silver, the *parure* tended to be austerely classical in form, the diamonds being either rose- or brilliant-cut or a mixture of the two.

For daytime wear there existed a type of semi-precious *parure* which was set either with lesser-known gemstones or with pastes. Shell cameos inevitably enjoyed a great popularity, since the cameo was the favourite form of jewellery of the Empress Josephine. It is interesting to note that England here repaid some of her debt to France in the matter of jewellery. Wedgwood cameos and plaques after the classical manner had long been familiar favourites in this country; they now enjoyed a similar favour in France whither a great number of them were exported. It is not at all uncommon to find Wedgwood cameos in mounts that are undoubtedly French, and it is reasonable to assume that in most cases they were exported to France unset and then turned over for mounting to the French jeweller. These Wedgwood cameos were largely used for brooches, although they are also found in *parures*.

The goldwork of the Empire was largely influenced by the prevailing classicism. It is not particularly fine in execution, being often rather coarsely modelled and cut. Exceptions can always, of course, be found to every rule; there were, for example, a number of charming pendant ear-rings in gold, after the Roman style.

The excavations at Pompeii profoundly influenced the jeweller's craft at this time. Although the excavations at Herculaneum in the middle of the eighteenth century had aroused great interest throughout Europe and had produced many motifs which were incorporated in the classical revival, it was the discoveries at the site of Pompeii which gave rise to an enormous vogue for 'things antique' in the sphere of jewellery. It was not until 1748 that the first really important work was done on the site of Pompeii, and systematic archaeological excavations were carried on during the last quarter of the eighteenth century. Between 1806 and 1814, however, under the French government, the extent of the ruins and the treasures of the devastated city were really uncovered. The influence of the Pompeiian murals and of the articles discovered in the houses cannot be overestimated in tracing the history of the crafts during the nineteenth century. Almost immediately French jewellers were producing imitation mosaic work—as were, of course, the jewellers of Rome and, finally, those of England. Forms and motifs embodied in the European jewellery of the first twenty-five years of the century include, apart from mosaic work, pseudo-classical cameos with gold, granulated borders, and such individual items as the rams' heads which are found principally in furniture but also as finial pieces on hair-combs, brooches and pins.

The hair-comb was an important piece in the jewellery of the period and was often decorated with Pompeiian motifs. The combs—quite a number still exist and can be found in many French provincial jewellers' shops—are of what is commonly termed the 'Spanish style'. They stand up high from the head in an arc and are usually fashioned with seven teeth for gripping the hair. In addition to mosaic work, pearls, ivory, tortoise-shell and, above all, coral are found as materials used in hair-combs. Although usually of little value in themselves, they make charming adornments if cleaned and repaired.

The Restoration in France did not affect the jeweller's craft to any very marked extent. The return of the exiled aristocracy did not mean that there was a return of sumptuous extravagance in jewellery, since so many of them had either lost, or had their fortunes depleted during the years of exile. The semi-precious jewellery which had come to the fore during the Revolution, and which had remained consistently popular even throughout the Napoleonic régime, was still in great demand. Turquoise and topaz, two of the semi-precious or lesser-known gemstones which had been much used both in France and England during these years, were still as popular as ever, although the amethyst may be considered the stone especially associated with this period. The granulated goldwork is often extremely fine and collectors should look for this, particularly where it is used with topaz and turquoise. Some of the most attractive French Restoration pieces consist of brooches and ear-rings of this nature. A *millegrain* setting with these minute gold beads on a ring or brooch is an attractive feature of this work. The granulation is never as fine as the early Greek and Etruscan, and is not always too well finished. But it has a distinct charm of its own and a delicacy which is not found to the same degree in other jewellery of the century.

Originating in France during the eighteenth century and found also in English jewellery is the ear-of-wheat motif. This, to some extent, took the place of the *genre casse de pois* favoured in the seventeenth and early eighteenth centuries. The ear of wheat, as with the peapod, lent itself admirably to delicate, flowing designs and was used largely for hair ornaments. Fashioned in silver and set with small diamonds, these 'wheat-ear' brooches were worn at the breast, sometimes as small single sprays and sometimes as more elaborate sheaves. The slight, fragile quality of the brooch when made in silver was an ideal setting for diamonds, which were usually brilliant-cut.

Another popular setting of the day was the *pavé* style. This is most suitable for a wide area of stones, which are set close together and fairly low down, being held in place by small, turned-over beads of metal. The effect produced, when the selection of stones has been good, is of a shimmering expanse of stones picked out here and there by small beads of gold or silver.

The Second Empire witnessed a revival of diamond jewellery which brought the stone back to a prominence it had not enjoyed since the previous century. The emphasis was placed almost entirely upon the stone itself, which was set in simple mounts designed in crescent and star shapes. The coronet for evening wear, which had been revived by the Napoleonic Court, was again reintroduced, but this time with a more lavish display of diamonds. There is little originality about this jewellery and little of it has, in fact, survived. The preponderance of diamonds in the settings has inevitably meant that they have been broken up at a later date and reset.

During the reign of Louis Phillippe there was a vogue in France for imitation medieval and Renaissance jewellery. Part of the general trend away from classicism, this had its counterpart in the Gothic revival in England. Little of this jewellery survives, and what there is of it does not make one greatly regret the loss of the rest. In common with the Gothic revival in architecture and furniture, it did not attempt to copy the original very closely but to approximate to the mood. The collector need have little fear of being deceived by any of these 'semi-copies'—for that is all they were. The modern craftsman, with his better knowledge of styles and with his greater reverence for historical accuracy, can produce far finer direct imitations of the antique.

In the imitation of the antique, particularly of Renaissance work, there were two outstanding jewellers, Lucien Falize of Paris and Giulanio in London, who must be exempt from these criticisms. These two, by paying attention to the originals, did evolve some striking examples of imitation work. Falize, in particular, produced some excellent enamelling on gold which is worthy to rank with that of the sixteenth-century craftsmen. He also managed to evolve a much wider palette in enamels than had previously been used.

The achievements of an Italian jeweller, Fortunato Castellani, far outshone, however, those of any other copyist or revivalist of the time. Inspired by the fashionable appeal of granulated work, he set himself to unravel those secrets of the craft which appeared to have died with the Etruscans. It is impossible to say whether he did in fact achieve his results by the same methods, since there is no record of the Etruscan manner of working. It is certainly true, though, to say that Castellani produced in his Roman workshop pieces which are far from unworthy of comparison with the Greek and Etruscan originals. He had two sons who followed him into his business and who also produced a number of fine copies and pieces of pseudo-Greek work. Their technical knowledge appears to have died with them, although a number of Roman jewellers still specialize in this filigree, granulated type of work. The tradition of fine goldwork has, of course, existed in Italy since the Italian Renaissance.

The mid-century was a time when the wealth of Europe was rapidly increasing, particularly in France and England. The background to the rise of our own wealthy middle class we know well. Their story in France has been immortalized in the novels of Balzac. This rise of a comparatively uncultured bourgeoisie, coupled with the repercussions of the Industrial Revolution, naturally meant a lowering of standards of taste. The craftsman was the first to be affected. But, despite this and despite the rise of a new type of popular, manufactured jewellery, there still existed an almost unprecedented demand for precious, gem-set pieces. The French journals describing the marriage of the Emperor Napoleon III in 1853 contain detailed descriptions of the jewellery worn by those present at the ceremony and at various concurrent festivities. It was many years since Europe had witnessed such a *concours d'élégance*. Eugénie de Montijo, Comtesse de Téba, the new Empress, was twenty-six and at the height of her beauty. Her influence upon the fashions of France and consequently of all Europe did much to revive the art of the jeweller. Apart from a predilection for diamonds in lavish settings, the Empress Eugénie set the seal of her favour upon the pearl. Long pearl necklaces with elaborate diamond clasps restored the pearl to a popularity which it had not enjoyed for over a century. As well as in the plain necklace, the pearl was now used again for pendant ear-rings. A number of brooches and lockets with their surrounds formed of seed-pearls date from this time. The style remained generally popular throughout the second half of the century.

While the beauty and taste of the Empress were an undoubted inspiration to the French Court and thus to the French jeweller, it cannot be said that Queen Victoria exerted anything like the same beneficial influence upon the craft of the jeweller in Great Britain. The majority of the fashions for gem-set jewellery were still largely derived from France. No great beauty herself, the Queen seems to have had little personal interest in jewellery. Her taste appears to have been largely formed by her Consort. Prince Albert's contribution to the English scene and his attempt to raise the general standards of taste from the abyss into which they had been plunged by the Industrial Revolution are facts beyond dispute. No one could accuse of lack of taste the man who, during the heyday of the Victorian Academy, had the judgment to buy—and to enjoy—the masters of the Early German School. Trinkets and *bijouterie* (and the temperament which enjoys them) are, however, things which appeal to a certain elegance of mind that one is tempted to call Gallic. The Germanic, somewhat Gothic, cast of a mind like Prince Albert's, combined with a high moral seriousness, is not likely to lead to an appreciation of the lesser delights of life. Be this as it may, there is no doubt that Queen Victoria gave little inspiration to the craft of the jeweller—although this is not to say that she did not wear a great many articles of jewellery.

The opening of the diamond mines in South Africa was one of the major events of the last quarter of the nineteenth century. Diamonds at once became more readily obtainable and the stone's popularity was even more firmly established. Following the prevailing trend from France of lavish display together with an almost complete absence of 'visible' setting, the coronets, brooches and head ornaments of the period show a profusion of gems. Although many of these pieces are set entirely in silver, a common practice was to mount the diamonds in gold but to set silver in the front where it would be visible and intensify the stones' brilliance. Designs in the shape of stars and crescents, which had been fashionable in Paris for nearly thirty years, remained a standard form and were copied and recopied until there was no possible variant left. Necklaces made of a row of large single stones called *rivières* were fashionable for both day and evening wear. Quite a number of these, set with amethysts and topazes, are still to be found in jewellers' shops. Provided that the goldwork is good, they have a certain simple charm. Most of the more important *rivières* set with diamonds have been broken up in the past fifty years.

Trade with South America played a large part in the jeweller's craft both of France and England. From 1870 onwards there are many references to the business done with clients from South America, Mexico and the West Indies. These wealthy customers tended to prefer large and sumptuous stones to the somewhat cold and indifferent classicism of the European mode. (The same preference is still noticeable today—for, now as then, the Parisian and London jeweller finds a number of his clients in these countries.) The influence of the non-European buyer upon the jewellery fashions of Europe, from 1880 onwards, plays quite an important part in determining the jewellery that Europe itself will buy. A jeweller, for instance, who has made a large, colourful brooch for a South African customer will be tempted to see what reaction he will get from his local clientele by making up a similar article and displaying it in his shop.

It was, perhaps, a combination of the foreign demand for large single stones together with the greater availability of good-quality diamonds that made the solitaire so popular from about 1880 to the end of the century. The solitaire is, as its name suggests, a single stone of such quality that it needs no other artifice to draw attention to its beauty. It was usually a diamond and was set either high-mounted on a ring or at the end of a pendant where its unique position drew attention to it. Next to diamonds the favourite for solitaire setting was the pearl. The individual beauty and lustre of a ripe, Orient pearl was ideal for this treatment. As opposed to the Renaissance fondness for baroque, irregular pearls, the pearl solitaire of the nineteenth century is invariably perfect, i.e. symmetrical.

From 1875 the growing importance of the United States was evident to the European jeweller. Many of his customers were American and many of his compatriots migrated across the Atlantic. It is natural therefore to find the jeweller, and particularly the English jeweller, keeping an eye on fashion trends in the States. In the *Watchmaker, Jeweller and Silversmith* of 1875 (the year in which this trade paper was founded) we learn that 'long, heavy pendant ear-rings are coming into fashion again in America. . . . The diamond solitaire, set in platinum clamps, are popular as are single pearls. . . . In coloured ornaments, the "Bonanza" [large painted porcelain brooches and suites of jet] are most in demand. In jet, these sets cost from three to fifteen dollars apiece.'

Jet, which is dealt with at greater length elsewhere in this volume, was an important material in the English jewellery trade during the latter half of the century. The Queen's long widowhood and lengthy mourning for the Prince Consort exerted almost the only influence of the Sovereign upon the jeweller's craft during the long years of her reign. Mourning jewellery became more widely worn than ever before, and the first to benefit from this were the Whitby jet-cutters. Although a great deal of this Whitby jet jewellery is over-large and ugly to present-day taste, there are still quite a number of necklaces and pendant ear-rings which, when cleaned, can look smart and distinguished against a simple costume.

Towards the end of the nineteenth century the watch-case, which had previously afforded so much scope for jewellers and enamellers, had become a completely utilitarian object, 'Science and Fashion having together banished all decoration from watch-cases and dials'. At the same time, unfortunately for the English horological trade, the short-sightedness which seems to have been one of the characteristics of the Industrial Revolution had almost entirely lost the clock and watch trade to Switzerland. This was, indeed, a great loss for the country that had pioneered most horological discoveries, and it was also to the detriment of the British jeweller. It was not until the twentieth century—until the last ten years, in fact—that a re-established watch industry was able to provide the working jeweller with commissions in the shape of gold and gem-set watch-cases.

Novelty was the cry during the close of the century. Novelty had superseded excellence of workmanship as the criterion by which most articles of jewellery were judged. It is amusing in this respect to read the remarks of an English traveller newly returned from Paris: 'The newest thing out in brooches are live beetles, a fashion which Mlle Judic, the Parisian *soubrette*, has just introduced from America . . . the insect lives on sugar and water, and can go for several days without food.' Not very long afterwards, a correspondent to the *Watchmaker, Jeweller and Silversmith* was protesting indignantly: 'Who but a Parisian would conceive the idea of bejewelling

Below: *late eighteenth-century diamond-enriched frame containing a fine miniature by John Smart. Signed and dated 1776. The diamonds are brilliant-cut.*

Right: *English-made rose- and brilliant-cut diamond bow-and-feather brooch, c. 1770.* Below: *silver star brooch and necklace of the eighteenth century, set with red garnets. The clasp of the necklace and its connecting links are of later date.*

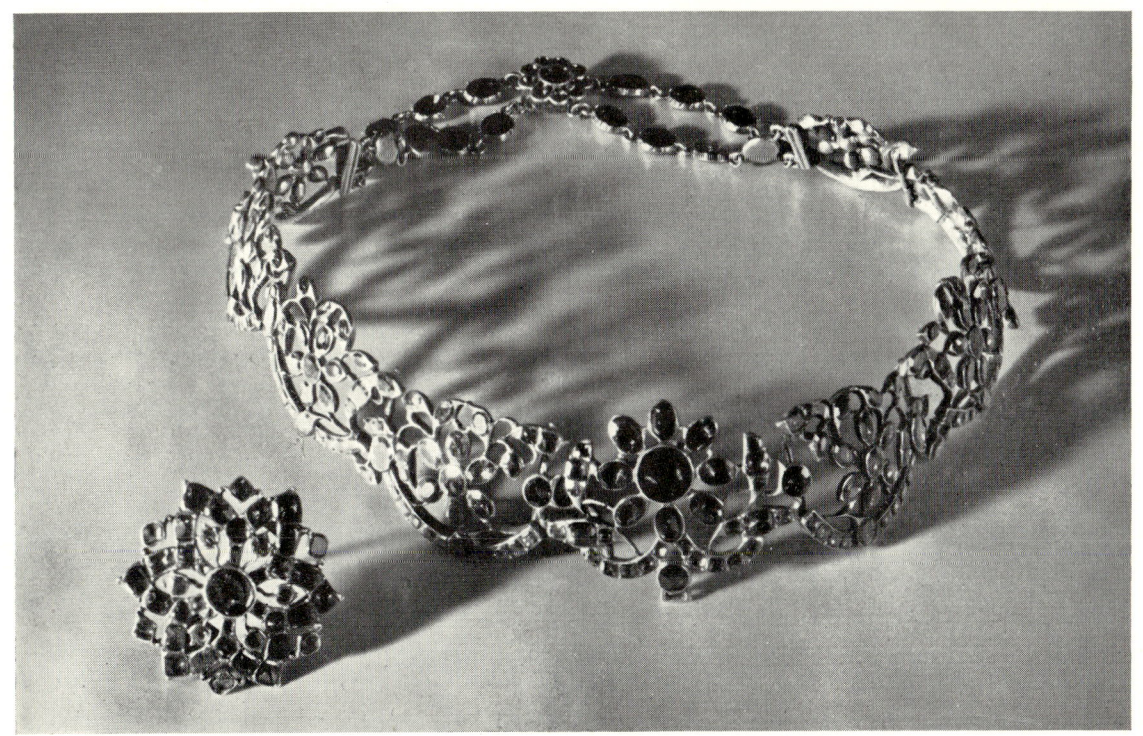

Large flower-spray brooch of diamonds pavé-set in silver. English, eighteenth century.

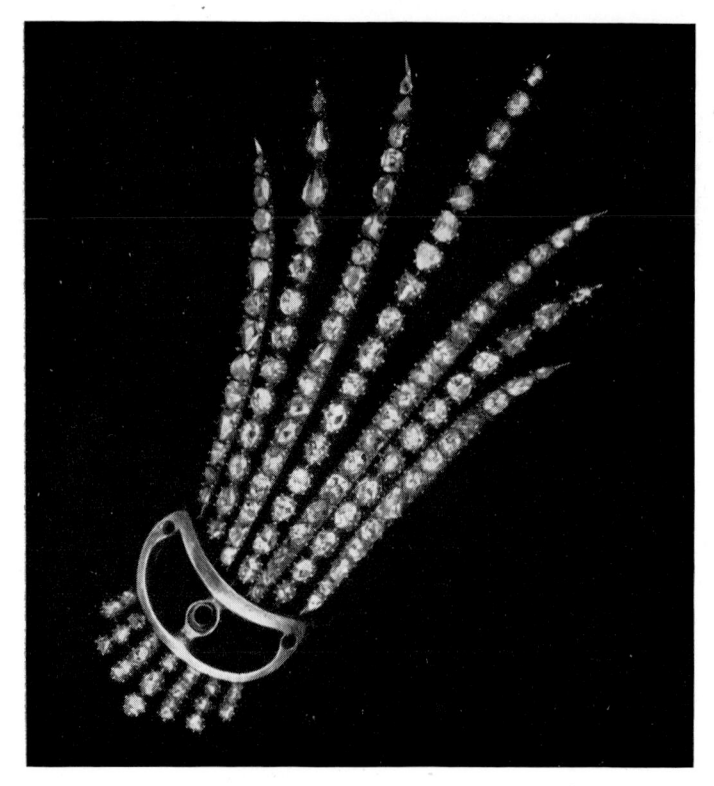

Silver and diamond aigrette, showing the various styles of cut used for individual diamonds. Each stalk of the ornament is flexible and vibrates at the slightest motion. Of late-eighteenth-century workmanship.

a miniature live tortoise? ... Not because the tortoise is not applicable to jewellery, because it has been used for a generation or more as a motif for jewellery, but because we cannot conceive that such a craze could find adherents anywhere else. Indeed we cannot fully understand why any delicate lady, no matter what her nationality, could enchain a live animal, bejewelled as ever it could be, to her bosom. The little animal must obey the dictates of nature and consequently the very idea of wearing a live thing on the person is repugnant.' Not the first—or last—time that Parisian fashions have shocked the English!

The growth of a large, prosperous middle class in Great Britain occasioned a great demand for all the lesser-known gemstones such as peridot, Alexandrite, tourmaline, spinel and garnet. Much of this semi-precious Victorian jewellery is still to be found in jewellers' shops throughout the country. Here again, the discerning can find many attractive pieces—even if of second-class workmanship—at reasonable prices. The Victorian use of filigree gold is seen at its best in some of these items. Pinchbeck and gold imitations were also used quite commonly with paste and semi-precious stones.

A stone which is found in much of the late-Victorian jewellery is the opal. The discovery of the great opal mines in Australia gave England a particular advantage in this respect. Some of this Victorian opal jewellery is extremely fine, the only disadvantage of this stone being that it is sensitive to temperature and is liable to contract or expand in its setting.

A final quotation tells of the close of the nineteenth century in the jewellers' quarters of Birmingham: 'Mafeking night will never be forgotten by those who witnessed the overflowing jubilation of the citizens of the metropolis. Many shops were closed for the day and workshops with open doors received no workpeople. Among those who celebrated in right royal fashion were Messrs. — and Sons who closed their premises and paid their workpeople and assistants in full.'

Thus, with 'Mafficking' and rejoicing, the nineteenth century closed. Although an age of great wealth for England and much of Europe, it had not been one of great good taste. Nevertheless, the collector who is prepared to dig and delve among its vanished splendours will find much that will repay him.

CHAPTER SIX

The Twentieth Century

THE revolution which has taken place in the jeweller's art during the first half of the twentieth century is similar to that which has affected every other branch of the European arts and crafts. The triumph of industrialization has led inevitably to a new conception of jewellery, so that, while the individual hand-craftsman has not been entirely dispossessed of his livelihood, he has nevertheless become a comparative rarity. This is not to deny that there are many craftsmen in jewels and precious metals at work in the world today, many of them the equal of their forebears. It is, however, fair to say that they are no longer as important as they were fifty or a hundred or two hundred years ago.

The great change has been the rise of a completely new type of jewellery, the so-called 'fashion' or costume jewellery. This is, of course, a product of the new conditions obtaining throughout Europe and the western world. The existence of a comparatively prosperous class of industrial worker, the destruction of ancient fortunes coupled with their more equal distribution among the great mass of people, have occasioned a need for a type of jewellery that is inexpensive and can be discarded after a short season. A further spur to the production of this type of jewellery has been provided by the great fashion houses which dictate what is to be the 'line' and the style for the season. Whereas previously in Europe a certain mode of dress might remain fashionable for several years, today, with fashion itself a major industry, it is natural that those in the position to dictate it should arrange for as many seasonable alterations as possible. These seasonal alterations have tended to call forth a type of jewellery which can be easily discarded. In the early history of European jewellery a necklace or brooch, if of value and fine workmanship, would be worn with daytime or evening dress. The modern conception of jewellery is that it should belong to the costume with which it is worn and, therefore, should be changed accordingly.

During the opening years of the twentieth century, however, the state of the arts and crafts was essentially the same as that which had existed during the later years of Queen Victoria. London was still the richest capital in the world and Paris still the arbiter of fashion. The passion entertained by King Edward VII for that most beautiful of cities led to a demand for all things Parisian in style. While the French themselves—or at least those of the upper class—tended to adopt a cult for all things English, the English, as if to return the compliment, turned towards France for the products of luxury and good taste. From this time onwards dates the ascendancy of the French *haute couture* and the jewellers' shops which sparkle around the Place Vendôme. It is interesting to note that the craftsman whose work aptly summarizes the Edwardian age was himself French by descent, although his birthplace and his main workshop was in Russia. The artifice of Peter Carl Fabergé so perfectly represents this era that it would be impossible to describe the Edwardian scene without giving a summary of his life and work. If Cellini is thought of as the representative Renaissance goldsmith and jeweller, Fabergé stands for those last brief years of European brilliance before the first World War—years whose image has been so clearly evoked by Sir Osbert Sitwell in his memoirs. The lassitude of great wealth, the drowsiness of country-house afternoons and the sheen on the coats of perfect horses—Fabergé's jewels, in their different way, evoke these images.

He was born in St Petersburg on May 30, 1846, the son of a jeweller. Like so many of the great artificers—Paul Lamerie for one—he was a Huguenot by descent. He was at the height of his powers in the prosperous 1890s, but one is tempted to associate him more with the Edwardian era, since it was during this time that he opened a London branch and thus introduced the products of his craftsmanship to the British public. Although it is tempting to compare Fabergé with Cellini, the fact remains that Fabergé, although a jeweller himself and principal designer for his firm, was the manager of a vast business whose scale and scope would have amazed the Renaissance craftsman. Besides the London branch, he maintained four workshops—in Moscow, St Petersburg, Odessa and Kiev—and employed 700 workmen. His was, in fact, an enterprise larger, perhaps, than had ever been seen before and which has certainly not been rivalled in the lean years since the first World War. It is true that there are in Europe and America today manufacturing jewellers who employ as many and more workmen, and the ramifications of whose business is world-wide. These, however, are manufacturers of costume jewellery, while Fabergé, it must be remembered, was working in precious stones and metals. His success must be largely attributed to the fact that he was working in that fortunate era before the fabric of Europe and of the Europeanized Court of the Tsars was rent, and ended—to reverse Mr T. S. Eliot's words—'not with a whimper, but a bang'.

Many of the products of the House of Fabergé are still in existence today, despite the depredations of two world wars and the dissolution of many great fortunes. Unfortunately, as would be expected, it is the jewellery which has suffered most. Enough remains, however, to judge of the exquisite workmanship of this master craftsman. Fabergé's chief contribution to the art is his blending of a certain type of Russian fantasy with a French delicacy and charm. Much of his jewellery is set with rose-cut diamonds as opposed to brilliants and it is worth noting that during the early years of the twentieth century the rose-cut diamond enjoyed a revived popularity. Rose-cut diamonds were, in fact, being quoted on the London market at a higher price than brilliants. It is this fact which often accounts for the disappointment of owners of Edwardian diamond jewellery when they find that their pieces are not considered as valuable as had been expected. Today the brilliant is triumphant and the rose cut is out of favour.

Fabergé was also adept at blending many colourful, semi-precious stones to achieve an effect that was not garish but soft and rainbow-like. A small jewelled figure of the type so popular at this time is composed of the following materials: rhodonite, sapphires, Caucasian obsidian, lapis-lazuli, black Siberian jasper, white quartz, Kalyan jasper and, finally, gold. Two categories of Fabergé's work which, although not strictly jewellery, can only be listed under this heading are his 'objects of fantasy' and his smallwork.

The 'objects of fantasy' consist of imitation flowers and the jewelled Russian Easter eggs which were made as presents from the Tsars to the Tsarinas. These eggs are miracles of fine enamelling and gem-setting, while the goldwork is exquisitely wrought. They contained inside them 'surprises' such as enamelled portraits of the Royal children which sprang out of the egg when a catch was pressed.

Fabergé's imitation flowers achieved a great popularity during the Edwardian era and were widely copied by both French and English jewellers, although these copies rarely if ever achieve the same quality of delicacy and naturalism. They were made for the boudoir table or a lady's writing-desk and usually consist of a miniature rock-crystal vase in which are arranged a spray or two of a flower or plant perfectly copied *au naturel*. These flowers are ingeniously contrived in gold, pearls and precious or semi-precious stones, and are triumphs of craftsmanship. In similar vein are certain spray brooches from the House of Fabergé, although again, unfortunately, there are now fewer of these than of the small *objets d'art*.

Smallwork—which is the craftsman's name for all objects such as cigarette- and cachou-boxes, cigarette-holders, parasol handles and similar articles—is a branch of the jeweller's art in which Fabergé excelled. If it is not too much to trace a personal ancestry through workshops which employed Russians, Finns, Swedish-Finns and Germans, it would seem that in these articles there is a vein of Gallic taste and discretion which is lacking in some of the other Fabergé products. The ancestors of these cigarette-cases and their like can be found in those snuff-boxes and other *minuterie* made in the Court of Louis XIV.

Peter Carl Fabergé lived on until 1920, but, alas, many of the products of his own hands and of his craftsmen disappeared during the Russian Revolution. In common with those of so many jewellers, his workshops were taken over for the manufacture of small arms. The god Ares has no use for precious metals—except as plunder.

If Fabergé and his work have been considered at some length, it is because he so truly represents this period before the first World War. The passion for small trinkets, *objets d'art* and diamond work which existed during those prosperous times produced many similar craftsmen, but none who can be quite reckoned as his equal. Apart from Paris and London, where so many of the most distinguished jewellers had their workshops and their showrooms, Rome and Berlin remained two focal centres. Across the Atlantic the ever-increasing wealth of the United States encouraged many European jewellers either to migrate there or to set up American branches of their firms. This migration of artists and craftsmen to America is, of course, one of the most prominent features of the past thirty years, and American jewellery, in common with the other American arts and crafts, can certainly be considered largely European in origin.

The Edwardian era was, above all, a period when a lavish display of wealth was indulged. The most favoured stone remained the diamond, and the metal platinum was already to hand as its perfect setting. Diamond necklaces and collars, diamond tiaras and pendant ear-rings provided a fire of brilliance that has never been seen since in the courts of Europe. The collector of antique jewellery in the future will, however, most probably find that little Edwardian jewellery remains intact in its orginal settings. So much of it has been broken up and converted during the past thirty years. So much of it has also been sold to other countries where, no doubt, the same process has taken place. A certain lavishness, a certain ostentation, marks most of the jewellery of this era. Aesthetically much of it is, perhaps, no great loss.

It is in scientific progress in the use of new metals and methods that the jeweller of the twentieth century excels. In common with all other workers in metals he has benefited by the developments of the research laboratory—developments only too often occasioned in the first place by the demands of war. The seventeenth and eighteenth centuries were the ages when the major advances in the lapidary's craft were made. It was left to the twentieth century to develop the scientific study of gemstones known as gemmology. In the nineteenth century this study was confined to a comparatively small number of mineralogists and scientists, but today there are a great number of skilled gemmologists whose skill in testing mounted stones is often greater than that of the mineralogist himself. The importance of this study to the working jeweller and his customer can readily be seen. In former centuries it was often possible for the jeweller and the customer to be mistaken about the quality and value of a stone. It was also, of course, only too possible for the fraudulent to work his way. One of the most notable examples of a mistaken classification of a gem is the so-called 'Black Prince's Ruby' among the Crown Jewels. It was only the modern gemmologist who could reveal that it was, in fact, a spinel.

Before 1900 a jeweller's equipment for testing gemstones was comparatively simple, and he relied a great deal on eye for his judgments. This resulted in great confusion of nomenclature, a confusion which has still not been satisfactorily cleared up among many members of the public. The invention of a machine called the refractometer which tests the refractive index of gems has been an important step forward. So too has been the endoscope, which was devised during the 1920s and by means of which distinction can readily be made between real and cultured pearls.

Metallurgical advances have also benefited the jeweller greatly, the most outstanding of these being the widespread adoption of platinum mountings and findings for jewellery. Although the properties of platinum were known during the nineteenth century, its price was prohibitive. The discovery of large veins of platinum ore during the mid-1920s resulted in its widespread use in the jewellery industry of both Europe and America. The use of platinum as a setting and mount for gems is, in fact, one of the distinguishing features of the past half-century. Its brilliant white colour and the fact that it does not tarnish render it the perfect metal for use with diamonds. Another member of the platinum group of metals, palladium, has also in recent years become available in quantity. Palladium has achieved great popularity in the United States in particular, and much of the precious jewellery made there in recent years has been in this metal.

Another development which has had a profound effect upon the manufacturing jeweller has been the growth of specialized bullion dealing. It has been seen how the jeweller in the past was at once goldsmith, silversmith, lapidary, gemmologist and, to some extent, metallurgist. Then, with the development of the various branches of his craft, these aspects of it resolved themselves into completely separate trades. But he had also to refine and alloy his own metals for himself. Today he receives these metals direct from his bullion dealer, whose workshops and scientific research centres can produce the perfect metal as it may be required for any particular article. A modern piece of gem-set jewellery, in fact, has a higher nicety of finish, and more perfect gemstones and metal, than was ever possible before.

The Twentieth Century

Linked with the technicians' better understanding of metals has been the twentieth-century evolution of costume jewellery from the 'imitation' jewellery of the 'nineties. Whereas previously there existed throughout Europe various types of peasant jewellery, much of it extremely attractive, it was not until the twentieth century, with its well-paid artisan and factory worker, that there could exist any large-scale demand for such articles. Costume jewellery became, in a sense, jewellery in its own right when methods of gilding and plating base metals were perfected. With the advance of mechanical piercing, stamping and finishing processes, production costs were reduced so as to place jewellery of this type within the reach of every pocket.

The term 'costume jewellery' includes all those pieces which are made of base metal or silver and which are set not with precious stones but with pastes, marcasite or other imitations. Plastics, pottery or glass can also provide basic materials from which costume jewellery can be manufactured. Designed as it is for a comparatively short life, the essence of costume jewellery is novelty, and it is dominated by dress fashions, styles of hair-dressing and topical events.

There are two main categories into which the costume jewellery of the past twenty-five years falls. First of these is the cheaper variety, which is made for the most part of plated base metals and which relies for its effect largely upon some fashionable appeal or novel treatment. In this class of work will be found all the necklaces, bracelets, ear-rings, etc., which are designed to accord with some aspect of current dress fashions.

The second and more important category may be termed the 'gem-set imitation'. Jewellery of this type is designed to approximate as closely as possible to 'real' or precious jewellery and is accordingly better finished and made. Silver is the metal usually employed for this better-quality work, and the modern use of rhodium plating has greatly added to its prestige, since rhodium plating preserves the silver from tarnishing. Formerly used as the metal for diamonds, silver is today invariably found in company with those diamond 'substitutes', paste and marcasite. Its natural colour provides an admirable reflector for the glitter of these stones. Although the majority of paste stones and marcasites are held in their settings by a form of cement, some of the more expensive pieces are still hand-set in exactly the same manner as is precious jewellery and old pastes. Where this hand-setting is used, the quality of the paste is always, of course, far higher than in the cheaper articles.

Silver is a responsive metal in the hands of the craftsman, and it is accordingly much used wherever a sculptural, 'in the round' effect is required. Heads and figures in relief after the cameo style have long been favoured; often where the silver is thus used without any attendant stones it is oxydized in order to give it an antique effect. In the mid-1920s, when there was a vogue for heavy and barbaric jewellery of a mock-oriental style, silver set with pastes or semi-precious stones was used a great deal, particularly with this antique finish.

The jewellery of the decade after the first World War was much influenced by the cinema, and the oriental motifs of much American and European jewellery of the semi-precious or costume type, came largely from this source. The Eastern 'vamp', the loves of the 'Sheikh' Valentino—themes such as these led to the widespread demand for long bead necklaces, heavy Oriental bangles and bracelets, pendant ear-rings and large rings set with stones cut in the antique manner. This was a transitory vogue, however, and did not to any great extent affect the worker in precious stones and metals. Design in precious jewellery was, however, affected by the abstract and cubist paintings of the Paris School, particularly by such artists as Picasso, Juan Gris and Fernand Leger. From this period date the many brooches of platinum set with rubies, diamonds and emeralds which employ abstract and cubist motifs. It is interesting to note again how the art of the painter is closely linked with that of the jeweller. The embodiment of these abstract themes in the jewellery of the 1920s has a parallel in the floral themes used by the seventeenth-century jewellers, taken from the Dutch painters whose influence was then paramount.

Among the most favoured materials during this decade were amber, coral and jade. Their colours went well with the fashionable oranges and greens, while their suitability for carving and bead-work naturally allied them with jewellery fashions. The long pearl necklace was another favourite and a great spur to pearl-wearing was given by the success of Mikimoto's experiments with cultured pearls (see Chapter Sixteen). These were now being imported into Europe in considerable quantities and their relative cheapness meant that strings of pearls were now available for a far wider market. The pearl, indeed, dominates these years.

In the 1930s a broader and heavier treatment of precious metals introduced an opulent style that matched the dress fashions of the period. Gem-set rings, necklaces and bracelets tended to be fashioned with an almost monumental heaviness and much use of coloured golds. From this time date the 'cocktail' rings and watches which merit description, since they are a distinctive feature of the period.

The 'cocktail' watch is, as its name suggests, a watch designed to be worn with cocktail or evening dress. While the usual ladies' watch is designed to be light, neat

Brooch with brilliant- and rose-cut diamonds in a setting of silver and gold, c. 1800.

Left: watch and chatelaine made by John Wilson of Peterborough and dated 1772. The watch-case is of enamelled gold; the chatelaine of pinchbeck enamelled with classical motifs. Right: Georgian Maltese cross set with diamonds and a central topaz.

Basket-case of gold housing a three-train cylinder watch with hour and quarter strike and calendar. By Mudge; London, 1765.

113

Left: *early Victorian brooch set with brilliant-cut diamonds and four rubies, with a good quality emerald in the centre.* Below: *Regency watch dated about 1820. The case and fob, with seals and tassels, are of gold and enamel set with pearls. The watch-dial is of pale blue and white enamel bordered with pearls. The hands are set with rose diamonds.*

Portrait of Queen Adelaide (1792–1849) by W. Beechey. She wears pearl and pendant jewellery. (In the National Portrait Gallery, London.)

Early Victorian necklace of flower and leaf design with rose diamonds in cut-down settings.

and comparatively unobtrusive, the 'cocktail' watch is designed to be as outstanding as a gem-set bracelet—its function as a watch being kept hidden as far as possible. Made often in gold, and set with diamonds, rubies, sapphires or emeralds, the 'cocktail' watch is in fact a bracelet rather than a 'watch'. As might be expected, many of the best examples of these were—and are—made in Switzerland. Paris, London and New York have also produced a number of fine examples.

The 'cocktail' ring, companion to the watch, is a return to the style of the ostentatious rings of the sixteenth century. The majority are too large to be worn under gloves; indeed, their extravagant beauty is best set off when worn over a black evening glove. Constructed in gold, platinum or, today, in palladium, they provide the jeweller with a magnificent opportunity for a display of his skill. Indeed, it is among these cocktail rings that some of the finest pieces of twentieth-century jeweller's work may be found. High-mounted stones are contrasted against the airy delicacy of pierced shoulders; much use is made of gold wire; the shoulders themselves may be gem-set; differently coloured golds intensify the colourful effect.

Composite suites were among the other pieces of jewellery which were brought to perfection in these pre-war years. In these suites the jeweller produced some of his best pieces and, in addition, a fine elaboration of his art. The composite suite may, perhaps, be a diamond and sapphire necklace. This can be worn by itself in the evening. For daytime, however, it is so constructed that the necklace pendant uncouples, forming a spray brooch. Some composite suites can be further dismantled to provide a pair of ear-clips. A large brooch designed for evening wear can be broken down to reveal two completely different, smaller brooches suitable for the daytime. There is practically no limit which can be placed upon this exercise of the modern jeweller's ingenuity. It is, in fact, not only an interesting elaboration of his craft, but also a concession to the modern customer's pocket. Providing the option of, say, three pieces for little more than the price of one, it is not surprising that these composite suites have remained in favour.

A simpler version of the composite suite, but one which is among the most popular productions of the past twenty years, is the double clip. This is, in effect, two brooches held upon one central bar and carrier. These can be uncoupled and worn either separately or one at either side of the dress neckline. These double clips are usually fashioned in platinum, and set with diamonds and other precious stones, although they are also to be found in costume jewellery. They range in size and price from the comparatively small and inexpensive to large classics of the jeweller's art. The design of the two interlocking halves of the brooch need not necessarily be similar; many, in fact, are completely different, but complementary to each other when assembled together.

It is only during the past fifteen or twenty years that the precious metal palladium has become readily available. Its importance to the jeweller and to the customer lies mainly in the fact that palladium is only a little more than half the weight of platinum. The comparative lightness of palladium has therefore made it possible for the jeweller to construct larger clips and brooches than was formerly possible—a great advantage in this age of light dress materials. The jeweller of the fifteenth and sixteenth centuries did not have to worry himself about the 'drag' of a large brooch upon velvets and heavy materials. To the modern jeweller the problem of avoiding damage to light silks, shantung, cotton and rayon is clearly a major consideration.

The pre-war years witnessed also the successful large-scale production of imitation pearls—an industry which was first established in Czechoslovakia and France. These imitations, produced at a popular price, led to a revival of the fashion for pearls. Since the second World War, these imitation pearls, and with them, of course, the cultured and the real pearl, have been fashionable all over the world. Never, since the Elizabethan Age, have pearls and their counterfeits been so widely used as both jewels and fashion accessories. Ear-rings, necklaces, brooches and bracelets have all been fashioned of imitation pearls, many of them ingeniously coloured in various tones of pinks and blues and bronze.

The industrial development of plastics during the recent war has led to the adoption of plastics as a material for the less expensive type of costume jewellery. The cheapness of production, combined with the many colour combinations available and the ability to produce new patterns without expensive die-casting has inevitably endeared plastics to the manufacturer. Although jewellery of plastic material is inexpensive, much of it is extremely attractive, while the material's lightness has made it ideal for summer necklaces and ear-clips. Not being confined, as is a natural material, to a limited colour range, plastic jewellery has been able to accord with whatever colour scheme prevailing dress fashions demand. A particularly pleasant treatment of plastics is the application of metallic films to the surface. Silver, gold and platinum finishes can thus be given to a comparatively cheap article and achieve an illusion that can otherwise only be obtained by the more expensive plating of base metals.

Aluminium, which was considered almost a precious metal towards the close of the nineteenth century because of its price, is another material that has been used in modern costume jewellery. Today, the treatment of aluminium by a process known as anodizing—whereby the metal can be given an attractive coloured surface

—has given it new possibilities for use in costume jewellery. It shares the advantage of plastics that it is very light and therefore particularly suitable for necklaces and other pieces designed to be worn with summer clothing.

Looking back over the last fifty years from this mid-century viewpoint, is it possible to assess what contributions the twentieth century has so far made to the craft of jewellery and is it possible to estimate in what direction the jewellery of Europe is likely to move? The main contributions are technical advances in the use and refinement of metals, the discovery of new techniques and the rise of a new class of jeweller, the manufacturer of mass-produced costume jewellery. It is this last development that suggests an answer to the question of the future of European jewellery. Viewing the situation without pessimism and without, as far as possible, nostalgia for the past, it would seem unlikely that Europe will again witness the profusion of fantastic and beautiful jewellery which has been hers at one time or another during the past four centuries. Where there is little or no wealth there can be little or no real jewellery. The conditions which produced it have disappeared, as have the conditions which produced the Court of *Le Roi Soleil* and the rich, bourgeois domesticity of the Dutch school of painting. In states where a division of wealth results in no one having too much money and no one too little, it is to be expected that what jewellery there is will be of the 'costume' variety. There will, of course, always be a limited number of craftsmen working in the old manner for their limited number of clients, but it seems reasonable to expect that there will be less and less of these. Across the Atlantic, where so many of Europe's craftsmen now practise their trades, the vast wealth of the New World is calling into being new masterpieces of the jeweller's art. But that is another story.

It may, perhaps, be considered strange that a chapter dealing with the jewellery of the twentieth century should have omitted all reference to the many brooches and badges that are associated with the two World Wars. Despite their sentimental interest, they are, however, of little importance in evaluating the changes and the progress of the jeweller's art. Naval crowns set with small brilliants, Royal Air Force wings in platinum and Army brooches fashioned with stones that copy regimental colours—these will be preserved long after their more expensive cousins have been broken up and reset. For the antiquarian and the jewellery-lover of the future they may well possess something like the same associations—if not the same merit—which Elizabethan ship brooches have for ourselves.

CHAPTER SEVEN

Diamond Jewellery

THE diamond is undoubtedly the most popular precious stone used in jewellery today. Its glamour and brilliance, set in the white metals platinum or palladium, make the diamond the most distinctive and distinguished of all the stones.

Throughout the history of jewellery the diamond's cutting and setting have varied considerably. Owners of old jewellery are sometimes dismayed to find that the value of their pieces is considerably less than they expected. This is occasioned by those changes in fashion and technique which have dispossessed silver of its pre-eminence as a setting for diamonds and have also improved the brilliance of the stone by modern methods of cutting. Whereas antique jewellery of pre-1830 making has an especial value of its own, late-Victorian diamond jewellery often, unhappily, falls between two stools.

All the famous diamonds of antiquity came from the mines of India, the first European to describe which was the Portuguese, Garcia de Orta, in 1565. It was in India that the possibilities of the diamond in jewellery were first revealed as the Indian lapidaries became skilful enough to facet the stone. But the brilliance of the diamond as we know it today was never seen in these early gems. As late as the fifteenth century all that the lapidaries could do was to remove the diamond's gum-like skin and polish whatever natural surfaces it possessed. Wherever flaws or discolorations occurred the lapidaries imposed a facet in order to disguise them. The result was that an imperfect diamond of this nature might be distinguished by its haphazard faceting.

In Renaissance Italy, the diamond was accorded high place; but here, again, its true qualities and brilliance were never revealed. In his autobiography, Cellini describes how a large diamond was set in Pope Clement's cope-button (see Chapter One). Bertoli's drawing of the cope-button in the British Museum makes it clear that this diamond was cut into pyramid shape with four main facets. Since the setting was of gold, it is likely that the diamond was backed with a reflective foil in the manner which was common at the time. Even with this backing, however, it is unlikely that a diamond of such cut would have much brilliance.

Although the traveller Tavernier, when he visited India in 1665, found a considerable number of diamond-cutters at work, it does not appear likely that their skill at this time was any greater than that of their European *confrères*. It was not until the rose form of cutting was discovered that the diamond acquired its present importance in European jewellery. The most perfect rose form is a hemisphere which is covered with twenty-four triangular facets; these are arranged in a regular fashion, the diamond having a flat base. This type of diamond cut has been popularly attributed to Cardinal Mazarin, but it seems more likely that the discovery originated in India and was brought to Europe by traders. It became, immediately, the standard form of diamond-cutting, and its popularity lasted right up to the early years of this century. There are six or seven variants of the rose form, but all are alike in the hexagonal arrangement of the facets and in the flatness of the base.

The full beauty of the diamond was revealed towards the latter end of the seventeenth century when a notable Venetian lapidary, Peruzzi, discovered the brilliant form of cutting. With the advent of the brilliant cut—as its name suggests—the true 'brilliance' of the diamond was revealed. The immediate effect upon the craft of the jeweller was to give the diamond predominance over other stones.

A descendant of the old table cut, the brilliant possesses a great many more facets, although the overall shape is not so different. As introduced by Peruzzi, the brilliant has not changed considerably over the centuries except in minor details and an increase in the number of facets. The modern brilliant has thirty-three facets on the crown (the top section) and twenty-five on the pavilion (the lower section). These include the table (the flat area on top) and the culet (the small flat facet cut at the base of the pavilion to prevent chipping). Several variants of the brilliant cut exist, among them the American brilliant with forty-one facets in the crown, and the Jubilee cut with the eighty-eight facets in all. The latter was an American innovation, introduced at the time of Queen Victoria's Jubilee. Victorian and early Edwardian diamonds may be found cut in this manner. The Star of Africa, which was cut from the largest diamond in the world, the 3,106-carat Cullinan diamond, has sixteen additional facets, totalling seventy-four facets in all.

Although the brilliant cut tended to supersede the rose form, examples of the latter are not difficult to find in both eighteenth- and nineteenth-century jewellery. Indeed, as late as the beginning of the present century the rose form, returning once more into general favour, was even more popular than the brilliant. This accounts for the fact that owners of diamond jewellery made in the years just prior to the first World War may find that the diamonds are rose-cut.

As has been indicated, it was not until the late seventeenth and early eighteenth century that the diamond achieved its predominance in European jewellery. This delayed recognition was, of course, occasioned by the stone's hardness which defeated the insufficient mechanical technique and knowledge of the early workman. On Mohs' scale the diamond is marked as 10—the hardest substance known. Corundum, which is marked as 9 on the scale, falls well short of the diamond in this respect, the latter being as much as ninety times harder than corundum. This quality of the diamond was naturally well known to the ancients and it was the stone's chief attraction in medieval and Renaissance days. (It is known that one of the amusements of Tudor gallants was to trace inscriptions, love-poems, etc., on glass with diamond points.) This knowledge of the diamond's hardness led to the misconception that a true test for the stone's authenticity lay in its ability to withstand the blow of a hammer. It is quite possible that a number of genuine stones were destroyed by this elementary procedure.

Right up to the twentieth century diamonds were invariably set in silver, which was recognized as the metal with the best reflectivity. Diamonds are also found set in gold, but here again, as in Cellini's cope-button, the diamonds were usually backed with a foil.

In the eighteenth century one of the most popular forms of diamond jewellery was the spray brooch, the revival of which has been one of the features of fashion within the last ten years. The elegance of the typical eighteenth-century brooch of this type has never been surpassed, the workmanship of both the English and Continental craftsmen being of a very high order. The silver is moulded so that a most attractive three-dimensional effect is achieved, carved or claw settings being used.

Unfortunately, as with all objects of the jeweller's art, a very great number of these have been broken up during the passing years. There remain, however, for the collector of antique jewellery many good examples of this period. Some of the most elegant are the openwork bracelets, fashionable towards the close of the eighteenth century, which embody designs of bows and lovers' knots. Also returned to favour today is the pendant ear-ring, examples of which, dating from the late eighteenth and nineteenth centuries, are comparatively easy to come by.

Diamond settings have varied considerably over the past three centuries. The methods used during the sixteenth and seventeenth centuries have already been discussed[1]: the diamond jewellery which is most likely to come the way of the collector, however, dates from the eighteenth century. During this period the two principal types of setting were *pavé* and claw. *Pavé* setting, which is still employed today, is designed to embrace a group of stones. It is generally found in diamond brooches, or in large pieces where it is not the individual stone which counts so much as the

[1] See pp. 42–3 and 65.

general display of a group of small stones. The diamonds are held in holes cut in the precious metal, the raised edge round each hole being burred over to hold the diamond in place.

Claw setting, on the other hand, was primarily designed to display individual and important stones—although nowadays it is often used where an eighteenth-century jeweller would have employed *pavé* or carved setting. The name 'claw' is self-explanatory. The advantage of this setting is that it is very secure; the only disadvantage is that it allows dirt to infiltrate behind the stone. An experienced jeweller, however, can easily clean up a claw setting.

Millegrain setting will be found in many nineteenth-century pieces, generally used in conjunction with small stones. A crenellated or 'milled' edge round the stone increases the apparent area of the diamond. It has a modern counterpart in the illusion setting, which is used for small or undistinguished stones and may often be seen in the less expensive types of engagement ring. The carved setting, akin to *pavé*, except that the diamond rests in a hollow scooped out of the metal and is enclosed at the back, was fairly commonly used during the eighteenth century, particularly in large floral brooch-sprays.

The process by which the diamond achieves its brilliant appearance out of the rough should be known to every collector or admirer of fine jewellery. Nowadays the rough diamond is generally sawn to make two smaller stones, these being more practicable for polishing and setting.

A phosphor-bronze wheel, charged with diamond dust and oil, is used to saw the stone along a predetermined line. The expression 'diamond-cut diamond' explains itself—only the diamond's own powder is sufficiently hard an abrasive to effect the stone's cleavage. After the diamond has been sawn, there follows the second process, known as 'roughing', in which the approximate shape of the stone is roughed out. Next, the facets are applied and the diamond is transformed into those familiar shapes, brilliant, rose or baguette. (Few other forms of diamond cut are used today, and even the once-popular rose cut is rarely seen in modern jewellery.) Finally the stone is polished, its 'skin' is removed, and the full brilliance of the gem revealed.

The high cost of the diamond is not, as is so commonly believed, entirely due to the rarity of the stone. There are some rarer gemstones in the world—the ruby for one. It is largely the long hours of skilled labour and craftsmanship involved in its cutting and faceting which make the diamond so expensive a gemstone.

It was not until the close of the nineteenth century that the precious metal platinum became the accepted setting for diamonds. Silver settings are still found in early twentieth-century pieces. With its very high reflectivity, good working qualities and untarnishability, platinum provides today a setting of which the early jeweller could only dream. Its sister metal, palladium, has similar qualities.

It is almost impossible to date antique diamond jewellery exactly, although an approximate date can usually be given on the basis of style, mounting and cutting of the stones, and so on. Even here, however, it has to be born in mind that jewellery is often made to an individual order, and this may specify a reproduction of some earlier motif or style. (A very popular device among jewellers in the late eighteenth century was the diamond floral spray in which one or more of the diamond-set flowers was affixed to a silver coiled spring so that the flowers vibrated when the wearer moved. Comparatively recently, a modern piece, incorporating the same idea, was hailed as an achievement of the twentieth century!)

Since the technique of making diamond jewellery has remained almost unchanged throughout the centuries it may prove of interest to the collector to follow such a piece through a jeweller's workshop, from its inception on the drawing-board to the finished article.

In our modern, mechanized age the making of precious jewellery remains one of the last handcrafts. That it should remain so essentially a handcraft is understandable since, if the design is not to be repeated, no advantage can be gained by the introduction of machinery. Wherever an article of jewellery is to be made in precious metal and set with precious stones, the skill of the human hand becomes the major factor.

It may seem, perhaps, a paradox that even the most modern styles of precious jewellery, those designed to accord with the latest dress fashions, are made by age-old methods employing tools that have been in use since the beginning of history. Yet, with very few exceptions, there is little in a modern jeweller's workshop which would be unfamiliar to an Egyptian gem-setter or a craftsman of the Renaissance. The main difference between a twentieth-century European workshop and its ancestors lies in the application of modern planning to the traditional tools and methods. The sequence of operations which go to the making of a modern diamond necklace illustrate this aspect of planning as well as the continuity of the craft.

As always, the first on the scene is the designer. He may, perhaps, have specific directions from his clients as to the style and motifs required in the work. If this is so, his knowledge of fashion and of the limitations of his material must guide him to weave the special requirements into a design that will fulfil the client's order, while at the same time achieving a fashionable effect. Alternatively, the designer may be working not to an order, but to produce a piece that must catch the eye of a potential buyer in a jeweller's shop. Here again each piece will be individual and unique, but it must also contrive to meet the fashion of the moment. Not only dress fashions, but also such things as changing hair-styles must be watched by the designer. Every piece of jewellery is, in a sense, 'signed' and it is possible for one acquainted with the craft to distinguish the work of many contemporary designers. Antique jewellery can similarly be distinguished—mainly through the volumes of jeweller's designs that are still extant.

Working on a drawing-board in a room and atmosphere that has the precision of an architect's office, the designer considers his problem. If the piece is to be a diamond necklace he must first of all decide which of the precious metals shall be used. He has today a choice of three—gold, platinum and palladium. These can of course be combined and used to contrast with each other, while differently coloured golds can be employed to produce a rich effect. On the other hand, if the necklace is primarily to be diamond-set, it is likely that he will decide on platinum or palladium, since their white colour intensifies the diamond's brilliance. The necklace may also be part of a suite, in which case the designs for the matching ear-rings, bracelet, ring and even, perhaps, brooch must be evolved at the same time. If the necklace is to be of the monumental and extremely elaborate style, then the designer may give preference to palladium, since it is considerably lighter than platinum or gold.

The resemblance of the modern designer's office to an architect's has already been mentioned and the resemblance goes even farther, for jewellery is in itself architecture in miniature. The stresses and strains of individual strips of metal, the airy cross-sections which support a high-flung bridge of precious stones, the amount of under-cutting to which a piece of metal may safely be submitted—these are typical of the problems which the jewellery designer and craftsman encounter every day.

After the design is completed it leaves the drawing-broad and passes to the issue office. Here modern planning obviates waste and eliminates time-lags. The amount of precious metal which will be required is carefully weighed out. Wires, strips and sheets of metal are assembled and their individual weights entered on a card bearing the job number of the piece in question. When the finished mount is returned, these will again be checked against any metal left over.

The mounter, who is the next man on the scene, plays a primary part in the fashioning of the necklaces. It is his job to prepare out of the strips and sheets of metal the completed mount into which the gems will be set. Working at a scalloped bench with a leather apron spread over his knees to catch any 'lemel' or scrap metal which falls from the piece, the mounter is surrounded by tools so simple and yet so perfect that they have never been improved upon. Among them are the hand-saw which shapes the outline of the metal to the design and cuts it out to the required size, the drill which pierces it where stones are to be set and the hammer which beats and raises it into shape. Most useful of all his tools is the file, so perfectly responsive to every movement of the human hand. This is used for rounding off corners and for shaping and finishing. The mounter's feet rest on slatting through which fall any scraps of metal that are not caught by his apron. At the end of every day these covers are raised, the floor swept and the residue stored for return to the refiners.

The poetry of craftsmanship is implicit in the very names of the tools at the mounter's disposal, such as scorpers, gravers, triblets, swage blocks and doming punches. Over the swage blocks the metal mounts are hammered to evolve the required shape. The doming punches are used to produce a raised part, while the scoopers and gravers are sharp-edged tools which raise and 'bring up' the metal or cut it where stones are to be set. These hand tools are traditional. The mounter today possesses only one advantage over his ancient predecessors—the gas-fed blow-pipe. This is employed in all soldering operations, of which there may be a great many in the construction of a diamond necklace. Wherever outlying bridges of metal may be required to rise higher than the main design, strips or sections of metal will have to be soldered on. Since the construction of the mount may call for several successive solderings, it follows that these solders must have progressively lower melting points or all previous work will be destroyed. The solution to the problem of obtaining these successive melting points without changing the solder's colour—the piece must have a uniform appearance—is but one of the many technical achievements of the refiner. Previously it was the jeweller himself who had to determine these points. Like the modern painter, the modern jeweller has the resources of great industries at his disposal, to which he can go for his materials. He does not, in fact, like the old craftsmen, have to 'mix his own paints'.

Before a strip of metal can be soldered on to the main piece, the surfaces of both must be scraped and filed until they are perfectly clean. They are then laid together and held in place by lengths of thin wire that are resistant to heat. Small pellets of solder, known as *paillons*, are laid in and against the required join which is then effected by the blow-pipe and with the aid of flux. Not only is the mounter a craftsman, he must also, to some extent, be a scientist. While the dexterity of his hand must be impeccable, his brain must contain a working knowledge of the chemistry and physical properties of metals.

After the mount for the necklace has been made, it passes to the polishing shop where again the human hand takes over to give it the preliminary polish. Internal surfaces which no machine can reach are polished by pulling the pieces through strings that have been rubbed with jeweller's rouge. For the exterior polish, pumice is used. In some large modern firms a little of this hand work may be eliminated by submitting the piece to a rotary buffer—the only mechanical process in the whole sequence. Even here, however, hand polishing is not entirely superseded.

At the issuing department the stones for the necklace are now selected. Bright, gleaming heaps are poured from their surgical-looking, white-paper packets, and the table glows with those products of the lapidary's craft—faceted and polished gemstones. The necklace may be entirely of diamonds, baguette and brilliant cut, or it may contain sapphires, rubies and emeralds, arranged so as to intensify the diamond's purity and, in contrast, to display their own richness of colour.

When the stones have been selected, the setter takes over. Holding the mount in a gemstick (a stick whose top is covered with shellac), the setter raises the small beads of metal which will grasp the stones, or bends over the claws where single stones are sited. The mount is held firm against the tarry shellac, so that the setter can apply the necessary force for his work while the metal remains uniformly supported.

Bent over the necklace, his shadow cast by the suspended light across his scalloped bench, the setter is, like the mounter, a figure symbolic of the continuity of his craft. Whether in Egyptian wall-paintings or in sixteenth-century engravings, the setter's figure is essentially the same. From the practice of this craft many notable painters have learnt the first lesson of their art—the necessity for painstaking and perfect workmanship. It was a lesson which neither Holbein nor Dürer, both of them acquainted with the jeweller's workshop, ever forgot.

After the stones have been set, the necklace is almost complete. One more stage remains, the final polishing and finishing. Where machine polishing is used, fan shafts over the rotary buffers suck away the fine particles of waste metal into a cabinet where they are collected for refining. After the final hand polishing the necklace is washed. Here again the same methods of recovery are employed and the water from the basin passes into a filter plant.

The diamond necklace—product of designer, lapidary, mounter, setter and polisher—is now laid in its silk-lined box. Behind it lie hundreds of working hours, perfect craftsmanship and skill, while from thousands of miles away, mined out of the earth, have come its metal and its stones. Its ancestry is as old as is the history of human civilization. Apart from the few modern improvements which have been noted, the making of an antique diamond necklace followed exactly the same process.

CHAPTER EIGHT

Rings

No article of jewellery is more readily accessible to the collector than the ring. Whether one's purse is large or small, there are rings available in jeweller's stores, antique shops and salerooms which can give pleasure and delight to the discerning. First-class specimens of fifteenth- and sixteenth-century European rings are, of course, outside the reach of the average collector. Even here, however, examples of *niello* rings can sometimes be had for comparatively small sums.

Here a warning may be given which applies particularly to rings but also to many other items of jewellery. Unless a would-be buyer has considerable knowledge of the subject, together with some experience of the manufacturing jeweller's methods and techniques, he should not buy from other than reputable sources. Apart from the work of the deliberate faker, there are many copies of antique jewellery in existence, copies which have been made deliberately as such, but which may well be passed on as originals by either the unscrupulous or the ignorant. (It must be remembered that many of those who have antique rings among their stock may not possess any specialized knowledge of the subject. They may quite genuinely think that a certain piece is of sixteenth-century origin when it is, in fact, a nineteenth-century copy.) As a general rule, then, the wise man will not buy from sources other than those which have a reputation to keep up and which specialize in antique jewellery.

At this point, and as a *caveat emptor*, let me record the story of a friend who is an expert craftsman and a manufacturer of jewellery—rings particularly—in a style which is based on the antique. His pieces are not copies but rather 'derivations', and are usually set with cabochon- or antique-cut stones in the same manner as their sixteenth-century predecessors. Shortly after the war, on holiday abroad, he chanced to meet a lady who was very fond of antique jewellery. Upon one of her fingers she had a silver ring set with antique-cut garnets, the shoulders embellished with figures 'in the round'. He was told that it was a sixteenth-century Italian ring, and that it had been recently bought in one of the capitals of Europe. My friend recognized the ring. It was one which he himself had made before the war and which had originally been sold for what it was—a modern ring designed and made in the antique style. To an expert, of course, the solders used in its fabrication would alone have been enough to betray its modern origin. Judging by its style, however, it might well have been taken for what it was later sold as—a sixteenth-century piece of jewellery. Here, in fact, was a ring which had never been intended to deceive, but which had passed into unscrupulous hands. It should be remembered, moreover, that the deliberate faker would have taken care to use appropriate solders, style, setting and the like. If the Dutch painter Van Meegeren could deceive many of the world's acknowledged art experts and historians with his fake Vermeers, how much easier must deception be in the simpler sphere of jewellery. For it must be remembered, too, that jewellery has never been the subject of the same intensive research as has the art of painting.

Lest this anecdote should in any way deter the aspiring collector, let me repeat that if he buys from a recognized source he has little to fear. Moreover, it must be clear that there is not likely to have been much deliberate forgery of the less expensive pieces of antique jewellery since the net returns would have been so small. On the other hand, the history of important pieces of early jewellery is likely to be known at least in part, together with some record of the collections through which they have passed. This, of course, applies mainly to articles which may be termed 'museum specimens'.

Rings are today universally connected with engagements and marriages. In a period when even women wear comparatively few rings, it is almost inevitable that the word 'ring' should have such associations, since for most people these are the only rings worn. That this was not always the case the study of the early history of European jewellery has demonstrated.

The history of the betrothal ring can be traced back to Roman times. It was a custom which was adopted and continued by the early Christians. During this era it would appear that the ring was worn on the third finger since a current superstition (referred to in Macrobius' *Saturnalia*) was that a vein from the finger was directly connected with the heart. The ritual of placing the ring upon the bride's third finger can be traced back to the eleventh century. Most pictures delineating wedding ceremonies show the ring being placed upon the right hand, although there does not seem to have been any hard-and-fast rule. In 1549 the position was clarified by the Book of Common Prayer of Edward VI which specified that the ring should be placed upon the third finger of the left hand. Even after this in England the ruling was not strictly followed, and wedding rings were still worn on other fingers and also on the right hand.

The plain gold ring which is now traditionally associated with weddings is a comparatively modern innovation. It is practically impossible to tell from a collection of antique rings which were wedding rings, which betrothal rings and which were merely given as a token of affection—although the problem can sometimes be solved where there is an inscription inside the hoop.

The modern engagement ring finds an ancestor in the Roman *anulus pronubus*. This was given as a definite sign of the plighting of the troth. But, during the early Christian era, this *anulus pronubus* would appear to have been absorbed, as it were, into the wedding ring. We do not know when the custom of a separate engagement ring originated; in England it does not appear to have become generally accepted until the nineteenth century.

A reference to the marriage of Mary Tudor in 1554 makes it clear that the plain gold ring was associated with an earlier custom, for we learn that she wore 'a plain hoope of gold without any stone in it because maydens were so maried in olde times'; yet despite this Royal precedent, the gem-set wedding ring was still widely used. It is interesting to note that today, particularly in the United States of America, the gem-set wedding ring is again in fashion and that engagement and wedding rings set with diamonds are made in matching pairs. Even in England, where tastes are more conservative, there is an increased liking for more ornate wedding rings, faceted, inlaid and engraved, and made in coloured golds, platinum and palladium.

One of the most interesting types of ring associated with marriage and engagement is the gimmel ring (Latin: *gemellus*, a twin). A considerable number of these rings was made by Italian Renaissance craftsmen, with the result that the collector will still find them in salerooms and dealers' cases. The gimmel ring has two hoops which 'marry' together so that they appear to be one single ring. It would seem that some of them were actually worn separately by the bride and bridegroom until the wedding ceremony, when the ring was symbolically joined together. Most gimmel rings, however, were clearly never intended to be so separated. What in fact may have happened was that, at the appropriate point in the wedding ceremony, both bride and groom inserted their fingers into the two opposed halves of the ring. This possibly took place at the same moment when, in the modern ceremony, the groom places the ring upon the bride's finger.

The majority of gimmel rings are of Italian workmanship and the metal in which they are usually made is silver. They are often ornamented with *niello* work. Seventeenth- and eighteenth-century gimmel rings, whether of Italian, German or English workmanship, tend to be engraved with inscriptions on the two flat, facing halves of the hoop. These inscriptions are either of the 'posy' or lover's motto type, or contain the names of the two who have plighted their troth.

Closely associated with the gimmel ring is the *fede* ring and, indeed, they are often one and the same thing. The *fede* ring (Italian: *mani in fede*) has as its motif two clasped hands which form the head of the ring. Where the *fede* is also a gimmel ring, these two clasped hands separate with the hoops; when the ring is joined together the two hands interlock, one thumb above the other. Apart from their use in wedding ceremonies, it seems reasonable to suppose that these *fede* rings may also have been used in swearing brothership or in pledging a contract. It should always be remembered that jewellery, until comparatively recent times, possessed many semi-mystical associations that are today only retained in engagement and wedding rings.

The subject of mystical rings and the intimate connection of rings with magic and religion is an important one. Pre-Christian examples abound, as do those of the Christian era. The Christian symbol of the fish (*ixthus*) was but the originator of a whole series of rings having engravings of saints and martyrs and objects with religious associations upon the bezels. Later, in the seventeenth century, as we have seen, a whole range of mourning jewellery made its appearance, among which are, naturally, to be found *memento mori* rings engraved with death's heads. These reminders of the owner's mortal lot also became connected with the familiar seventeenth- and eighteenth-century rings that served as memorials to the dead. Some of these have the initials of the deceased engraved upon the bezel. Usually the rings are engraved inside the hoop with the full names of the deceased. Some of the most attractive examples have the bezel formed of a painting representing a woman leaning upon an urn. This is either painted in enamels or in colours which are protected by a glass cover. In common with all mourning jewellery, these rings experienced a great revival during the latter part of the nineteenth century. Many of these pieces are enamelled with shades of violet—a colour often associated with mourning—and contain lockets of hair belonging to the deceased.

One of the most charming decorative rings that has ever been made is the floral *giardinetti* ring. As its name suggests, it is constructed so that its bezel forms a flower-like garland. These rings became popular during the last quarter of the seventeenth century. Often enamelled, they are set with a variety of coloured, precious or semi-precious stones. The settings are usually of delicately pierced silver openwork that enhances the light, colourful nature of the arrangement. Owing to their popularity at the time, quite a number of these rings are still to be found. Apart from the fact that many more rings are made than any other article of jewellery, rings are often spared from destruction since their comparatively small amount of precious metal and stones does not render them worth breaking up. This, of course, does not apply to diamond rings which have constantly been re-set to accord with changing fashions.

Signet or seal rings have, ever since classical times, played a major part in official life. It was not indeed until the nineteenth-century invention of the gummed envelope that their importance began to diminish. They constituted a signature, an authority and a token of good faith. Their importance to the owner can readily be gathered from the description of the death of Gaius Petronius, the author of the *Satyricon* and former favourite of the Emperor Nero. One of Petronius' last actions was to destroy his signet ring so that it could not be used by the Emperor to endanger either his household or his friends.

During the Middle Ages the use of signet rings in England seems to have been restricted to civic dignitaries and aldermen but, with the Renaissance and the Italian revival of gem-cutting, the signet ring became once more an important part of the jeweller's trade. Their bezels were adorned with numerous devices which associated them with the owner. Initials and monograms were among the most common, since they could clearly admit of no confusion. Portrait heads in imitation of classical work were comparatively rare in the sixteenth and seventeenth centuries. With the classical revival of the eighteenth century, however, stylized heads were common, some of them, presumably, designed to represent the owner. For those entitled to coats of arms the armorial seal was often inscribed or engraved upon the bezel. Apart from the signets whose bezel was formed of an intaglio, the majority of signet rings, then as now, were fashioned in gold. For tradesmen who needed the signet for use in their business, the gold or silver signet must have proved invaluable. It indicated to illiterate employees and others who could neither read nor write the identity of the despatcher of the goods in question. Parcels and bales could be thus sealed and impressed.

Many of the finest signets, above all intaglios, belong to the eighteenth century. This is particularly true of English work. The inspiration given to the English arts and crafts by this revival inevitably left its mark upon the jeweller's work. From the middle of the eighteenth century date many of the best intaglios carved to represent classical heads.

The subject of the so-called 'papal' rings is one that has occasioned much controversy. The term has been loosely used to describe any large ecclesiastical ring. In fact, papal rings form a separate category of rings. Their outstanding feature is their great size. They are, indeed, far too large ever to have been worn in the ordinary way. Even worn as thumb-rings they could not have been retained long upon the hand. Their other distinguishing feature is that they are all made of base metals such as bronze and copper, and are set with common, poor-quality stones or pastes. Although there are examples of these rings which seem to date from the eleventh and twelfth centuries, the majority, judging from the arms they bear, date from the times of the fifteenth-century papacies. The fact that some of the rings bear the arms both of a pope and a king has suggested to some that they were connected with the transference of letters of importance from the pope to the king in question. This conjecture seems worthy of consideration. If these rings were used to indicate that the messenger was an emissary of the pope it would seem reasonable that they should be of little intrinsic value. They would offer little temptation to the thief or bandit upon the messenger's route. No definite explanation of their use can, however, be given. As examples of the jeweller's craft they are of little interest to the student or collector, being coarsely worked and cheaply set.

The true papal ring is that which is conferred upon the pope at his investiture. Its correct name is 'the ring of the fisherman' (Latin: *anulus piscatoris*), so called because it is engraved with the figure of St Peter casting a net into the sea from a boat. The ancestry of 'the ring of the fisherman' can be traced back only as far as the thirteenth century. From the middle of the sixteenth century dates the ceremony, still observed today, whereby, on the death of a pope, his *anulus piscatoris* is broken in front of a conclave of cardinals. A new ring is prepared before the election of the new pope with a space for his name left blank. When the pope has chosen his name, the ring is returned for engraving. The Victoria and Albert Museum is fortunate enough to possess an *anulus piscatoris*. The space for the name has here been left blank, so it is possible that this example had been prepared for an election and never used. Another possibility is that an astute Roman jeweller made the ring for an English traveller, knowing well what unique value it would have. The fact that the ring has been ascribed to the eighteenth century makes this supposition more reasonable since, of course, it was during this period that Rome was invaded by the wealthy English in search of works of art, antiques and souvenirs.

Episcopal rings are those conferred upon bishops at their consecration. Their use can be traced back with certainty to the seventh century. From the seventh century, too, dates the injunction that they shall be made of pure gold and set with a plain (i.e. not engraved) gem. A number of examples have survived and, allowing for the simple character of the gem-setting, many of them are fine examples of workmanship. The stones which have been traditionally used in England for episcopal rings are the ruby and the sapphire. The amethyst has also been employed in these episcopal rings.

Apart from these specialized categories of rings, there remain that vast number which can only be loosely labelled 'fancy' rings. Among them are to be found every type and style of design and the employment of every gemstone. Until the beginning of the twentieth century the jeweller had, of course, the choice of only two precious metals in which to work—gold and silver. These two metals are often used together in 'fancy' rings, the gold being nearly always used for the hoop or haft, and the silver for the collet and setting. It may be pointed out that a wide field of attractive rings is available to collectors of moderate means from those made during the nineteenth century. Although the official ruling of the British Antique Dealers' Association is still that an article, to be defined an antique, must have been made before 1830, this ruling is certain to be amended as the century advances. The collector of Victorian jewellery will thus be ensuring the preservation of pieces that will in due course be officially classified as antique. By the use of his own taste and discretion he can also secure for moderate prices rings which are very often of exquisite taste and workmanship. Much of the Victorian jewellery which was despised, broken up and re-set during the past thirty years is already becoming fashionable again. The quality of the craftsmanship in many of the Victorian rings which are set with semi-precious or lesser-known gemstones cannot be bettered.

Amethysts and garnets, which enjoyed widespread popularity during the eighteenth and nineteenth centuries, are stones admirably suited to ring design. A favourite form was the ring whose bezel was shaped like a dome into which were set small, faceted garnets held in rub-over settings. Cabochon-cut garnets were also favourites. In ring settings these stones were often drilled through the centre and held in place by a snake's head of gold rising from the shoulders and supporting a gold pin through the lower side of its head, thus securing the stone to the mount.

The amethyst was popular not only in England but also in France. Table-cut, it is a most beautiful stone if set in a well-designed, gold 'fancy' ring. The quality of Victorian gold filigree work is seldom given the praise which it deserves, but the collector who takes an interest in nineteenth-century jewellery will soon discover that, next to Etruscan work, gold filigree has probably rarely been better employed than by the Victorian jeweller. Although this applies especially to necklace settings, it will also be found true of rings, particularly where the stone is surrounded by delicate, wire filigree or where the shoulders are so decorated.

The fabrication of rings has always played so important a part in the jeweller's trade that a few notes upon the processes employed may assist the collector. Most important in the manufacture is the use of the drawbench and drawplate. These are two simple forms of the same tool, the use of which can be traced back with certainty to the fourteenth century, but which was probably known as early as 1000

B.C. The drawplate is a metal plate pierced by holes of various dimensions through which the precious metal is drawn to emerge as wire. The drawbench is merely an extension of the drawplate and is designed for drawing out the heavier gauges of wire. Before the invention of the drawplate a tool similar to the beading tool described by Theophilus was used. The metal wire, of course, forms the main part of a simple ring such as the wedding ring. In the manufacture of modern wedding and signet rings it is rolled out from gold sheet to the thickness required and is then passed through the drawplate in the traditional manner. If the ring is to be a gold wedding ring the wire will next be cut into the required lengths and soldered into hoops with gold solder of the same carat-quality as the ring. The ring is then ready for the polisher.

In the case of signet rings the method of manufacture has changed little in the course of centuries. Indeed, it seems likely that the shape of the signet with its flat bezel was suggested to the early jeweller by the very simplicity of the operation required. The gold strip needed only to be flattened at one point, and thus the table was formed upon which could be engraved the required name or device. Modern signets differ in their manufacture only to the extent that they are stamped out of rolled sheet metal, the blanks then being soldered together in exactly the same manner as the wedding ring. The flat top or table of the signet is filed by the jeweller into the shape required, and the ring is now finished except for polishing and engraving. In antique rings where an intaglio was to be set, the necessary hollow was cut in the metal to receive the stone. When the stone was ready it was placed in position and the surrounding edges of metal burred over to hold it in place—the 'rub-over' setting.

In gem-set rings the jeweller's principal object is, as always, to enhance the quality of the gemstones, and it is here that his skill both as designer and as craftsman plays its part. The stone or stones must not only be held securely, but also displayed so as to show themselves to the best advantage. The discovery of the beauty of faceted stones led to the claw setting which allows the maximum play of light through the stone with the maximum security. Previously, when stones were merely cut *en cabochon*, the rub-over setting was usually employed. In the claw setting, which is still most commonly used today, small strips of metal hold the stone securely, the top of each claw being turned over the stone just above the girdle (the stone's widest part). Many varieties of the claw setting are to be found and, as is to be expected, the jeweller tended to employ the one which he himself found most effective. Although there are a number of modern variants on the claw setting, their common ancestry is always apparent. The coronet claw is one which collectors will meet with in a number of nineteenth-century pieces. During the present century the mass-production of jewellers' 'findings'—as settings, clips and so on are called—has led to a standardization of types. The student of modern jewellery is advised to refer to any of the catalogues issued by British and American firms who specialize in 'findings'. There he will find all the modern variants of the claw listed and illustrated.

A type of setting which was popular during the nineteenth century was the *millegrain*. Minute beads of metal are pushed up to grip the girdle of the stone. This is thus held very securely, while the stone's depth of colour is intensified by the exclusion of light from the sides. Where the mount or head of a gem-set ring was required to be intricately pierced it was often made separately. The piercing was carried out in the usual manner with the hand-operated bow-drill, and the head then soldered on to the shank.

In conclusion, mention must be made of those rings which have acquired a romantic reputation through their association with the family of the Borgias—poison rings. Although we live in an age when few illusions are left to us—and it would be a pity to destroy those few which we have—yet it must be stated that no evidence exists to show that there ever were rings of this type. It is true that some rings have been found which have a hinged bezel that opens to disclose a small cavity within. But there is no evidence that these ever contained poison. It seems more probable that they did, in fact, contain some essence of perfume and thus constituted miniature pomanders. Fr. Rolfe, in his unusual book *Chronicles of the House of Borgia*, devoted a chapter to a consideration of this aspect of the Borgia legend. He was finally compelled to conclude that their knowledge of the subject was most probably insufficient to enable them to fabricate any drug that could both be deadly and concealed in so small a space as a ring.

CHAPTER NINE

Enamels and Enamelling

THE term 'enamel' is derived from an old form of the word 'to smelt' and is applied to vitreous glazes. It means the process of fusing powdered glass on to a surface that is capable of bearing red heat, such as metal. Enamels can be fused upon pottery, brick and many other substances, but so far as jewellery is concerned, the term is usually applied to articles treated in this manner that are made of gold, silver or copper.

The process of enamelling has been familiar to craftsmen for many centuries. The Egyptians were skilful enamellers and, apart from their excellent work upon brick and pottery, used enamels to enrich their jewellery. Greek and Roman jewellers were also acquainted with the process and used it for personal articles of jewellery, as well as for other types of decorative work.

The essential basis of all enamels is a transparent glass-like compound which is known either as paste or flux. This is usually composed of potash, silica and minium and can be coloured by the addition of various metallic oxides. The range of colour available is almost limitless, while, by various processes, the depth and density of colour can be most sensitively controlled. It would not be untrue to say that, of all the techniques available to the jeweller, enamelling gives the widest possible scope. It can be used not only for personal items of jewellery such as necklaces and brooches, but also for snuff-boxes, watch-cases, hair-combs and brushes. It presents a hard durable surface that is as suitable for the article which will be worn only occasionally as for the article which is in everyday use.

The reputation of British enamels was established as early as the second century A.D. by the Greek sophist and writer Philostratus who writes in his *Icones*: 'It is said that the barbarians, who dwell in the ocean beyond the pillars of Hercules [Gibraltar], pour colours into bronze moulds, and that the colours adhere, and become as hard as stone and preserve the designs made on them.' This technical skill was preserved by British jewellers throughout what are commonly called the 'Dark Ages'. Many of the best examples of Anglo-Saxon jewellery are enamelled, and the Kentish school of jewellers were adepts at the art. The Kingston brooch in the British Museum is not only one of the finest pieces of jewellery of its school, but is also a magnificent specimen of enamelwork.

Both clear and opaque enamels have been in use since the Middle Ages, and six main types of enamelling have been practised. One of the most important of these is *champlevé*. Although this method has freely been used by the goldsmith and jeweller, it has most commonly been practised by the worker in copper. In *champlevé* work the molten glass, or paste, is poured into hollows cut in the bronze or copper. The craftsman has first, in fact, to execute his design by digging out trenches or grooves in the metal. The form imposed by the *champlevé* technique is inevitably less delicate than that which is possible with other methods. It is likely that any assessment of a piece of *champlevé* will tend to 'over-date' it at first sight. Even if a piece was worked only yesterday, the method of working will inevitably suggest a style reminiscent of the Middle Ages. A certain angularity and coarseness of treatment is unavoidable. At its best, work in this medium can have something of the naïve grace of a Douanier Rousseau painting. It can never have the elegance with which the term 'enamel' is commonly associated. For by 'enamels' most people mean the exquisite work of the eighteenth century, of Battersea enamels, and of those associated with Limoges.

Niello work, which has been discussed elsewhere, has a great deal in common with *champlevé*. The main difference, of course, resides in the fact that, whereas in *champlevé* work the engraved or incised areas are filled in with vitreous glaze, in *niello* a compound of lead, sulphur and copper is used. One form of Renaissance *champlevé* work, however, which is most distinctive is that in which white enamel-work is contrasted with gold filigree or arabesques.

In the final analysis *champlevé* remains, principally, the method employed by the coppersmith and worker in bronze. It does not admit of the delicacy required by articles of jewellery for personal use. On the other hand, for articles such as crucifixes and religious emblems it has the advantage of boldness. Its wide areas of enamel stand out clearly and are distinctive even at a distance.

Cloisonné, or cell, enamelling is achieved by pouring molten enamel into cells or sections which are divided one from another by narrow strips of metal wire. It is, *par excellence*, the method employed by the jeweller and goldsmith. The ductility of gold makes this metal admirably suited for *cloisonné* work. The gold can be drawn into thin strips, which are then used for building up the cells or *cloisons*. This type of enamelling was used by classical goldsmiths and was later copied by the craftsmen of the Renaissance. Its advantages are obvious, for the fluid enamel can be contained within lines so fine that they are scarcely visible to the eye. Some of the most magnificent *cloisonné* work is Byzantine, the Byzantine jewellers having been greatly influenced by Eastern craftsmen and thus prone to the use of colourful enamels. The brilliant, fine lines of the gold strips were carefully employed by the Byzantine workmen to form a major part of the design. This spider's web of bright gold combined with the masses of enamel produces something of the same effect as a stained-glass window.

Apart from their decorative value the gold *cloisons* have a major rôle to play on the technical side. They contain the enamel and—enamel being glass—they prevent it from being chipped. The larger an area of enamel, the greater is the danger of cracking or chipping. The cells in *cloisonné* work thus fulfil three functions: they contain the enamel, they prevent it from being chipped or broken, and they can also be used to form a most decorative part of the design.

In making *cloisonné* enamels, the artist first of all traces his design upon the surface of the piece he is fabricating. After this, the strips of gold wire are drawn and are cut to form the cells. These strips are then soldered to the surface, the background of each cell sometimes being slightly 'roughed' to give the enamel something to grip on. The coloured fluxes are then poured into their cells, and, after firing, the whole is polished. In certain types of Oriental enamel of the *cloisonné* type the strips are not soldered to the base surface but are only glued. During the fusing of the enamels these glues melt and the metal strips are then held in suspension by the hardened enamels. This method, however, was not practised in Europe before the nineteenth century, and is unlikely to be found in any of the articles of jewellery which the collector is likely to meet.

Basse-taille, or translucent, enamelling is very similar to *champlevé* in that the areas for the enamels are scooped out of the metal. At this point, however, the resemblance ceases, since in *basse-taille* work the whole area—not only the scooped-out section—is covered with enamel; even the highest parts of the design are so covered. Silver or gold bases are usually employed for this type of work, and the effect achieved by it is most attractive. The colours of the enamels appear shaded according to their depth as it varies over the high and low parts of the design. A magnificent example of this type of work is the 'King's Cup', now to be seen in the British Museum. The process appears to have originated in Italy during the fourteenth century and from there to have been transferred to the other countries of the Continent. Some of the finest *basse-taille* work was executed in France.

The possibilities of translucent enamelling were fully developed with the discovery of the method known as *plique-à-jour*. In this the cells of enamel are treated rather as if they were themselves gemstones. No longer is the effect that of coloured glass held between walls of metal, but the attention is deliberately drawn to the enamel which is set in high relief and accorded the same type of treatment as if it were a stone. The main feature of this work is that the enamel has no base—it is held at the sides by a metal setting but is not backed with metal. Naturally, the fact that it is suspended 'in the open', as it were, makes for extreme fragility. This accounts for the fact that very little of this type of work has come down to us.

The resemblance between *cloisonné* work and stained-glass windows has already been commented upon. *Plique-à-jour*, however, is the only type of enamel which really deserves this description, since the effect arrived at is almost exactly the same as of a stained-glass window. An outstanding example is to be seen in a fifteenth-century cup in the Victoria and Albert Museum where the artist has deliberately stressed the stained-glass effect by making one of the main motifs a miniature church window.

The basis of work of this nature is a flux which has sufficient consistency to hold together when fluid, without, as it were, 'pouring through' the setting. It must, in fact, have somewhat the same consistency as treacle. Another and easier method is to pour the enamel into the setting but to leave a thin metal backing to hold the enamel until it has set. As soon as the enamel is hardened, the backing can be scraped away, leaving a perfect, transparent example of *plique-à-jour*. In his treatises on the art of goldsmithing, Cellini has left us with a description of his own methods for *plique-à-jour*—methods which were probably common to many craftsmen of the Renaissance. The design was laid out in strips of gold on a layer of clay lining an iron caisson. The clay prevented the enamel from adhering to the iron during the firing process. When broken away afterwards, it left the gold setting with the enamel contained in the centre exactly like a gemstone.

Towards the close of the fifteenth century in Europe, two major discoveries were made in the art of enamelling. First it was found that enamel could be fused on to both sides of a metal surface without being contained by wires, strips or *cloisons*, and secondly, that different shades of colour could be obtained by applying different coats of enamel upon one another after each had been fused; that is, if a green ground was applied first and then fused, it was found possible to apply another colour over it without causing either to break away from the surface or to mingle with each other. The basic principle of this work is, of course, to work with enamels which have different melting points. Provided that sufficient differentiation can be made between the melting points of the various enamels applied, there is practically no limit to the variety of colours that can be used. This type of enamelling is known as 'painted enamel' and has remained the most popular of all the methods. Its suitability for decorative work on boxware and similar objects can readily be seen. The term 'Limoges enamel' is commonly applied to this type of work, although there can be no certainty that it was originally discovered at Limoges. Many of the

Victorian ornament of amethysts and gold, showing the heavy style of setting and massive stones typical of the period.

Nineteenth-century topaz necklace set in pinchbeck which shows the delicacy of Victorian filigree work. From a suite which also includes earrings, and a cross which may be suspended from the necklace.

Above, left: *the Victorian love for opulent and massive jewellery is expressed in this pendant of yellow amber mounted in gold. The gold is chased with a foliate pattern.* Right: *another example of the delicacy of nineteenth-century filigree work—a gold butterfly brooch set with opals and other gemstones.*

The nineteenth-century jeweller made lavish use of richly coloured gemstones. Purples, pinks and yellows were highly favoured. This pendant cross is of deep purple amethysts set in gold.

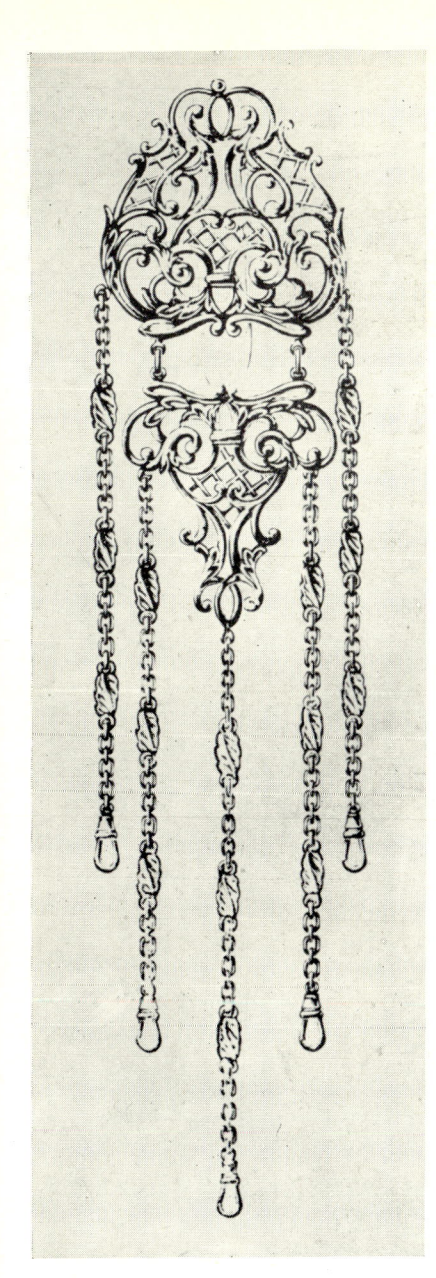

Nineteenth-century gold brooch bordered with pearls and garnets. The large central stone is a mixed-cut cairngorm.

Almandine garnet brooch mounted in gold, of mid- or late-nineteenth-century Central European workmanship. The garnets are backed with silver foil to reflect the purplish-red of the stones, which would otherwise appear almost black.

Jewellery of the 1880s was often intricate and elaborate in style. The chatelaine shown above comes from a jeweller's design-book of 1886.

Panagia by the Russian jeweller Peter Carl Fabergé, in enamelled gold set with pearls, cabochon rubies and brilliant-cut diamonds. The ikon is surmounted by the Russian crown.

traditional secrets of the Limoges enamellers owed their origin to the enamel-workers of Germany, particularly those of Cologne, whence they were transferred to France.

The work of the sixteenth-century French enamellers was of such a quality as to establish a great school and tradition in this type of work. Outstanding among these craftsmen were the Penicauds—Nardon, Jean Premier and J. B. Penicaud. Nardon Penicaud, who worked in the early sixteenth century, was a very fine artist, and a number of his works are still preserved in France. A magnificent example, which shows painted enamels used in conjunction with *paillons*, or small pieces of foil, thus giving a gem-like effect, is to be seen in the Cluny Museum. This use of *paillons* is only one of many small variants on the main types of enamelling. Each master had his distinctive 'tricks', if so one may term them, and there are so many of these minor variants that little would be gained by cataloguing them.

A follower of Nardon Penicaud was the famous Léonard Limousin, a considerable amount of whose work still survives and is to be found in many collections. Limousin was a master of painting in *grisaille*, or monochrome, and one of his most interesting works in this style is a plaque now to be seen in the Waddesdon Bequest Collection at the British Museum.

The technique of *grisaille* is similar to that of all painted enamels. The difference lies mainly in the fact that the painter first of all coats the surface of the piece upon which he is to work with a black enamel. This is fired and is then coated with white. After the second firing the artist is left with a grey enamel surface. Between the first and second firings the artist very often transferred his design on to the black enamel. His whole picture was finally built up by successive over-paintings—the whole emerging as a picture in graduated tones of white, grey and black. *Grisaille* work is most suitable for the reproduction of engravings and for other work where delicacy of execution is important. Even about the best *grisaille* work, however, there is, to the true lover of enamelling, a certain austerity which does not seem to belong to the medium. Enamelling, after all, is principally a means of introducing colour into a metal surface. To reduce it to monochrome seems almost a contradiction in terms.

An important variant of true *grisaille* work was painted *grisaille*, a style in which Léonard Limousin and Jean Penicaud were both skilled. The effect produced in this way is somewhat similar to that of a coloured print. Upon the *grisaille* foundation the artists worked with various shades and tints. Washes or glazes were also laid on in much the same manner as a painter may lay a glaze over some passage in order to change its tone or to accentuate its colour.

There remains a sixth and most important form of enamelling, usually referred to as 'encrusted enamel'. This term is used to cover enamelwork on jewellery, where the colour is painted upon the raised or modelled surfaces without being contained in cells. It is, in fact, very similar to Limoges or painted enamelwork with the difference that Limoges enamels are laid upon flat surfaces such as boxware, mirror backs, etc. Encrusted enamel is, then, that type of enamelling which is automatically associated with Renaissance jewellery. By the sixteenth century the goldsmith and jeweller were employing this type of enamelwork on every type of jewellery. Where the enamel was not held in place by a fine edging of gold wire or metal in relief, it was painted on to a roughened surface which thus possessed the necessary 'bite' to secure the enamel. Successive layers of enamel, each separately fired, were an added precaution whereby the jeweller prevented the enamel from chipping away. Inevitably, however, some of the jewellery which has survived has lost its enamel in the course of time. It is to the credit of the sixteenth- and seventeenth-century craftsmen that so much of their enamel jewellery still retains its colours.

The variety of colour which can be achieved by enamel processes is immense. The materials upon which enamel is laid have, of course, a considerable effect upon the tones. Pale yellow gold, for example, imparts a subtle mellowness to enamels, somewhat similar to the patina which age produces in a painting. Where silver is used as a base, great care has always to be exercised to prevent the silver from melting during the fusing process. (In modern work a furnace heated to 1,400 degrees F. is used.) For the enamel composition flint glass has long provided the essential basis. This flint glass, which contains between 25 and 40 per cent of lead oxide, is crushed and mixed with water and various colouring substances until a fine paste is produced. The minerals which have been used to produce the colour of enamels are many and varied. A bright blue, for instance, can be obtained by adding 2 per cent of oxide of cobalt to the glass paste. Dark red is made by adding ·01 per cent of gold chloride. Among other colours which have long been popular with the enameller are emerald green, achieved by adding 10 per cent of oxide of iron; purple by 15 per cent of permanganate of potash; yellow, by ·15 per cent of uranate of soda; and a light blue by adding 3 per cent of bichromate of potash. Oxide of tin when added to the lead glass base will produce an opaque enamel.

After his paste is ready the enameller spreads it over the surface, taking great care that it is laid on evenly and that the various colours do not overlap. The enamel is then ready to be fired. The old craftsmen had to spend a considerable time over the firing process, since their ovens could not attain anything like the temperatures which are so readily available today with the modern gas-fired furnace.

After each coat of enamel is laid, the piece must be refired. After the fusing process, the surface of the enamel is rough, so, between each separate firing, it must be smoothed on a carborundum wheel kept moist with clean water. The final polishing is done by holding the enamel surface against a rotating felt buff which is usually charged with pumice, this being one of the softest polishing agents.

It will be clear that in the making of enamel jewellery, much work goes into the enamel process alone—quite apart from the original designing of the piece, the gold work and the gem-setting. Every colour must be separately fired in order to prevent any spreading or overlapping, and an enamelled pendant may have required as many as nine or ten separate firings, in between each of which the piece must have been stoned and cleaned.

The craft of the enameller is today sadly neglected by those who buy jewels. Enamel jewellery is not fashionable and, inevitably, the lack of demand has meant that few enamellers are produced from the schools and training colleges. But the fact that there is little new enamelwork being made does not mean that the modern craftsman is not sufficiently skilled. An inspection of any of the exhibitions of contemporary craftsmanship held in the Goldsmiths' Hall, London, will reveal remarkably fine work. Unfortunately, the quality of the execution is not always matched by equal quality in modern design. It is to be hoped that a turn of the wheel of fashion will restore enamel jewellery to popularity. Encrusted enamelwork is one of the most delightful aspects of European jewellery and should not be allowed to become relegated only to museums and private collections of antique jewellery.

Although enamelwork is little found in contemporary European jewellery, it is still widely used for decorative articles such as brush sets, compacts, vanity-cases and similar objects. These articles are not strictly jewellery, and the enamelwork which is used on them certainly cannot be compared with the individual examples of master craftsmen such as those already referred to. Nevertheless, since the term 'enamel' is so much associated today with articles of this type, it may be of interest to describe the process whereby a modern enamelled brush or toilet set is manufactured. Although the approach is somewhat different from that of the craftsman who is making up an individual brooch, and although the modern manufacturing plant is alien to the conception of enamels as works of art, yet the skill and technique which lie behind the mass-production of such articles must still be respected.

First the designer evolves his pattern, bearing in mind the limitations of the plant of the firm for whom he is working and the price at which the article is required to sell. After the design has been approved, metal and other items are allocated and dies are cut. If the article is a brush or mirror, bristles and mirror glasses must then be ordered to fit the pattern. Most modern enamels are made on a silver base, and the sheet silver must therefore be marked out so as to avoid waste of the metal. Cutting machines, hand-operated, rough out the shapes, which are next passed to the die-stamping shop. Hand-cut in steel, the dies are placed upon the bed of the stamping block, putty is set around the recession in the die, and a molten alloy—usually of lead and tin—is poured in. As soon as this metal is beginning to set, the hammer of the stamp is lowered and picks up, on its toothed edge, the metal impression left from the die. The rough-cut silver metal shape is now laid upon the die, and the hammer, holding the impression, is lowered. The silver is thus 'forced' into the die by the metal impression or 'force' held on the toothed hammer. Even today in work of this type the hammer is hand-operated, since only the skill and knowledge of a trained workman can gauge exactly how hard the hammer must be lowered. This method of impressing precious metal with a die is far from being a twentieth-century or even a nineteenth-century invention. Although modern techniques of die-stamping are a considerable advance upon those known to earlier jewellers and goldsmiths, the principle has remained the same.

The excess metal surrounding the impression must be trimmed away before the article is ready for the polishing shop. (A clean, polished surface is essential before any article can be treated with enamel.) The most common modern type of enamelware is of the translucent variety, laid over an engine-turned design cut into the silver. This design shows through the enamel surface coating and produces an attractive patterned effect. Although most of the work is of a coarser nature, the idea behind this use of engine-turning combined with translucent enamel is somewhat similar to that of *basse-taille* enamels.

After the engine-turning is completed the piece is ready for the enamellers. The 'paste' is first of all mixed in a mortar and pestle and then spread on the mirror-back, brush, compact or whatever the article may be. If a single-colour, plain enamel surface is required—and this is most likely to be the case if the article is engine-turned—a first layer will be spread and fired, then a second and then a third. The three thicknesses of enamel give the article a greater degree of protection and will therefore last for a long time under any normal conditions. After their third firing the articles are ready for their final pumicing and polishing.

In the case of painted enamels, where a design or a scene is to be delineated, the technique remains the same as in the days of Léonard Limousin. The area to be painted is first of all covered with an opaque matt enamel in much the same way as an artist may 'tone down' a canvas before beginning his picture. This matt enamel provides the background on to which the design is transferred after the matt surface enamel has been fired. Each of the colours used must be fired successively. The colour range of a piece determines the time which must be given to the making of an article and, therefore, its cost. When the painting is completed it is given a final coat of colourless enamel, in the same way as a painting is varnished, in order to keep the dirt off its surface.

It should be said that nearly all enamels can be safely cleaned by washing, although the owner of a piece should, of course, take care not to use water anywhere near boiling point. A little lukewarm water and a very soft rag will do much to clean up a piece of enamel that has become dirty or discoloured. Every care should be taken with enamel pieces to see that whatever duster or cloth is used to clean them, it is perfectly clean and free from any grit or hard particles.

CHAPTER TEN

Cameos and Intaglios

THE delicacy, ingenuity and craftsmanship to be found in cameos and intaglios are qualities which appeal to all collectors. These engraved gems are sculpture in miniature. They deserve this title even more than other types of jewellery. At their best, cameos and intaglios possess a precision of workmanship which differentiates them from all other articles. The combination of stone-cutting and life-like representation, together with skilful setting, requires so high a degree of art, not to mention technique, that they deserve more adequate consideration than can be given to them in a brief chapter.

Definitions are important and it is essential first of all to be sure that the words 'cameo' and 'intaglio' are fully understood. The principal difference between the two is that the cameo is cut in relief, the design being sculptured so that it stands *above* the surrounding background. The intaglio is cut so that the design lies *below* the surface of the surrounding stone. Those who are familiar with silverware will see that the difference between the cameo and intaglio is much the same as that between embossed work and engraving.

Unfortunately, the term 'cameo' has become corrupted and has lost its original value. Recently, a friend was delighted to receive an invitation to inspect 'a large collection of cameos', and went off in eager anticipation. Returning, he said disgustedly, 'Nineteenth-century shell cameos'. The story is not told to excuse what may be regarded as a superior attitude to shell cameos: indeed, many shell cameos—and nineteenth-century work at that—are excellent. The point is that a definite distinction should be made between shell cameos and cameos carved in hard stones. The true and best cameo is one which is carved in precious or semi-precious stone. The shell cameo, while it has its own merits, is a definite type of its own, not equalling the best of the gemstone cameos.

While it is beyond dispute that during the past four centuries major technical improvements have been made in the lapidary's craft, it must be conceded that the quality of cameo and intaglio work has never been as good as that of the ancients. The gradual reduction of importance of the seal in everyday life has largely accounted for this. Once a man can sign his own name and write his own letters, the importance of an engraved symbol naturally declines.

It is to the early days of Near Eastern and Mediterranean jewellery that one must look in order to find the cameo and intaglio at their best, and at their most functional. The magnificence of so many of these early pieces lies in the fact that they are not only delicately and most precisely worked, but also that they have a certain grandeur about them—a boldness of conception which can only be compared to a Rubens working within the limits of a Nicholas Hilliard.

The art of stone engraving and cutting originally flourished in the Mesopotamian civilizations. Marble was the material chiefly used for these seals, which were fashioned in cylindrical shape. The advantage of the cylinder is obvious. It could be rolled over the seal that was to be impressed and could thus give a long impression —that is, of the whole of the circumference. Its use in this context is somewhat similar to the Chinese 'roll' paintings which, while being reducible into a convenient form, can at the same time give the maximum representation of a subject. In England, collectors are fortunate in having the magnificent collection of the British Museum at their disposal. Here, not only can the original seals be seen, but also, alongside them, are carefully-taken impressions. One of the most interesting of these is the very fine seal of Darius, King of the Persians, *c.* 500 B.C., which is an admirable specimen of the period.

The art of seal-cutting, however, was well developed by the fourth millennium B.C. Its greatest period during the Sumerian civilization was *c.* 2700 B.C., when the delicacy of the work reached a height that was not to be surpassed until the best period of the Greek and Roman lapidaries. These seals were not jewellery in the sense that we understand it today. They were circular rolls of marble or other stone which were pierced through the centre and slung on strings, their purpose being almost entirely functional; although there is no doubt that the quality of the best cut seals was appreciated as something admirable in itself—as a work of art, in fact. Haematite, quartz and rock-crystal were other materials which were used by these Mesopotamian lapidaries. Seals of this period of history are, of course, essentially 'museum pieces', and are most unlikely to come the way of the collector. Their importance must not, however, be forgotten. Apart from beaten gold and goldwork generally, they are the earliest examples known of what may well be called the 'ancestors of European jewellery'.

The Egyptians were quick to follow the methods of the Mesopotamian lapidaries. The scarab itself is one of the earliest types of seal, its base being cut in intaglio fashion with the owner's name, rank and so on. Unlike the Sumerians and Akkadians, whose seals were mainly pictorial representations of subjects such as hunting and religious ceremonies, the Egyptians mostly used script engravings on their seals. This makes them, in general, of lesser interest to the student of the craft. Their more frequent use of script was most probably dictated to them by their more easily worked system of notation. The cuneiform alphabet of the Mesopotamians was awkward and unattractive from the engraver's point of view, while the Egyptian hieroglyphic, with its semi-representational system, had a certain pictorial attraction of its own.

Many materials were used by the Egyptians for their seal-cutting. Most common, as one would expect, is *faience*, which was widely used for all articles of jewellery and for seals, particularly of the small scarab type. The Egyptians also used semi-precious stones for this purpose, of which the variously coloured members of the quartz group were most popular. Cornelian was another semi-precious stone which the lapidary found suitable for cutting and engraving.

How did these early gem-cutters and engravers work? The answer is—in almost the same manner as the craftsman today. It is this essential continuity in the jeweller's craft which helps to make the subject so fascinating. Even in the age of atomic power and of the electric brain nothing has yet been discovered which can equal the co-ordination of the human hand and eye when it comes to delicate precision work. When it is remembered that the hand which shapes and the eye which guides must also be controlled by a brain in which the details of the required design are held, it seems a reasonable prophecy that it will be a long time yet before the craftsman can be eliminated.

Besides shells, the technique of whose cutting is different and which is discussed later in this chapter, many materials are available to the cameo- or intaglio-cutter. Almost any of the hard, precious or semi-precious stones will serve the purpose. The opal, for instance, is one stone which, because of its soft nature, is clearly unsuitable. Amethyst or emerald are two of the principal gemstones which have been used by lapidaries for cameos and intaglios. The garnet, agate, jasper, haematite and turquoise are others.

The stone is first of all selected for its suitability for the cameo design. Different layers and areas of colour can be utilized in the design in the same manner in which the Renaissance craftsman elaborated his design around a baroque pearl. In this sense the art of cameo and intaglio work is different from that of the modern lapidary, whose concern is to bring out the faceted beauty of a perfect stone. The gem-cutter and engraver may well find that a stone, which is in a sense 'imperfect', may yield the best results. After the stone has been selected it must be 'roughed' into the shape required. For a ring, for instance, it must be cut into an oval or round shape as the setting may require. The table, the flat top surface of the gem, must now be cut and rough-polished.

At this point one may visualize the lapidary as being in the same situation as an artist who has primed his canvas. He now has the flat, bare surface before him, on to which his design must be transcribed. He may either—depending upon his method of work or the size of the gem—transfer his design to the table before starting to cut the stone, or he may work direct upon the stone, keeping his design beside him for reference. If the stone is soft, he can work by hand with cutting tools in exactly the same manner as the engraver. In most cases, however, the stone will be too hard for this treatment and the cutting wheel will be required.

In the early days of classical cameo-cutting the work appears to have been largely done with the bow-operated drill and with various shaped cutting-heads. Sapphire dust and sapphire points were in common use by the Greek lapidaries of the sixth and fifth centuries B.C. The use of the wheel was also known, the wheel being turned by a foot-operated treadle in much the same manner as the potter's wheel. The modern gem-cutter and engraver works in the same way, with the difference that he now has electric power which enables him to regulate the speed of his cutting discs more easily than was formerly possible. (It is worth remarking that modern advances in dental surgery have proved of great assistance to the lapidary. The modern dentist's drill, equipped with appropriate heads, is an admirable tool for some lapidary work.)

The technique of working is to hold the gem on a gemstick and apply it to the disc or wheel. The wheel can thus be made to turn at a predetermined speed, while the hand does the shaping by applying the face of the gem when and where necessary. It seems probable that, in the days before mechanical power was available, the procedure was reversed. The stone would be kept stationary and the drill held in the hand. This would appear to be a logical arrangement and one which would have its advantages when the drill was motivated either by hand or by foot. As with all gem-cutting, a mixture of oil and fine-ground, hard powder must be used on the cutting edge. Diamond powder was probably used by Roman lapidaries; references to the diamond's quality of hardness in Pliny reveal that its properties were well known. Before this, sapphire powder is likely to have been the principal medium employed in lapidary work.

For the precise detail required by gem-cutting and engraving the modern lapidary works with an eye-glass lens of the type commonly used by jewellers. There seems little doubt that even as early as the Greek and Roman era some form of lens must have been used. A number of references exist in ancient literature to the properties of magnifying glasses, one of the most specific being in Seneca's *Naturales Quaestiones*, Book I.

The full realization of the possibilities of gem-cutting came with the Minoan civilization, whose contributions to the cult of jewellery were very great. Engraved gems played an important part in Minoan culture and we find that in the work of these lapidaries the stone was considered in its context not solely as a means of identification—as a seal, in fact—but as a jewel, a work of art itself. The legacy of this Cretan work was bequeathed to the Greek lapidary, and it is from the sixth century B.C. onwards that we find the production of those masterpieces which have never been surpassed in the history of European jewellery. Lapidary work of the cameo and intaglio type is sculpture in miniature, so it is not unnatural to find reflected in Greek and Roman cameos and intaglios the various phases through which the art of these civilizations passed. It is enough for our purpose here to say that it is possible to trace the course of Greek intaglios from the early 'Archaic smile', through the full, serene glory of the Pheidian era, to the deliberate and dramatic style which is associated with the sculptor Scopias. The stiffness of the early carvings is superseded by a perfect and faithful naturalism, becomes charged with virtuosity, and then declines into a sugar-sweet sentimentality.

Apart from mythological subjects, many of these gems are carved with representations of everyday life. It is this which gives so many of them their great charm. Here we can see for ourselves a woman playing with a bird or taking a bath, a man pouring out a libation, an athlete combing off the dust with a strigil, or a huntsman pursuing his prey. These minute portraits of life are carved in many stones, among them the amethyst, cornelian, garnet and topaz. Rock-crystal, also, which had been used for this type of work since Sumerian times, was popular. Some of these intaglios will be found signed, others are inscribed with the name of the owner. Of the many fine artists who worked in the medium during the fifth century B.C. one of the finest was Epimenes, a number of whose signed pieces are in public collections throughout the world.

It must be remembered that all of these early carved gems were intaglios, the cameo as such not making its appearance until the Hellenistic period of Greek art. The reason for this is not difficult to find. So long as the cut gem was considered primarily in its function as a seal or signature, the intaglio was the obvious form to use. As soon, however, as the cut gem came to be considered as an item of jewellery, something more was needed, something bolder, making an immediate appeal to the eye. The appearance of the cameo was not delayed by technical difficulties. (It is, in fact, often a more difficult task to carve in intaglio than in relief.)

During the days of the early Roman Empire a passion for engraved gems absorbed all who were rich enough to indulge in this form of collecting. References to the whims and extravagances of collectors are scattered throughout Roman literature so widely that, if no gem had survived, it would still be possible to estimate how many varieties must once have existed. Fortunately, gemstones themselves are unlike the composite article of jewellery. The hardness, which is one of their chief attractions and which preserves them in the earth, preserves them also after the artifice of man has turned them into works of art. The amateur of gems, though he may never be able to possess any of these early masterpieces for himself, is fortunate in that he can enjoy many of them in the magnificent collections of the British Museum. The Roman period of gem-cutting and engraving is notable not only for the numbers of examples which still exist, but also for the variety of materials in which they are carved. The skill of the Roman glass-maker was also turned to account and many paste cameos and intaglios were made.

The story of the decline and fall of the Roman Empire is also the story of the decline and fall of the glyptic art. Although there is no doubt that some cameos and intaglios were made even during the Dark Ages, the art of gem-cutting and engraving was not revived until the Renaissance in Italy.

One result of the enthusiasm for all aspects of classical art which possessed the artists and craftsmen of the Renaissance was the rediscovery of classical gems. The amazement at the perfection of execution of these early masters was, of course, a spur to the craftsman of the day. No better picture of the enthusiasm which these early gems aroused can be found than that given by Cellini in the first book of his *Autobiography*. With his usual vitality he brings the whole atmosphere of the time vividly before our eyes:

> '. . . [This] was also the cause of my making acquaintance with certain hunters after curiosities, who followed in the track of those Lombard peasants who used to come to Rome to till the vineyards at the proper season. While digging the ground, they frequently turned up antique medals, agates, chrysophrases, cornelians and cameos; also sometimes jewels as, for instance, emeralds, sapphires, diamonds and rubies. The peasants used to sell things of this sort to the traders for a mere trifle; and I very often, when I met them, paid the latter several times as many golden crowns as they had given giulios for the same object. Independently of the profit I made by this traffic, which was at least tenfold, it brought me also

into agreeable relations with nearly all the cardinals of Rome. I will only touch upon a few of the most notable and rarest of these curiosities. There came into my hands, among many other fragments, the head of a dolphin about as big as a good-sized ballot bean. Not only was the style of this head extremely beautiful, but nature had here far surpassed art; for the stone was an emerald of such good colour, that the man who bought it from me for tens of crowns sold it again for hundreds after setting it as a finger-ring. I will mention another kind of gem; this was a magnificent topaz; and here art equalled nature; it was as large as a hazel nut, with the head of Minerva in a style of inconceivable beauty. I remember yet another precious stone, different from these; it was a cameo, engraved with Hercules binding Cerberus of the triple throat; such was its beauty and the skill of its workmanship, that our great Michel Agnolo protested that he had never seen anything so wonderful.'

Besides making copies of antique cameos and intaglios, the craftsmen of the Renaissance naturally executed their own designs. These can be detected as such by their subject matter which, even if it is not contemporary, is noticeably different from the work of the classical artists. A classical scene executed by an Italian sixteenth-century craftsman will usually tend to have an individualistic treatment that is quite distinct from early work. Where a deliberate imitation or even forgery has been attempted it is more difficult to differentiate. If the forger has copied some Roman or Greek gem with perfect fidelity, even down to the signature, the possibilities of detection are remote. In many cases, however, signatures have been wrongly copied, Latin or Roman characters being mixed with Greek, and so on. In the final analysis only experience can tell. The ability to distinguish between the genuine classical gem and the Renaissance copy is something which cannot be learnt in books, but only by handling and examining numbers of pieces. It must also be remembered that, if an intaglio is set in a sixteenth- or seventeenth- century setting, this does not necessarily mean that the gem was cut at that date. It was a very wide practice to set antique gemstones in Renaissance rings. It is a practice which has been carried on in European jewellery up to the present day.

Intaglios were also cut in precious metals, particularly during the fifteenth and sixteenth centuries. Both gold and silver were engraved with inscriptions, heads, rebuses and initials. These could be made by a mould system in much the same way as glass intaglios were made in Roman times. An individual motif or inscription would, of course, have to be engraved since there would be no advantage in making a mould. But it was obviously of advantage to the jeweller to be able to turn cameos or intaglios of popular figures or inscriptions out of a mould. Today similar cheap cameos and intaglios are mass-produced in much the same manner, though in far greater number.

The revival of the glyptic art was only temporary; by the seventeenth century the fashion had waned. The lapidary was now engaged almost entirely in the newly discovered methods of faceting precious and semi-precious stones. The decline was, as always, caused not by the lack of competent craftsmen but by the lack of demand.

The eighteenth century witnessed a further revival, particularly in France, where a number of excellent craftsmen distinguished themselves in this branch of lapidary work, and copies of classical cameos and intaglios were again made. They can usually be distinguished by their particularly 'French' interpretation of classicism. That is to say, they resemble in mood the paintings of François Boucher rather than, for instance, the wall paintings of Pompeii. Many of these cameos and intaglios have a definite charm and quality of their own. The majority of the best artists signed their names to them, among whom the Pichlers and Natter should be singled out for mention. Where deliberate forgery was intended it is usually possible to distinguish some anomaly or innovation which marks the gem as eighteenth-century work.

The modern collector is further safeguarded by the many museums and their specialized officials to whom he can apply for information and help. It was not until our own century that the scientific study of antiques was developed. The articles which deceived a dilettante Englishman on the Grand Tour two centuries ago are unlikely to deceive the modern expert equipped with a specialist knowledge of the subject and with the modern methods of testing and examination that the gemmologist has placed at his disposal.

Among the less valuable cameos dating from the eighteenth century are those made by the famous pottery and porcelain firm of Wedgwood. These must be considered one of the graceful but minor aspects of eighteenth-century jewellery, although they are by no means to be despised on that account. The cameos will be familiar to nearly all collectors, being cast in what may be called the traditional 'Wedgwood classical' style, the figures and heads being in white relief against a background of pale blue, green or buff. Set as brooches and surrounded by marcasites or cut-steel borders, they are often attractive.

Of somewhat similar nature and value are the glass cameos which were made by the Scots craftsman, Tassie. These were set in a variety of ways, as ring stones, as brooches, in combs, in bracelets and necklaces. As with the Wedgwood wares, they are usually set with surrounds of marcasites or cut steel. They were mounted in both silver and gold, as well as in pinchbeck and other gold substitutes. A considerable number of these still survive. This is not surprising, for a catalogue of the Tassie designs compiled by Professor Raspé lists several thousand different varieties. They cannot, however, be considered in the same light as true cameos or intaglios since they were not individual products of the craftsman's skill but were cast in moulds.

Shell cameos have enjoyed a steady popularity from the eighteenth century to the present day. Because of the cheapness of the material and the comparative ease with which it can be cut, the shell cameo, even if a good specimen, remains comparatively inexpensive. The cameo is carved in the mollusc shell with hand-tools and does not require the wheel or disc treatment essential for the hard-stone cameo or intaglio. Similar tools to those used in silver chasing and engraving are suitable for work on shell cameos, the material being cut or sliced quite easily.

These cameos have been made in such large numbers and by so many workmen throughout the world that it is practically impossible to provide any hints as to what to look for. Very few of them are signed and, even where they are, the name of the artist is usually unknown. The collector must be guided entirely by his own taste and judgment. So many shell cameos are on the market that it is safe to say that the majority are of little worth or value. Many of them are, however, exquisitely carved and should be judged by the quality of the work and the pleasure which can be got from them rather than from any financial consideration. Shell cameos will be found in every type of setting and decoration—from rings and brooches to ear-rings and hair-combs. The quality of the setting is often an indication of the quality of the cameo carving, since the cheap articles which have been produced in such great numbers in Italy and elsewhere are usually coarsely and simply set. The craft of cutting these cameos has been practised in Italy since the fifteenth century and still gives employment to a considerable number of craftsmen. Modern work is usually coarser in quality than the early specimens, the articles being produced quickly and cheaply for tourists.

Within the past ten years a form of imitation shell cameo has been widely marketed by modern manufacturers, against which the collector should be warned. These imitation cameos are mass-produced by injection-moulding in plastics and have at first sight a resemblance to the real article. They can, however, be quite easily detected. Firstly, the settings tend to be rather coarse and are often of base metal plated to resemble gold. Secondly, the cameo has quite a different feel from the true shell. Thirdly, visual inspection will soon reveal that the cameo is not 'cut' into the material, but that it has all been moulded in one piece. These cameos are, of course, sold as imitation and with no attempt to deceive. It is possible, however, that second-hand examples may be encountered and may be sold as genuine articles by people having little knowledge of gems and jewellery.

CHAPTER ELEVEN

Paste, Marcasite and Cut-steel Jewellery

'BETTER a diamond with a flaw than a pebble without'—so runs a Chinese proverb. The European reply to this might well read, 'Better a pebble that resembles a diamond than none at all'. Substitutes for diamonds and other precious stones have been used by jewellers since the craft existed. The Roman jeweller was an expert in the manufacture of paste or glass substitutes, and this traditional skill was preserved in Italy. During the sixteenth and seventeenth centuries the manufacture of pastes was widely practised, particularly in Milan, where the glass-makers were famous for their work. Paste was also used by the early British craftsmen, and much of the jewellery of the Anglo-Saxon school is set with pastes. In those early days little or no distinction was made between precious, or semi-precious, stones and pastes. (The Kingston brooch, for example, is set with both garnets and paste.) English skill in glass-making and particularly, during the eighteenth century, in the manufacture of flint glass, provided the jeweller of this country with a very fine-quality glass that could be cut and faceted much like a precious stone.

Paste, the most common and the most popular diamond substitute, is a glass product with a refractive index of about 1·5. It is often harder than window glass, but can still be quite easily scratched, and for this reason should be treated with some care. Two types of glass are commonly used for imitation gems. Flint glass, already referred to, is so-called because, in the early days of its manufacture, crushed flints provided the silica. It is a compound of silica, lead oxide and potash or soda. The second type of glass is commonly called bottle glass and is a compound of silica, lime and potash of soda, together with various oxides which are used for colouring the glass.

Paste used as a diamond substitute is usually flint or lead glass, since it is brighter and more suitable for faceting. It is often referred to as Strass after the name of its supposed discoverer, Josef Strass or Strasser. Strass or Strasser is a fairly common name in Austria and it may well be that Josef was a Viennese, since there was a tradition of fine-glass manufacture in Vienna. He appears to have resided in Paris during the mid-eighteenth century and there is a reference to his name in connection with paste in 1758. The word 'paste' itself is a reminder of the old Italian glass-makers, since it is derived from the Italian *pasta* (pastry). This was undoubtedly a mocking term bestowed upon it by the lapidary and jeweller in allusion to its softness compared with most real stones.

The paste-set articles which are of most interest to the collector are those made during the eighteenth century. There are two main reasons why these pieces are particularly attractive. Firstly, they are most skilfully set in direct imitation of precious, gem-set jewellery and, secondly, the paste itself is usually of good quality. A considerable amount of eighteenth-century paste still survives, a fact which may seem strange in view of its comparatively cheap quality. It is, however, just this cheapness which has protected it. When fashions changed, it was not worth breaking up a paste necklace and having it reset. A new necklace was bought, and the old one relegated to a cupboard, given away, or sold to a dealer in second-hand jewellery. Moreover, so many articles set with paste were made during the second half of the eighteenth century that a large number must survive today.

The manufacture of so large a quantity of paste jewellery was due to changed social conditions. In England, particularly, the rise of a prosperous middle class provided a vast new market for the jeweller. The bourgeois tradesman and merchant could not, however, afford to rival the upper classes in his display of diamonds, and found in paste an admirable substitute. In addition, the fashions of the time called for shoe-buckles. Few men, whatever their wealth, could be disposed to have such articles set with diamonds, so shoe-buckles were almost invariably set with paste.

The styles and the settings in which paste jewellery was made follow closely upon those evolved for precious jewellery for the same period.[1] Bow brooches, openwork bracelets and necklaces, and floral sprays were carefully copied. The jeweller who was making a diamond-set, silver bow brooch, was also making much the same article set with paste. The same skilled workmanship went into both, and it is this fact which gives eighteenth-century paste jewellery its importance. Apart from the substitution of paste for diamonds, there was often little difference between them.

Two misnomers for paste which the collector may meet are 'rhinestone' and 'Bristol stone'. The term rhinestone is one which is commonly used today. The use of the term as applied to paste appears to have originated in the United States and was presumably designed by the enterprising jeweller or advertising agent to capture the public by its more romantic associations. Rhinestone, however, is a completely different substance and the term should be applied only to cut rock-crystal. Bristol stone, again, is truly a natural stone, a colourless quartz, and has in fact been used for jewellery in the same way as the rhinestone. It is easy to see how

[1] See pp. 78–80, and 83–89 *passim*.

Towards the close of the nineteenth century the tiara, de rigueur for the ball or the opera, grew ever more elaborate in design. For the up-to-date the new white metal, platinum, set off the dazzling display of diamonds.

Peridot, yellowish-green in colour, was one of the fashionable stones of the 1880s. This pendant brooch has a step-cut peridot bordered with diamonds above the bow, and a pendeloque peridot drop below.

The excellence of modern diamond-cutting is shown in this composite necklace of baguette, marquise, brilliant- and square-cut diamonds. It divides to form two bracelets, ear-clips and a brooch (M. P. Greengross).

this term became confused with paste in England, for Bristol was a great centre of the glass industry and a considerable amount of paste was made there. The well-known coloured Bristol glass used for sapphire and amethyst substitutes quite naturally, but incorrectly, became known as 'Bristol stones' or 'Bristows'.

Eighteenth-century paste has often been praised for its soft colour. It is true that this mellow colour is undoubtedly attractive, but it was no more intended by the original jewellers than is the patina on an old master. The principal cause of this mellow lustre is that the pastes have tended to lose some of their polish during the course of years. Being of glass, they are also liable to discolouration by the sulphur content of the smoke in our modern cities. Another reason for the colour of old paste is that the foils which back it have become tarnished or discoloured with age.

These foils were used to back paste stones in much the same manner as, in the sixteenth century, they had been used to back diamonds. They were used to give the imitation stone something like the same brilliance as the brilliant- or rose-cut diamond. Even where these foils have become discoloured or broken with age, it would not be correct to have them removed or replaced. Admittedly, by doing so and by having the pastes and the whole mount cleaned, the brilliance will be intensified and something like the original effect restored. However, in articles like paste jewellery, this cleaning defeats its object. Although the cleaning of old paintings is a subject for dispute, it is possible to maintain that, by careful cleaning, the picture may be nearly restored to the condition in which it left the painter's studio. Even here, however, there is a school of thought which maintains that time and the patina of age improve a picture. But to clean minor articles of jewellery, such as paste, would not only invalidate their claims to be genuine but would also destroy that patina which, in the case of much eighteenth-century paste, is half its charm.

Paste stones held in claw settings were not often backed with a foil. Those set in *pavé* or rub-over settings, however, were usually backed. The pastework of the later eighteenth century tends to favour the *pavé* setting as does the diamond jewellery of the same period. The metal most commonly used is, of course, silver. This was ideal for the imitation diamond, particularly in the days when silver was also used for diamonds themselves. Today, when diamonds are invariably set in either platinum, palladium or gold, the use of silver is restricted almost entirely to imitation jewellery such as that set with pastes.

Gold was also used as a setting, especially where the paste stones were coloured. Good-quality paste, coloured to resemble sapphires, topaz and other fashionable stones, was common in the eighteenth century. Emerald colours were also successfully imitated. One stone which has to this day defied the copyist is the ruby. Although ruby-coloured pastes have been made since the last quarter of the eighteenth century, no one has as yet managed to produce a paste which has anything approaching the true colour and depth of the ruby.

One non-precious metal which is found used for certain paste articles is pewter. I myself have never come across it other than in shoe-buckles, although there seems little doubt that it was used for cheaper articles of every kind. The grey, smoky colour of pewter is particularly attractive in an article as simple as a buckle. Naturally it does not have anything like the same reflectivity as silver.

No one need be deceived by paste—in the sense of taking it to be the real stone which it imitates. The tests for paste are very simple and, although due care should be exercised, can easily be made. It can be readily scratched with a steel file, which should, of course, only be drawn across some part of the stone that is not visible in the setting. A piece of paste jewellery placed against the tongue will feel warm, while a diamond or other natural stone will feel cold. However, the qualities of paste are so well known and its appearance so different from the diamond—even to the comparatively inexperienced—that no fear should be felt on this score.

Another imitation of the diamond which may sometimes be encountered is made from fused beryl or quartz. This will be found only in articles of good quality. It was used during the nineteenth century and is still sometimes found today. Quartz, however, is considerably harder than glass and can be distinguished from it on this score alone.

A word of warning must be given about pastes that may have been used to give a false depth of colour to an indifferent but genuine stone. Suppose this stone to be an emerald or sapphire of poor quality; it is possible for a natural layer of real stone to be laid upon a coloured paste so that the effect will be that of a good coloured sapphire or emerald, while the top surface—being real—will pass the usual tests. A deliberate deception of this nature, however, is unlikely to be encountered by the collector in search of antique jewellery. Any jeweller equipped with the proper testing equipment can soon expose such an attempt at fraud. Indeed, there is little danger to the collector of being deceived or having such frauds practised upon him in Britain. The traveller to the East, however, should beware. It is an old saying that 'more scarab jewellery comes out of Egypt than ever the Pharaohs saw'.

The value of antique paste depends largely upon three things, the quality of the paste itself, the workmanship involved in the setting, and the fineness of the cutting or faceting. The best quality Strass or lead glass is usually well cut. Being comparatively soft, however, it has the disadvantage of discolouring more quickly than bottle glass. Paste is still made in the same manner today as it was in the eighteenth century. Most of it comes from France, Austria and Czechoslovakia, the good quality Strass being faceted in the same manner as are precious stones. Bottle-glass paste, on the other hand, is moulded, not cut, a cheaper method of manufacture.

During the period following the Revolution, paste enjoyed a wide vogue in France because it was comparatively inexpensive and because it accorded well with the simpler fashions of the *citoyennes*. Not as attractively set, nor so lavishly displayed, the paste of this era can be distinguished from the best eighteenth-century work mainly by reason of the fact that both follow the fashions predominant in other, more expensive, articles of jewellery.

Good-quality paste is still made today, hand-set in the same manner as precious jewellery and mounted in silver. Although many of these good paste brooches follow early designs, it is usually easy to distinguish them from eighteenth- and nineteenth-century pieces by their brilliance. Modern pieces of first-class quality, moreover, make more use of the claw setting than was customary in the eighteenth century; and they have no foil or backing. Almost all modern paste is backed with mercury or quicksilver, this being a simpler and cheaper method than fashioning an individual foil for each stone.

Plastics are also used today for cheap imitation stones. These have the advantage of being easily moulded as well as having a wide colour range. They are easy to distinguish from real glass pastes. Apart from the feel of plastic, the material is considerably softer. These plastic 'pastes' will be found only in the cheaper articles of modern costume jewellery, and there is no danger of the collector being deceived by them.

Two other forms of imitation jewellery used in the eighteenth century were marcasite and cut steel. Both were in use throughout the nineteenth century, and marcasite is still employed today. The term 'marcasite' is a misnomer, for it is not this mineral, but one closely resembling it, which is used in jewellery. The jeweller's 'marcasite' is in fact iron pyrites. This mineral has the same qualities as flint and, like flint, would appear to have been used by the ancients for fire-making purposes. Pyrites has the same chemical composition as marcasite, so it is not surprising that the two have become confused. It is possible that they were even further confused by the use of iron pyrites for 'marquise' rings, a confusion which has led to marcasite being sometimes spelled as 'marquisite'.

The main source of iron pyrites in European jewellery has been, and remains, Central Europe and France. The cutting of the mineral into facets was done by hand, and a traditional industry of this nature still exists in France, from where most modern cut 'marcasites' are imported into Britain.

The popularity of marcasite jewellery in the eighteenth century may be traced to much the same sources as that of paste. In addition, the financial retrenchments of the reign of Louis XV accelerated its use. M. de Silhouette, who was one of the Ministers of Finance during the reign of Louis XV, was credited with causing the widespread adoption of marcasite. His name indissolubly linked with the portraits that were presumed to be another off-shoot of his economies, M. de Silhouette goes down to history as an astute minister whose unpopularity resulted from trying to make the French pay their taxes and from trying to curb their desire for elegant living. If one of the results of his economies was the widespread demand for marcasite jewellery, then he deserves the collector's blessing. Many of these items—though inexpensive in themselves—are very charming and beautifully worked. By its nature, marcasite could not be used in the same manner as paste. The 'stones' themselves are very small, while the dense nature of the substance meant that there could be no play of light *through* the 'stone'. However, as they were hard and took a good polish, marcasites could be faceted and polished so that they reflected the light *off* their surfaces. They are usually rose-cut, this being the most suitable form of cutting. In eighteenth-century work the marcasites are usually *pavé*-set, the small burred edges of metal intensifying their sparkle. They were usually mounted in silver. Besides forming a most attractive surround to lockets, cameos, enamels and mosaics, marcasites were set in a narrow row to form bow and knot brooches.

Throughout the nineteenth century marcasite continued to have a steady, if more limited, popularity. These later examples are usually not as well set and are more coarsely mounted than eighteenth-century work. They had now degenerated from being a fashionable gem-substitute to being jewellery for those who could not afford better. At the same time, marcasites used as borders for pendants, brooches and ear-rings are still found in fine-quality nineteenth-century work. During the vogue for pendant ear-rings they were often set as surrounds for small enamels or miniature mosaics of the Tonbridge-ware type.

Marcasite is still used in modern jewellery and is set in silver in much the same fashion as in the early pieces. In the cheaper types of jewellery, however, the setting is not rubbed over but the stones are held in place by a form of cement. For the cheaper types of costume jewellery, the marcasites are often counterfeited by coloured glass or plastics. No difficulty exists in distinguishing between these cheap imitations and the genuine article.

Jewellery of cut steel enjoyed a great vogue in the eighteenth century. Somewhat similar to marcasite in appearance, it is formed of cut and polished pieces of steel about the same size as individual marcasites. A considerable amount of craftsmanship was used in the fabrication of these cut-steel 'heads'. Individually faceted and polished, they were held in their mounts by small rivets, an operation involving much work and skill. Similar types of articles to those set with marcasite were made in cut steel, principally belt- and shoe-buckles and clasps. Designs of great intricacy and delicacy were used and, since for its maximum effect a considerable number of individual steel 'heads' were required, these designs tended to follow contemporary bow and scroll motifs where long lines of polished 'heads' could be seen at their best. Cameos were also mounted with surrounds of cut steel. Some of the most attractive of these were made in Britain to surround the Wedgwood plaques and cameos which enjoyed so wide a popularity both in England and France.

The manufacture of this cut-steel jewellery was undertaken largely at Birmingham. Matthew Boulton was one of the Birmingham manufacturers who specialized in this type of work. Indeed, so important had this aspect of the jewellery trade become to Birmingham that, early in the nineteenth century, the manufacturers appealed to the Prince Regent to revive the wearing of shoe-buckles to save their trade from its decline. It is recorded that the Prince graciously agreed to assist his subjects by wearing shoe-buckles. Despite this Royal assistance, however, the trade continued to decline. It is possible that the Prince's influence on matters of fashion was less than he had anticipated.

A later development was the manufacture of sheets of cut steel in which the individual heads were simulated but were not in fact individually constructed. This mass-production completely removed the article from the sphere of quality jewellery. These cheaper manufactures are easy to detect, since in the genuine early work each individual 'head' is separately set and separately riveted. Steel jewellery is not made today, as it would be fairly expensive and so many other alternatives to it exist. Articles in which cut steel might previously have been employed can now be mass-produced in base metals.

The intrinsic value of paste, marcasite and cut-steel jewellery is usually small. It is the quality of the design and the amount of craftsmanship involved which counts. A hand-set paste necklace in silver may entail almost as many hours at the mounter's and setter's bench as a necklace of diamonds. This, of course, is true only if the necklace is of the first quality—the type which may be called the 'gem-set imitation'. Even today in England, France and elsewhere there are firms who specialize in such work. It should never be confused with the cheap, mass-produced article which has little or no hand-work in it, and in which the pastes are not held by individual settings but are secured by cements.

CHAPTER TWELVE

Birthstones

INTEREST in the supposedly mystical qualities of gemstones has been widespread in Europe for many centuries. The attribution to precious stones of powers such as preservation from disease, freedom from the evil eye, and so on, is pre-Christian in origin. It was, indeed, natural that the colour, shape and feel of different precious stones should suggest to the ancients that individual properties were latent in the mineral—properties either of a mystical or a sympathetic magic character.

During the Middle Ages, as the writings of the monk Theophilus reveal, many of the pagan legends regarding gemstones were preserved. These legends were grafted on to Christian and also Jewish traditions, so that it may be said that the modern list of stones associated with the different months of the year is a *mélange* of the customs and religious traditions not only of Europe but also of the Levant and the Near East.

The collector of antique jewellery may well find an interesting sideline in forming a small collection of, say, gem-set rings, each being set with the stone for the month of the year. Alternatively, he should at least revive the tradition of seeing that his wife possesses an item of jewellery set with her birthstone! Traditions of this nature have evolved over so many centuries that it would be a pity if they were allowed to disappear in our somewhat traditionless age.

The working jeweller is dependent for his existence largely upon the survival of traditions of this nature. Where would he be without the constant demand for engagement and wedding rings? Today, when few rings are worn as compared with the past, the revival of the wearing of birthstone rings and jewellery would prove of immense value. For, without demand, there can be no supply and, therefore, no craftsmen.

It was not until the eighteenth century that the custom of wearing natal stones became widespread throughout Europe. The associations of gemstones with specific months was originally conceived on the basis of colour, with the result that the type of stone allotted to any one month varied from time to time. One colour might well be represented by a number of different stones. This has resulted in some confusion with regard to birthstones, a confusion which has been finally cleared up by the researches of the National Association of Goldsmiths in Great Britain. The Association's list, established in 1937, has been followed in the British Dominions and in the United States of America. It reads

Month	Colour	Gemstone
January	Dark red	Garnet
February	Purple	Amethyst
March	Pale blue	Aquamarine; alternative, Bloodstone
April	Colourless	Diamond; alternative, Rock-crystal
May	Bright green	Emerald; alternative, Chrysoprase
June	Cream	Pearl; alternative, Moonstone
July	Red	Ruby; alternative, Cornelian or Onyx
August	Pale green	Peridot; alternative, Sardonyx
September	Deep blue	Sapphire; alternative, Lapis-lazuli
October	Variegated	Opal
November	Yellow	Topaz
December	Sky blue	Turquoise

The custom of wearing birthstone gems appears to have been first popularized by Jewish immigrants to Poland and Central Europe, for the two chief lists, on which the modern one is based, are the stones of the High Priest's breastplate and the twelve foundation stones of the New Jerusalem. Behind the theory of a link between a given gemstone and a given month of the year lies the neo-Platonic conception of a link between minerals and the planetary influence under which they are presumed to have been formed. The astrological theory of a connection between a human being and his planetary or zodiacal sign is, of course, very old—certainly as old as the Chaldean civilization. It is not unnatural that the two astrological or zodiacal ideas should have been combined; that is, that the stone appropriate to a certain planet will be appropriate to the human being born under the influence of that planet.

It is a strange fact that so many of the old lists of birthstones are similar. As they were worked out in different countries at different dates, their similarity must be due to something more than coincidence. Perhaps the answer is simply that the tradition passed from generation to generation and from country to country.

The principal source of this European tradition, which accounts for its continuity over the centuries in so many different countries, is the Book of the Revelation of St

John the Divine. In verses 19 and 20 of Chapter XXI, St John lists the twelve stones forming the foundation stones of the New Jerusalem as follows:

> 19. And the foundations of the wall of the city were garnished with all manner of precious stones. The first foundation was jasper; the second, sapphire; the third, a chalcedony; the fourth, an emerald;
> 20. The fifth, sardonyx; the sixth, sardius; the seventh, chrysolyte; the eighth, beryl; the ninth, a topaz; the tenth, a chrysoprasus; the eleventh, a jacinth; the twelfth, an amethyst.

It is interesting to compare this list with that other main source of Christian tradition, the Book of Exodus. In Chapter XXVIII there is a description of the twelve stones set in the Breastplate of Judgement.[1] This was the sacred breastplate in which were contained the mystical Urim and Thummim, and which was first worn by Aaron and subsequently by every High Priest of Jerusalem.

A comparison of the list in Exodus with the twelve foundation stones of the New Jerusalem reveals a similarity which seems more than coincidence. The most reasonable explanation would seem to be that, even in his mystical trance, the subconscious mind of St John was active. Familiar as he undoubtedly was with the Book of Exodus, it would be only natural that a similar list of stones should come into his mind when he was striving to interpret the glories of the New Jerusalem.

If we take sardonyx and sard to be similar or identical stones, the only difference in the lists is the mention of the diamond in Exodus and the ligure. The latter has never been identified. In the case of the diamond, however, the chrysolite given by St John seems a more reasonable choice, for we can be certain that no gem-engraver—at the time when the Book of Exodus was written—would have been able to engrave a diamond. The instruction that the stones were to be engraved, with its specific reference to 'like the engravings of a signet', leaves no doubt in one's mind as to the author's intention. But, as we know, it was not until the seventeenth century that the art of diamond-cutting was mastered. The diamond, therefore, can safely be dismissed in this context, and it seems reasonable to accept the chrysolite in its place.

---

[1] Exodus XXVIII. v. 17. And thou shalt set in it settings of stones, even four rows of stones: the first row shall be a sardius, a topaz, and a carbuncle: this shall be the first row. 18. And the second row shall be an emerald, a sapphire, and a diamond. 19. And the third row a ligure, an agate, and an amethyst. 20. And the fourth row a beryl, and an onyx, and a jasper: they shall be set in gold in their inclosings. 21. And the stones shall be with the names of the children of Israel, twelve, according to their names, like the engravings of a signet; every one with his name shall they be according to the twelve tribes.

The brooch which divides to form a pair of clips is one of the most popular forms of jewellery. This double clip is of platinum, set with well-matched rubies in collet settings, and baguettes and brilliant-cut diamonds (H. A. Byworth).

Daffodil ear-clip and cocktail ring from a modern suite which also includes necklace and brooch. In gold, set with diamonds and rubies (D. Shackman & Sons).

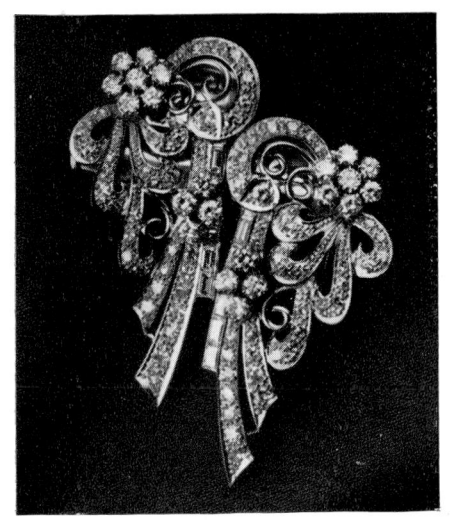

Another modern double clip, asymmetrical in design, set with diamonds (Wright and Hadgkiss).

Clusters of sapphires with baguette and brilliant-cut diamonds are used in this platinum bracelet. The open settings allow the maximum of light to be reflected (M. P. Greengross).

Left: *detail showing the central motif of a twisted gold necklace. The leaves are of palladium wire. The flower is a mass of rubies* (Roy C. King). Right: *a graceful spray brooch in platinum and diamonds. Brilliant-cut diamonds in claw settings form the flowers; the leaves are of platinum wire.*

The cocktail ring has enjoyed considerable popularity in recent years. The ring shown is of gold set with a yellow diamond surrounded by brilliants (D. Shackman & Sons).

Above: *an example of modern design in floral spray jewellery—a gold brooch set with rubies, sapphires and other coloured gemstones* (Whitehorn Bros.). Top, right: *a large pearl trapped by gold wires in a gold seashell is the motif for an unusual cocktail ring* (M. Bialkiewicz). Centre, right: *modern Creole-type earclip in gold with brilliant-cut rubies set in engraved stars* (Roy C. King).

An asymmetrical double clip which contrasts rubies in a gold setting with diamonds in platinum, and which shows the high standard of modern gem-cutting (D. A. Soley).

Necklace from a suite in palladium and diamonds made for the Festival of Britain, 1951.

It is pertinent at this point to warn the collector against the danger of accepting at their face value the nomenclature of gemstones in old documents and catalogues—at any rate, without a regard to the known history of stones and lapidary work. The diamond, as we have here seen, is described as a stone which can be engraved at a time when we know from all sources that it could not even be faceted. In assessing manuscript descriptions of gemstones it is always worth bearing in mind that the scientific means for testing gemstones did not exist until the late nineteenth and twentieth centuries. The one essential item in a jewellery collector's equipment is a working knowledge of gemmology and lapidary work, without which he is in the position of a pianist who aspires to play Bach without a knowledge of elementary finger exercises.

A brief commentary on the modern list of birthstones may assist collectors in determining what types of pieces are available and where the various stones are most likely to be found. The garnet comes first, being ascribed to January. Those with birthdays during this month are fortunate in possessing so attractive a stone, one which has long played a part in European jewellery. Garnets are not invariably nor necessarily red, but the rich plum-coloured almandine garnet is generally considered typical of the stone. It is found in European work from classical times onwards, cut first of all *en cabochon* and, later, table- or step-cut. The garnet has been used in a great deal of Bohemian and Middle European work, with the result that it is still possible to acquire a first-class specimen of eighteenth- or nineteenth-century garnet jewellery for ten to twenty pounds. Many of the nineteenth-century pieces are set with brilliant-cut garnets, a cut which particularly suits the red almandine.

The amethyst, a stone which was extremely fashionable in Victorian England, belongs to February. Its name is taken from the Greek and signifies 'not drunken'. As an emblem of sobriety and asceticism it has, therefore, long been associated with the Church and is one of the stones traditionally used for episcopal rings.

The aquamarine and the bloodstone, in that order, are assigned to March. Of the two, the variant bloodstone, although less well known, is most suitable for individual setting in rings. The aquamarine, on account of its light colour, usually appears at its best in conjunction with other stones in a bracelet or brooch.

Although there is less traditional authority for including the diamond in the birthstone list than for most other stones, it would be unthinkable to leave it out. It is ascribed in the modern list to April, while the month's alternative stone is rock-crystal. Besides being the traditional material for the crystal-gazer's ball, rock-crystal is one of the noblest diamond substitutes and has been popular in this respect since the eighteenth century. In the nineteenth and early twentieth centuries it was often polished into heart or crystal shapes and used as a pendant on a length of velvet ribbon.

The emerald belongs to May. It has been widely used in European jewellery since antiquity and is most commonly found in Renaissance Spanish jewellery. From the eighteenth century it will usually be found step- or trap-cut, very often in an individual setting such as a ring. Occasionally one may come across magnificent nineteenth-century *rivière* necklaces where the stone is used in contrast with the diamond.

The pearl, of which, according to St John, the gates of the New Jerusalem were formed, is the birthstone for June. Although not mentioned in the older lists, the position held by the pearl in European jewellery is such that, like the diamond, it cannot be omitted. The pearl's alternative for this month is moonstone, a soft stone of the feldspar group which is usually cut *en cabochon*. Moonstone was quite commonly used in Middle European peasant jewellery, and is seen at its best when contrasted in a ring or bracelet with colourful stones such as the garnet.

July's gemstone is the ruby. One of the world's most rare and lovely stones, it has played a great part in European jewellery, although it has never, perhaps, been used with such ostentatious grandeur as in Indian work.

Sardonyx, a type of onyx interspersed with red bands, is the alternative birthstone for August, of which the principal stone is the peridot. Neither of these stones belong to the more expensive group of gemstones, although the wise collector will not despise them on that account. There are a number of attractive Victorian pieces in existence set with peridots, and the stone's delicate emerald colour is most distinctive in a filigree setting. The peridot serves as a reminder that one should never despise any gemstone because it is not particularly expensive. Most of Fabergé's exquisite smallwork, for that matter, is composed of semi-precious materials.

Blue is the colour for those born in September and the sapphire is naturally the month's stone. The faceted sapphire will be familiar to most collectors. Not to be despised, however, is the cabochon-cut star sapphire, in whose milky blue depths a perfect star is reflected under the right conditions of lighting. This phenomenon, known as asterism, gives the star sapphire a unique beauty and makes it particularly suitable for ring-setting. Lapis-lazuli, the alternative stone for the month, has been used in jewellery since the beginning of European civilization and the collector can exercise his choice over a wide range of countries—and centuries.

It is unfortunate that the opal, one of the most fascinating stones, has an aura of ill-omen about it. This popular superstition would, in fact, appear to date back no earlier than the nineteenth century.[1] The opal, which has a colour range from jet-black shot with fire to a pale moony glow, provides those born in October with a wide range of choice. The settings of opals should always be carefully examined, since a disadvantage of this stone is that it is susceptible to changes of temperature. The fact that it is liable to contract and expand slightly necessitates a firm setting. (A 'claw' is as good as any other.) It may well be that it is the opal's responsiveness to changes of temperature which has given it in the past an ill name. One popular superstition has it that, during the great plagues in Europe, the opal was seen to change colour when a man was about to die. This is not entirely impossible, since the stone is affected by skin temperature; an interesting experiment in this direction is to take an opal which has not been worn for some time and to observe how it 'comes alive' shortly after being placed against the skin. In this respect it resembles the pearl, which completely loses its lustre unless it is in contact with the skin—and, indeed, reacts differently on different people.

The topaz, November's stone, is found in a great number of nineteenth-century pieces, usually brilliant-cut above the girdle and step-cut below. Large stones are particularly suitable for brooches and, when surrounded by Victorian filigree gold-work or bordered with small pearls, are extremely handsome.

December is represented by the turquoise. Being a soft stone, the turquoise is almost invariably cut *en cabochon*, the depth of its colour being determined by the depth of the cabochon dome. Although it has played a less important part in the history of European jewellery than most other birthstones, turquoise will be found in a number of antique pieces. During the nineteenth century, when semi-precious stones were lavishly used, the turquoise was often set in brooches and rings.

The legends and the mystical properties ascribed to gemstones provide an interesting by-path for the collector of jewellery. Half the interest, for instance, in a writer such as Theophilus lies in his digressions on the magical associations of stones. The modern science of gemmology, while of invaluable assistance to the student of antique jewellery, has, perhaps, removed some of the glamour from the subject. It is difficult to refrain from wishing that one still believed in the power of unicorn's horn to protect one against poisoning. (Instead, we know that the 'unicorn's horn', as found in antique *nefs*, is usually a narwhal's.) That sovereign remedy for most ills, the stone found in the brain of a toad, and the Philosopher's stone itself—these too have gone the way of other childhood illusions. Only the polished round globe of rock-crystal, still the traditional medium used by fortune-tellers, remains to remind us that gemstones were not always assessed in terms of their crystalline structure.

[1] Possibly originating in the ill-omened opal of Sir Walter Scott's *Anne of Geierstein*.

CHAPTER THIRTEEN

The Precious Metals

GOLD is undoubtedly the most famous and the most ancient of the metals which have been used by mankind in the manufacture of jewellery. Its place in the history of jewellery can be traced back to the earliest products of the metalworker and craftsman. Gold is plentifully used in Chaldean work and with a degree of skill that shows that it had long been in use. The magnificent quality of this early Chaldean and, later, Egyptian work reveals a well-established tradition of practice, experiment and achievement.

As a precious metal, gold has maintained its place in the fabrication of jewellery from these early beginnings right up to the present day. Throughout the past four centuries of European work gold occupies the predominant place among the metals employed by the craftsman. Although within the past fifty years platinum and palladium have become as important to the craftsman as gold, it still holds pride of place for many types of work. Even the jeweller whose main trade may be in platinum brooches and dress-clips will concede that gold has no rivals for certain types of necklaces, bracelets and other articles of jewellery. Gold, moreover, possesses a wide palette—a choice of colours which can be rivalled by no other metal.

Softer than silver, gold is alloyed to give it the necessary hardness required for jewellery. Its softness, however, is one of its attractions, since it is magnificently workable and can be chased and engraved with great ease. Gold's malleability means that it can be beaten down into thicknesses of no more than ·0000004 of an inch. This fact was well known to the ancient craftsmen of Europe and the Near East, who employed gold leaf for decorative purposes and for jewellery in much the same manner as it is used today.

Another quality possessed by gold, and one which has endeared the metal to the craftsman, is its ductility; it can easily be drawn at the drawplate or bench into wire of any thickness. The use of gold wire in jewellery can be traced back to the earliest European work. Its importance in ring manufacture, in the construction of necklaces, bracelets and ear-rings can readily be seen. Finally, the working jeweller can alter the colour of gold by the addition to it of other metals. Thus, by a careful juxtaposition of differently coloured golds he can achieve a most rich and attractive effect.

Red gold, which is one of the oldest types used by the jeweller, is formed by the addition of a percentage of copper. Other colours of gold used by the jeweller are white, green, blue and pink. Silver is added to gold to whiten its colour; it is also used to produce green gold. The addition of iron gives the gold a greenish tinge— a fact which was known as early as the sixteenth century. Gold of a whitish hue has also long been used by the jeweller. What would nowadays be termed white gold was known to the Greeks and termed electrum—the native source of which was reputed to be the river Pactolus in Asia Minor. Pliny defines electrum as an alloy of gold and silver in which the silver content is one-fifth of the total.[1]

The quality of gold is assessed in terms of 'carats'. This form of measurement assumes a completely pure gold consisting of 24 carats. This would be too soft for ordinary use in the field of jewellery, so the gold is alloyed to harden it. The standard gold usually employed by the jeweller is about 18 carats. This is used for fine work where precious stones are required to be set in the mount. For less expensive articles, 9-carat gold is commonly used today—although this is, largely, a form of gold economy.

Most of the gold used in early Mediterranean and European jewellery came from the mines of Asia Minor and Egypt. Later, the gold mines of Spain were exploited. Later still the Spaniards mined the metal in South America. During the nineteenth century the discovery of gold in North America and Australia led to the famous gold rushes. The richest deposits known today lie in the gold fields of South Africa.

Second to gold in order of historical importance is silver. In the twentieth century its place as a noble metal has been largely, if not entirely, taken by the metals of the platinum group. To the early craftsmen, however, silver was a metal ranking only second to gold and it was widely used for all types of precious jewellery. It became the favourite metal for diamond-setting and, from the eighteenth century onwards, almost displaced gold as the major precious metal in the jeweller's craft. Today silver ranks far below gold in the order of precious metals, while its place as a setting for diamonds has been taken by platinum and palladium. It is now mainly used in the cheaper grades of jewellery—the 'costume' or 'fashion' jewellery— where its reflective qualities are admirably suited to paste and marcasite. Its qualities have been enhanced by recent discoveries in plating, particularly in the use of rhodium plating. Rhodium, a precious metal of the platinum group, when it is

[1] *'Ubicunque quinta argenti portio est, electrum vocatur.'*

plated on to silver, preserves the silver from tarnishing. This was, previously, the metal's major defect.

Silver has many of the same properties as gold, particularly in regard to its malleability and ductility. It can be worked with ease and lends itself well to wire-drawing. Like gold, silver in its pure state is too soft for practical purposes and has to be alloyed to give it the necessary hardness for jewellery. This is done by alloying the silver with copper. British hall-marked silver contains 925 parts silver out of 1,000, indicated by the *lion passant* punched upon all silverware produced and assayed in England. The Britannia standard of silver, with which silver collectors will be familiar, was employed during a short period between 1697 and 1720 when the standard of silver was raised in order to prevent the fraudulent conversion of coin of the realm into articles of silverware.

Besides its use from the eighteenth century onwards as a setting for diamonds, silver has always played an important part in European jewellery. It has been widely used for rings and, during the sixteenth and seventeenth centuries, was attractively ornamented with *niello* work. Many of the minor articles of dress, such as the various items of the chatelaine, have been fashioned of silver. The techniques acquired by the silversmith, such as embossing, chasing and engraving, have been adapted by the jeweller to the smaller sphere in which he works and applied equally to jewellery of silver. As an excellent base for enamelling, silver has also played a part in the enameller's craft. It has been widely used too for those small *objets d'art* such as snuff-boxes, enamelled bijouterie, and the like, which cannot strictly be classified as jewellery but which belong rather to the sphere of the smallworker.

The collector of antique jewellery who possesses pieces set in silver should take great care to expose them as little as possible to the smoky air of our modern towns. Although the open surfaces of the metal can readily be cleaned, yet, if the metal behind the stones becomes tarnished, the task becomes considerably more difficult and should be entrusted only to an experienced craftsman. It must be remembered that during the eighteenth century, when silver was most used as a setting for jewellery, the problem did not arise to anything like the same extent. It is not exposure to air that tarnishes silver but the presence in the air of hydrogen sulphide, and it is smoke from coal fires that produces this condition. Before the exploitation of England's coal fields and the Industrial Revolution, the air of England and, indeed, of all Europe was comparatively free from taint. If worn in a modern industrial city, however, an eighteenth-century silver brooch will lose nearly all its lustre within a day or two.

Silver ore has been found in most parts of the world. During the Middle Ages the main source of silver was in Central Europe, a fact which contributed largely to the fortunes of such families as the Fuggers. But these European mines, as well as those in Spain which had been in use since Roman times, were far from inexhaustible. The discovery of the New World and the vast silver mines of Mexico—still the major supplier of the world's silver—led to the importation into Europe of quantities of silver such as had never been known before. It was mainly the great resources of South America that made possible the enormous expansion of European silversmithing during the sixteenth and seventeenth centuries. The comparative abundance of the metal meant that the sixteenth-century jeweller tended to neglect its use in his more important commissions. From this neglect silver was rescued by the discovery of the brilliant cut for diamonds. It remained the most favoured setting for diamonds until displaced by platinum in the present century.

Platinum is, perhaps, the most widely used precious metal in gem-set jewellery today. Together with palladium, another metal of the platinum group, it has become the accepted setting for diamond jewellery. Its brilliant white colour makes it an excellent reflector of light and, thus, most suitable for diamonds.

Platinum is not found in early European jewellery, since its existence appears to have been unknown until the Spaniards discovered it in South America. There is a reference in book 34 of Pliny's *De Rerum Natura* to a 'white lead' which sounds, from the description, as if it may have been platinum. However, the technical problems involved in the use of platinum for jewellery would have been likely to defeat the early jeweller. Chief of these is platinum's very high melting point (1773° C.). Apart from the necessity for a flame of this heat to reduce the metal to a state of flux, the high melting point would have involved the early jeweller in complex metallurgical problems connected with his solders.

Platinum takes its name from the Spanish *Platina del Pinto* (literally: Little silver of the Pinto—the river where the metal was discovered). Its colour is somewhat similar to silver, but it does not tarnish. Whereas the European jeweller working in silver had to reckon with this polishing problem, his modern counterpart does not have to worry. He knows that in all normal temperatures and conditions platinum will retain its brilliance. For use in jewellery platinum requires to be given a slight additional hardness. This is achieved by alloying it with either a small proportion of copper or of other members of the platinum group such as iridium or palladium.

Although most of the working problems of platinum had been solved before the close of the nineteenth century, little jewellery was as yet made in the metal. This was chiefly due to its rarity and, consequently, its high price. Much more platinum jewellery was made during the Edwardian era, but silver or gold still remained the usual settings for most precious pieces. It was not until the discovery of the great nickel-copper ore deposits in Ontario during the 1920s that platinum became widely known and used. To the collector of antique jewellery, therefore, platinum is of negligible interest. Its interest to the future student will be paramount, since the use of platinum has been one of the major features of twentieth-century work. It is found in ring settings, in necklaces and, above all, in brooches and clips. The diamond spray or brooch cannot be considered to have reached the highest peak—technically, at least—until the use of platinum. Although it may be true to say that the Georgian diamond spray set in silver is among the highlights of European jewellery, yet the very nature of the material in which most of these were set prohibited the jeweller from attaining technical perfection. As a setting for diamonds platinum must be considered unrivalled—unless, perhaps, by its sister metal, palladium.

Palladium is the most recent of the precious metals to be used in the manufacture of jewellery. It is a metal which the collector of antique pieces will never meet, but its importance today is so great that it cannot be overlooked. Palladium is not a 'new' metal, for it was first isolated by the metallurgist and scientist Wollaston as early as 1804. Like platinum, palladium was not available for general working until this century, when rich deposits of nickel-copper ore were discovered in Canada.

During the platinum famine occasioned by the first World War a certain amount of palladium was released for jewellers' work. But at this time insufficient research into the technical problems of using the metal caused the manufacturing jeweller some difficulty and he discarded palladium in favour of platinum when that metal again became available. During the inter-war years considerable research was devoted to the properties and qualities of palladium. This research was mainly undertaken in the United States of America, with the result that palladium was being used by the American jeweller long before it had become a familiar metal in European workshops. The last fifteen years, however, have seen palladium universally recognized as an excellent working material and one which possesses many of the qualities of platinum. At the same time, it has certain advantages of its own.

Palladium is very similar to platinum in colour—it is doubtful, indeed, whether any but the experienced can detect the difference on sight. It is ductile and malleable, both qualities of major importance to the jeweller, and is comparable in hardness to either gold or platinum. In common with these two precious metals it has one major advantage over silver, the fact that at ordinary temperatures it does not tarnish. One considerable advantage which palladium possesses over platinum is its specific gravity. This is approximately equivalent to that of 14-carat gold—a

Five examples of modern French jewellery.
Right: brilliant-set diamond and palladium leaf brooch and coiled ring set with a diamond, by *Chevrier-Huo-Diderot*.

Left: *leaf clip set round with graduated diamonds.*
Below, left: *bracelet by Uti in palladium and diamonds.*
Right: *diamond spray clip by Lesson.*

Modern Swiss jewellery designs are frequently connected with the watch. The ring above, in gold and diamonds, opens to reveal a tiny watch.

A graceful spray set with diamonds and freshwater pearls, a popular Swiss motif today.

Watch-case design is an important function of the Swiss jeweller. The simple gold case (left) by Omega has twisted lugs, gold hands and raised dot ciphers. Right: bird brooch by Weber, whose flowing lines are achieved by the use of gold wire.

The art of the Swiss jeweller. Right: *a covered watch by Gubelin of Lucerne in twisted gold wire and pearls.* Centre: *a magnificent baguette and square-cut diamond and palladium bracelet, also by Gubelin.* Far right: *an elaborate filigree gold watch-bracelet by Rolex.*

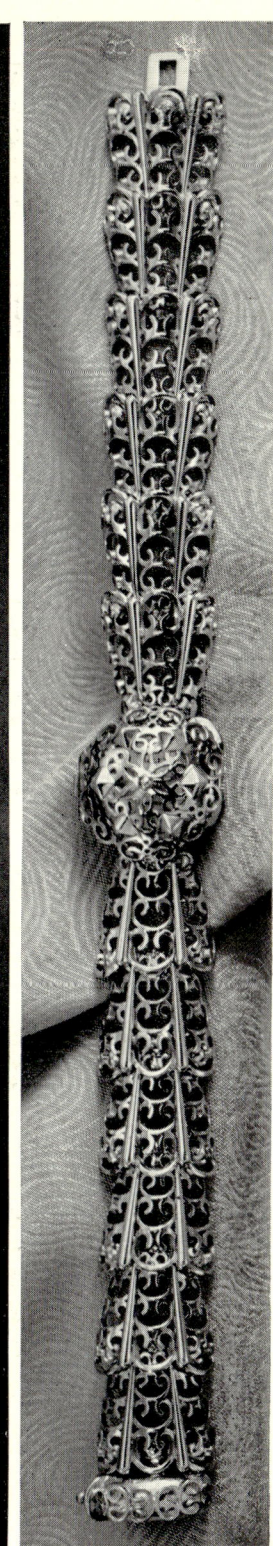

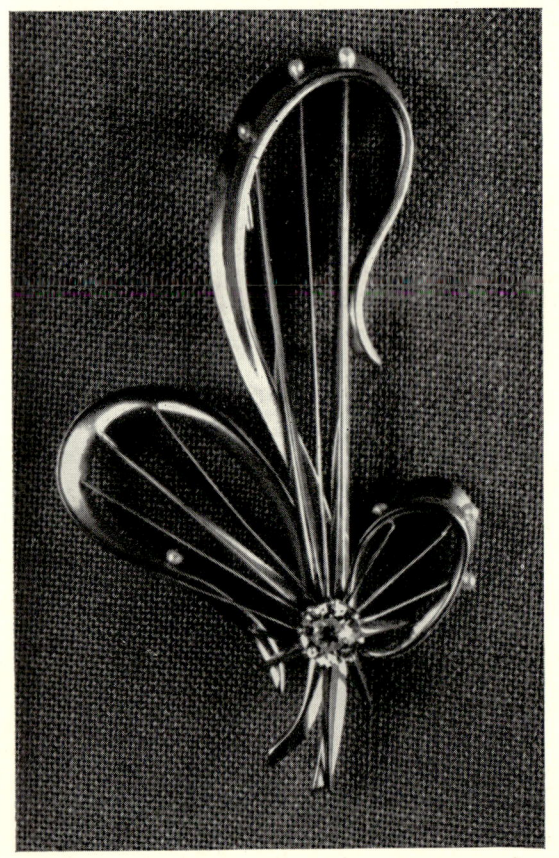

Modern costume jewellery takes on many forms. It is set with coloured gemstones such as amethyst and cairngorm, with marcasite, with white or coloured pastes, and artificial pearls. Sometimes mounts are of silver, sometimes of gilt metal or aluminium. Designs range from ultra-modern abstractions to reproductions and antique and modern gem-set pieces. *Above*: a twentieth-century hand-set paste brooch in silver, based on an eighteenth-century design (H. A. Lazarus).

A modern gilt brooch set with pastes and artificial pearls.

little over half that of platinum. In recent years a fashionable demand for large-size dress-clips has increased the importance of this attribute of palladium.

Like platinum, palladium is an ideal material for use in all types of diamond jewellery. Its high reflectivity, combined with its untarnishability, makes it a perfect setting for the diamond, since the main requirement of this stone is a maximum 'play' of light. This fact has for some years been realized in the United States, where palladium is as familiar a name to the jeweller and his public as is that of platinum. Since the second World War, particularly in Great Britain, palladium has become equally well known to the European jeweller. Another advantage of this metal is that its cost is considerably cheaper per ounce than platinum.

The metals of the platinum group comprise not only platinum but also palladium, rhodium, iridium, ruthenium and osmium. Although all of these metals have other and important uses in industry, they are all, in one way or another, intimately connected with the jeweller's craft. Where they are not used as precious metals in their own right, they may be used for plating and protecting metal surfaces—as in the case of rhodium—or—as in the case of ruthenium—used as a 'hardener' to give palladium the qualities necessary for jewellery.

The most important source of these platinum metals lies today in the region of Ontario, Canada. After being mined, the concentrate which contains the platinum metals, as well as gold and silver, is shipped to London. At the largest refinery of precious metals in the world, the raw concentrates are subjected to various processes which divide the different metals from each other. Wet chemical treatments separate the concentrate into its different constituents. A chemical reduction process takes place, which is continued until all the precious metals are precipitated. The platinum and palladium salts are packed in special, ashless paper and are placed in gas-fired furnaces. Here they are decomposed into the respective metals which, at this stage, take the form of grey sponge-like material. The pure palladium is then alloyed with a small proportion of ruthenium in a high-frequency electrical furnace. The jeweller's palladium can now be cast into an ingot which, in its turn, is hot-forged into a thick strip with a power hammer. The final stage is now reached, and the metal can be cold-rolled into a thin strip to whatever gauges may be required by the jeweller.

CHAPTER FOURTEEN

History and Properties of the Precious Stones

A GEMMOLOGIST's knowledge of the exact properties and qualities of precious stones is not necessary to the collector and student of jewellery. Some knowledge, however, is essential. Without it he has no basis for judgment.

First and foremost of all gemstones is the diamond, whose place in jewellery has already been discussed. Here our concern is with the history of the diamond and the diamond trade. As far as its chemical construction is concerned, the diamond is very simple—it is no more nor less than crystallized carbon.

After extraction from the mine, the diamonds are sorted out by numerous processes, in one of the last of which they pass over a moving band. During this process the concentrates are washed away and the diamonds themselves stick to the thickly greased band. They are still 'in the rough' and have a greasy look and feel about them. There is nothing to indicate to the inexperienced eye that these yellowish crystals, somewhat like ordinary soda in appearance, will one day assume their place in a necklace, bracelet or brooch. Aided by his long experience, the sorter grades the diamonds into their various sizes, as well as sorting them for colour. They are then weighed in readiness for the sales. Before being shown to the diamond buyers, the diamonds are washed in pans containing methylated spirit, and then pass to the skilled craftsmen who cut and polish them.

The position occupied by Great Britain in the diamond industry is of great importance—not only to the jewellery industry of this country but to the jeweller throughout the world. One of the main services which Britain offers is the collection of diamonds, their sorting and, finally, their resale. Although it is only the gem diamonds with which we are here concerned, it must not be forgotten that the procedure is similar with industrial diamonds, whose importance to the world of industry is ever-increasing.

Besides the Union of South Africa, the Gold Coast, the Belgian Congo and various other areas of Africa are the world's principal sources of diamonds today. From all the principal mines the stones come to London, where they are offered to the buyers at what are known as the 'Diamond Sights'. At these 'Sights' the cutter is able to examine the diamonds and to make his selection. Many of the rough diamonds go to the cutting centres of Amsterdam, Antwerp or Palestine, while a large percentage are flown to New York. It is an interesting commentary upon the present-day diamond trade that the greatest of all Britain's dollar-earning exports during 1947 was the export of diamonds to the United States.

How Great Britain has come to occupy this unique position in the diamond trade of the world is a fascinating story. Although diamonds had been discovered in a variety of places in the world, the traditional source of supply was India. Today the Indian mines are exhausted, but, until the eighteenth century, nearly all the diamonds found in European jewellery came from that source. By the end of the first quarter of the eighteenth century, however, the mines of Brazil had been discovered and these were then widely exploited. They are, in fact, still in production today.

In the early years of the diamond trade the prices of the stones fluctuated widely, depending upon delivery of shipments and inevitable variations of quality. These two factors were, as can be imagined, far from stable. The schedules of sailing vessels could not be co-ordinated as can those of modern steamships and aircraft. Insufficient gemmological knowledge and gem-testing instruments meant inevitably that the quality also varied considerably.

The discovery of diamonds in South Africa altered the whole history of the diamond trade and, thus, the production of diamond jewellery. The first diamond discovered in South Africa in 1866 was found on the banks of the Orange River, whence also came the second famous diamond, an $83\frac{1}{2}$-carat stone, which was subsequently called the 'Star of South Africa'. This discovery led to a great diamond rush—the rush to Kimberley. Among the diggers was one man whose greatness was afterwards proved in other fields—Cecil Rhodes. With his instinctive good sense and judgment, Rhodes realized that the prime need for the diamond workings was centralization. In 1873, together with several other financiers and backers, an amalgamation was effected out of which finally emerged the great company of De Beers.

The discovery of the Kimberley mine was, however, only the beginning of South Africa's diamond industry. Not long afterwards a number of other mines, whose names are now world-famous, were opened up. Among these were Bultfontein, Wesselton, Dutoitspan, the Premier and Jagersfontein. Other alluvial deposits were revealed from time to time elsewhere in Africa, until finally the Government of South Africa and the Administrator of West Africa respectively took over the control of granting claims and licences and the disposal of finds. The diamond dealers themselves and the producers had thus by somewhat different means established the principle of co-operation. The first were working for the maintenance of a steady demand at agreed prices, and the second for economy of production costs by centralization. The way was clearly open for the amalgamation of the two policies into one organization. Before this happened a number of other important discoveries were to take place. Deposits of diamonds were found in Portuguese West Africa, Tanganyika, the Belgian Congo and, on a smaller scale, in the French African colonies. These communities also realized the importance of maintaining a steady income rather than a series of spasmodic booms and slumps. In the period following upon the first World War almost all of these individual companies and governments co-operated in the wise policy of centralization.

The original 'Diamond Syndicate' came into being in the last years of the nineteenth century. It consisted of a number of London diamond-buying firms of considerable financial strength, between whom agreement was reached as to the number of diamonds which should be taken out of shipments of diamonds from South Africa. On the all-important question of price policy unanimity was also achieved. The 'Syndicate' was at no stage, however, an incorporated body. It was not until 1930 that the Diamond Corporation was formed under the guidance of Sir Edward Oppenheimer. From this time onwards the policy of centralized selling was rapidly pursued and in 1933 the Diamond Producers Association was formed. Its members were the Government of the Union of South Africa, the Administrator of West Africa, De Beers and its associated companies, and the Diamond Corporation. The latter was to be the channel through which the diamonds produced outside South Africa were handled. In 1934 came the formation of the Diamond Trading Company, whose task was the actual selling of both industrial and gem diamonds.

Such, in brief, is the recent history of the vast organization which has sprung out of this one stone. Apart from the industrial diamond, its primary concern is with that small brilliant or baguette stone that is destined for the jeweller's workshop. It is difficult to refrain from wondering what the craftsmen of the sixteenth century would have made of it—an organization with world-wide ramifications designed to mine, market and sell the very gem which they themselves were unable either to cut or facet adequately.

Associated with the diamond in the front rank of important gemstones are the ruby and the sapphire. They are both varieties of corundum, the material which is second to the diamond in the scale of hardness. The true ruby is sometimes called the 'oriental ruby' to distinguish it from the spinel ruby, which is somewhat similar in colour but considerably softer and of less value. The 'oriental ruby', however, is one of the finest gemstones. Its colour and its density have long made the ruby, whether faceted or cabochon-cut, a stone favoured by the jeweller and his public. The colour, which is the ruby's main attraction—particularly when it is used in contrast to the diamond—can range from a deep cochineal to a very pale rose pink. The word ruby itself comes from the Latin *rubeus*, red. The most favoured colour is the very deep, almost purple, colour which has been described as 'pigeon's blood'.

The fine ruby is a stone with a very limited distribution. Indeed, almost the world's entire supply of rubies comes from one small area, the Mogok mines in Upper Burma. Mogok is about ninety miles from Mandalay and has been mined for very many centuries. The Burmese rulers worked the mines originally under a royal monopoly but, following upon the British annexation of the country, the mines were taken over and worked by a British company. This company came into existence in 1887 and continued working the mines until the 1930s. At the present day the mines are worked by the local inhabitants, although to a lesser degree than formerly. Its very rarity makes the ruby a gem of great value. In perfect condition it is one of the world's most expensive stones. It is not, however, often of any great size, although exceptions have been known in the past. Outstanding among these was a ruby which in its original state is said to have weighed 400 carats.

In recent years the natural ruby has had to face increasing competition from the synthetic or artificial ruby. The method invented by Professor Verneuil has enabled synthetic rubies to be manufactured at an economic cost. At the same time it is possible to produce that richness of colour which has given the natural ruby its distinction. The much-desired 'pigeon's blood' colour is fabricated in the Verneuil furnace by the addition of 2·5 per cent. chromic oxide to the ammonia-alum and chrome-alum which are the other constituents. The collector of antique jewellery need not fear that he will be deceived by a forgery containing a synthetic ruby. Although the manufactured article possesses the physical characteristics of corundum, it can be distinguished by a gemmologist on account of certain characteristics peculiar to it.

The sapphire, which is a blue variety of corundum, will be familiar to collectors in both its forms, either faceted or cut *en cabochon*. The star sapphire, one of the most beautiful forms, is cut like the star ruby in a deep dome, or cabochon, so that the light falling upon it is reflected in the shape of a six-pointed star. It is almost invariably set in a ring where a maximum individual effect is achieved.

The sapphire, being a twin-brother of the ruby, is composed of aluminium oxide together with iron and titanium oxides that give it its distinctive blue colour. The range of colours which are found in corundum can certainly lead to some confusion, since the word 'sapphire' is automatically associated with the cornflower blue which belongs essentially to the Kashmir sapphire. Pink, green and yellow sapphires are also common. At what point one should start calling them 'pink' rubies instead of 'pink' sapphires it seems impossible to decide. It is, perhaps, best for the collector of jewellery to leave nomenclature to gemmologists and specialists and to take the word sapphire at its face value from its Latin derivation, *sapphirus*, meaning blue.

Like the ruby, the sapphire is found in the Mogok area of Burma. Sapphires from these mines have long been used in jewellery. Sapphires of ideal colour also come from Kashmir and from mines in Siam. Ceylon is also an important area for sapphires, although the Siamese mines have a greater reputation, largely, perhaps, due to the fact that they appear to have been the first sapphire mines known to have been worked for the stone. It is principally from Ceylon, however, that we have the cloudy blue sapphires which are noted for their asterism, that is, their ability, when cabochon-cut, to form a luminous star. The largest sapphires are usually step-cut. The majority are cut in a rectangular form, since this provides the maximum display of their colourful surface. One of the attractive qualities of the sapphire is its ability to change colour. This is particularly noticeable under artificial light: a sapphire which in sunlight will look sea- or cornflower-blue may alter to a deep violet or to a dark royal blue.

The emerald, known to the Romans as the *smaragdus*, is the fourth in the royal court of gems. Its rarity, however, has made it even more valued than the ruby. Indeed, an emerald of the best quality is more expensive than a brilliant diamond. The majority of the emeralds known to the ancients came from the mines of Egypt, which are believed to have been worked as early as 1700 B.C. They were certainly still being mined in Egypt during the Greco-Egyptian period and the emerald was a gem well known to the Greek jeweller. The rediscovery of these Egyptian mines is one of the most fascinating stories in the history of jewellery. For centuries it was known that they had existed, and many expeditions were made in attempts to find them. But it was not until the early nineteenth century that the remains of the early workings were discovered by a French traveller and explorer. Under Mohammed Ali the mines were reopened and appear for a short time to have been worked again. Internal troubles in Egypt obscure their history for fifty years after this. Today, however, they are still being worked, though to a limited extent.

The emerald is a bright green variety of beryl, beryl being the species which also contains the well-known gem, aquamarine. On account of its strange, green brilliance, it has long fascinated the lover of jewellery. It has been credited with strange powers, not least of these being its supposed ability to affect cures to the eyesight. This belief was probably some form of sympathetic magic, since it has long been known that the emerald—unlike the sapphire—is unaffected by changes of light or by artificial light. Whether held in daylight, in candlelight or under modern electric lighting, the emerald retains its colour. Impervious to the changes of light, it may well have suggested to the ancients that the stone had some curious property which could heal eyes that *were* affected. The Emperor Nero, it is recorded, carried an emerald. It has been suggested that this emerald was used as a lens—as an eyeglass—or even as a mirror in which the Emperor could watch the reflections of the spectacles and gladiatorial shows. It would seem more probable, however, that whether it was used for these purposes or not, it was principally carried as an amulet.

The main sources of emeralds in European jewellery were the South American mines discovered by the Spanish. These emeralds appear to have been mined in Peru, although the exact source of these early workings is still not known. Emeralds are still systematically mined in Brazil, the Urals, parts of South Africa and Australia. The famous Colombian mines near Bogota produced in the past many of the best-quality emeralds, but they are now closed. The best known of these was at Muzo; others were situated at Coscuez and Somondoco.

The rarity of the emerald is an added fascination. Its sources of supply are few, and it is this fact which makes the possibility of rediscovering some of the old Spanish mines even more tantalizing. There seems little doubt that, although the whereabouts of the Colombian mines are known, these in themselves could not have been the sole sources of the enormous quantities of emeralds which the Spaniards brought back from the New World. It seems possible that somewhere, overgrown and hidden in the jungles of Peru, lie the derelict workings from which were mined many of our finest emeralds. One day, perhaps, they will be rediscovered. In the meantime, the very possibility of their existence adds one more strange quality to the history of this most beautiful gemstone.

CHAPTER FIFTEEN

The Craft of Gem-cutting

THE development of the craft of gem-cutting has been one of the main features of European jewellery during the past four centuries. Until the fourteenth century, and even during the fifteenth century, most gems were cut *en cabochon* or polished and drilled like beads. Today, when one speaks of the lapidary's craft, it is largely of the plane-faceted cutting of stones that one thinks. Gem-engraving, unfortunately, is on the decline in Europe. This is largely due to the fact that seals and seal-rings play little or no part in modern life. It is worth remembering, however, that gem-engraving is an important part of the lapidary's work. Indeed it was brought to a high degree of technical excellence long before stones were faceted in the modern manner. Here we shall indicate some of the most important types of cutting which have been practised since the sixteenth century and describe briefly the manner in which this cutting is done.

The cabochon cut, which is still used for opaque and translucent stones such as the turquoise and the opal, was the earliest. The most usual and the simplest form of cabochon has the familiar raised dome and a flat base. Similar to this is the double cabochon, the difference being that here the whole stone is shaped like an egg. Another form used in jewellery from the sixteenth century onwards is the hollowed cabochon. The base is cut away so that the stone, seen in profile, is shaped like a new moon. The purpose of this hollowed cabochon was to enable a foil—similar to those used in sixteenth-century diamond jewellery—to be inserted behind the stone in order to improve its colour. If the stone was too dark a light reflective foil would be placed behind to brighten it. On the other hand, if a stone lacked depth of colour, this could be intensified by a coloured foil. A form of cabochon-cutting which will be found mostly in opal jewellery of the nineteenth century and onwards is a flattened version of the double cabochon. Other variants of the cabochon cut exist, but those we have described constituted the four main types which collectors are likely to encounter.

Early attempts at faceting gems resulted in haphazard cutting of facets without any particular order or symmetry. In some cases a gem would be to all intents and purposes cut like a cabochon with the exception that the top, instead of being rounded, would be ground flat. The sides around the domed top were also in some instances ground flat, while the back was left rounded. These, however, were no more than exercises in ingenuity on the part of the jeweller and did little to heighten the beauty of a stone. They certainly did not approximate to the mathematical brilliance of truly faceted gems.

Those who have handled gemstones in the rough know to what extent the jewellery-loving public is indebted to the lapidary. Who, handling the unpolished stones of the gemmologist, would be able to guess at the beauty which is latent in them? Cutting facets in a stone is far from being a pure exercise of technical skill, it is a means whereby the intrinsic quality of the individual gemstone is revealed. Not every stone will respond to the same treatment. Almost every stone within the species—with the exception of diamonds—requires a different approach and a different method. The major difference between diamonds and coloured stones from the lapidary's point of view is that the former must be cut with a mathematical precision in order to bring out their fire and brilliance. The cutting of one diamond hardly varies from that of another.

The craft of the lapidary still remains primitive, since nothing has yet been found which can improve upon the precision of the human hand for holding and adjusting the gemstick. The visitor to the workshop of a modern lapidary can see the craft being practised in the same way as it was in the fifteenth century A.D. or, for that matter, in the fifteenth century B.C. Almost the only change is the use of electricity to provide the power for rotating the polishing wheels, or 'laps' as they are known. The stone is still held in a gemstick, similar to those depicted in the earliest records of the lapidary at work. The co-ordination of the craftsman's hand and eye remains the most important factor. It is unlikely that anything else will ever supersede it.

When the lapidary receives the rough gemstone he must study its structure and consider how best to approach the problem of cutting. Very often the rough stone will need to be cut into a number of separate pieces by the process known as 'slitting'. The abrasive used by the modern lapidary for cutting the stone is a mixture of diamond dust and oil. In the ancient world sapphire powder or emery dust were probably the agents employed, although a reference in Book XXXVIII of Pliny's *Natural History* shows that diamond powder was known as an abrasive in his time.

The first task of the lapidary is to assess the rough gemstone and to determine the best method of cutting it. It is at this point that the lapidary is most in need of his specialized training, for, by careful cutting, he may be able to produce two or three separate stones suitable for faceting out of one large rough gemstone. His approach must be guided by his knowledge of the crystalline structure of the stone, while taking into consideration any particular flaws or idiosyncrasies it may possess.

The stone is cut or 'slit' on a small wheel, usually driven nowadays by electric power, though the old-fashioned foot-operated treadle has not been entirely superseded. Once the stone has been slit, the individual gemstones must be cut into the approximate shapes required. After this they are ready for the process of faceting—the most exacting part of the work and the one which will determine the final appearance of the gems.

The lapidary works with the gemstone held in a type of cement on the head of a gemstick. A horizontal wheel is used for the process of faceting, against which the lapidary manœuvres the gem to determine the individual facets. It is at this point that his trained precision of hand and eye is most needed; one error at this juncture may ruin an entire stone. Nowadays, particularly where gem-engraving is concerned, the lapidary has the advantage of working with precision-made magnifying and eye-glasses which enable him to examine his work at every stage. It has long been a matter of controversy whether the ancients possessed efficient magnifying glasses for their work. There do exist, however, a number of references which show that the principles of magnification were understood in classical times (*vide*: Pliny's *Natural History* and Seneca's *Naturales Quaestiones*). It seems reasonable to think, therefore, that magnifying glasses were known and used by classical gem-engravers.

Lapidary terms with which the collector should be familiar are those which distinguish the different parts of a gemstone. The table is the flat surface on top of the stone. The whole of the top surface above the girdle is referred to as the crown. The girdle itself is, as its name suggests, the widest section of the stone which lies between the crown and the pavilion—the latter being the underneath side of the gem. The culet is a small facet cut at the base of the pavilion to prevent chipping when the stone is being set.

Apart from any misapplication of the facets, the lapidary must also guard against heat generated by friction during his work on the gemstone. To obviate this, the cutting wheel is kept constantly wet with running water. Any considerable increase in the heat of the gemstone will lead to its expansion, with the result that either the facets will be cut 'out of true', or, if the rise of temperature is excessive, the stone may even split.

In addition to the cabochon cut, there are four main types of cuttings with which the collector should be familiar. The oldest of these are the table cut and the rose cut. The table cut is, as its name suggests, a cut in which the table or flat top of the stone is predominant. It was widely used throughout Europe in the sixteenth century not only for coloured stones but also for diamonds. The table itself is large and is surrounded by a simple, bevelled edge or a number of small facets. These may be cut irregularly in order to disguise imperfections or may be arranged in some symmetrical sequence. The table cut does not, of course, do the diamond full justice, but in the case of coloured stones it often proves effective. As a form of cutting it is quite often found in ring-stones from the sixteenth century onwards.

The history of the rose cut is described in detail in Chapter Three. From the point of view of the lapidary, it is enough to say that it is a logical development of the table cut, the table itself being replaced by six triangular facets. The crown has a further eighteen facets, thus making twenty-four in all. This is the perfect rose form, but many variants exist. The pavilion is usually absent, the stone having a flat base. In some cases the back of the stone may be a duplicate of the top, that is, a double rose.

The two other principal forms of cutting are the step, or trap cut, and the brilliant cut. The former is commonly found with coloured gems such as the emerald and other stones, where the revelation of the stone's colour is of major importance. The facets lie in long, inclined planes and are situated horizontally round the edge of the stone. The table is, in fact, surrounded by sloping steps leading down to the girdle. The pavilion may be cut into as many as four steps, although three is usual, and terminates with an oblong culet. The size and area of the table determines the effectiveness of the step cut. If it is too large, the reflections from the steps in the pavilion appear through the table itself. This does not make for as much brilliance as when they are reflected through the steps of the crown. The proportions of the step cut inevitably vary with different stones, since every stone presents its own problems. Because of its suitability for the emerald, the step cut is quite commonly known as the emerald cut.

The brilliant cut is undoubtedly ideal for the diamond. In its perfect form it contains fifty-eight facets in all, including the table and the culet. The table, which forms a perfect octagon, is the largest of the facets and it is through the table that the light rays enter and leave the stone.

Other forms of cutting which may be met with include the scissors cut, which is a modified form of the brilliant sometimes applied to square stones; the buff-top cut, which has a cushioned-shaped table and a step-cut pavilion; and the mixed cut, which is used to produce both colour and brilliance. The varieties of cutting are, of course, almost limitless, being dependent so much upon the problems which the lapidary has encountered with the stone. However, if the collector is familiar with the main types outlined above he will soon discover for himself what are the variants and in what way they differ from the principal forms.

The final act in the lapidary's work is to polish the stones. This is of very great importance, for, after cutting, the stones have a hard, glassy appearance which must be removed in order to reveal their beauty. The stone must first of all be carefully cleaned, since any grit on the surface will cause the stone to be scratched during the polishing process. The polishing wheel or lap is similar to that which is used in the cutting. For hard stones a copper wheel is used; softer stones are polished on pewter or lead wheels, while for very soft stones like opals a felt buff is used. The polishing wheel is kept perfectly clean, since any grit or oil would disfigure the stone. It is rotated in a clockwise direction. Rough sandstone is used to provide a 'bite' for the polishing agent, which is a soft, broken stone. As with the cutting operation, the wheel has to be kept well watered during polishing so that friction may not result in any expansion of the gem.

The lapidary's work is now completed. After polishing, the stones are graded ready for selling. Their destination is the jeweller's workshop.

CHAPTER SIXTEEN

Pearls, Amber, Jet and Coral

A NOTABLE feature of post-war fashion in Europe has been the popularity of the pearl. Whether real, cultured or artificial, it has occupied a position equalled only by its predominance during the 1920s and, previously, during the Renaissance. Seed-pearls are found in Roman and Greek jewellery, particularly in small clusters forming pendant ear-rings. (This, incidentally, is a fashion which has been revived recently.) It was not until the fifteenth and sixteenth centuries, however, that the possibilities of the pearl in jewellery were fully exploited. By the sixteenth century in Italian and South German work it was recognized as a major feature in gem-designs, and the baroque pearl was widely used as the central motif for pendants and brooches. Many of the seed-pearls used in Renaissance pieces came from the Adriatic coast, while the larger pearls and baroque pearls came from the Red Sea and the Persian Gulf.

The gradual extension of trade with the East over the course of centuries brought the European jeweller in touch with the great fisheries of the Orient. The Persian Gulf remains the principal source of the world's pearls, although the modern world has additional sources in certain areas off the Australian coast, some of the South Pacific islands, Ceylon, the Sulu seas and the South Americas.

Pearl-fishing is still carried on from small boats by native divers working to traditional methods. Usually two men form a team. One of the men remains on the surface and tends the lines, one of which is attached to a large weight or stone and the other being a signal cord. The diver is lowered to the bottom on the sink-weight, taking down with him the signal cord and the baskets. When he has filled the baskets with oysters he jerks the signal cord and they are drawn to the surface. Finally the diver himself comes to the surface, sometimes having stayed below water for as long as two or three minutes. In exceptional cases divers are known to have stayed below the water for as much as five minutes but, even when their stay underwater is comparatively short, the strain on their bodies is excessive. In the depths at which the divers work, depths to which few Europeans could descend without shallow-water diving-suits, the pressure of the water, combined with the lack of oxygen, is highly injurious. Pearl-divers are not a long-lived race. Those who have watched them at work will know that it is not uncommon to see a diver hauled to the surface bleeding from ears, nose and even eyes. In the Red Sea, and off Australia and Ceylon, the divers are, moreover, working in shark-haunted waters.

Climatic conditions, the density of the sea-water and the variety of the pearl-bearing oyster are all factors which govern the colour of a pearl. The fresh-water pearl is, however, quite different in that it is not found in the oyster but in the pearl mussel (particularly the type known as *Unio margariterferous*). Both European and American inland waters harbour the pearl-bearing mussel; in the United States the Mississippi is renowned for these fresh-water pearls, while in Britain the streams of Scotland, particularly the Tay and Spey, have long been famous for the quality of their pearls.

The substance from which the pearl is formed is basically the same as that which lines the inner shell of the oyster and which is commonly known as 'mother-of-pearl'. An irritation is set up inside the oyster (or mussel) by the intrusion of some foreign body such as a grain of sand. Round this initial centre there is deposited layer after layer of nacreous substance, each layer being microscopic in itself.

A perfectly formed round pearl is one which has grown inside the tissue of the oyster. These, of course, are the pearls which fetch the highest value, since they are required to form matching pearl necklaces. There are, however, three other main types of pearl with which the collector should be familiar, since they are commonly found in antique jewellery.

Most important of these is the baroque pearl, so dear to the Renaissance jeweller. These are usually formed by the deposit being laid over an irregularly shaped intrusion in the oyster, such as a minute stone or piece of wood.

The blister pearl, on the other hand, is produced by the attacks of a small parasite which bores its way through the oyster's shell. To protect itself against the attack the oyster forms a deposit round the point of entrance in the shell. This inevitably results in a hollow-bodied pearl, its shape being determined by the extent of the intrusion. The button pearl, *perle bouton*, occurs where the pearl, during the course of its growth, has become fixed to the shell by successive deposits and has thus grown on one side while remaining flat on the other. The quality of a pearl is judged by its skin and its 'orient'. The skin should, theoretically, be flawless, while the term 'orient' denotes the clear lustre which the pearl should possess.

The Chinese have cultivated pearls artificially ever since the thirteenth century A.D. by inserting an irritant inside the shell of the pearl-bearing mussel. Minute particles of sand, mud and wood are introduced into the mussel, which is then returned to its bed and kept there for about three years. The pearl market of Soochow was until recent years entirely engaged in the marketing of these fresh-water pearls. Whether or not the new Communist régime will allow the continuance of such 'capitalist exploitation' remains to be seen.

A major event in the history of jewellery was the successful application of this method by the Japanese scientist Mikimoto to the pearl-bearing oyster. Having started his researches as early as the 1890s, Mikimoto had laid the foundations of his commercial success by the end of the first World War. After experimenting with various irritants, Mikimoto found that a small mother-of-pearl bead was most successful: it possessed the added advantage that the whole of the cultured pearl was thus formed of natural secretions. A fall in the value of real or genuine pearls was the inevitable result of the commercial exploitation of Mikimoto's discovery. Although real pearls have subsequently regained their value, it seems unlikely that they will ever again command such high prices as they did in the nineteenth century.

These cultured pearls resemble the natural product very closely. To distinguish between them is largely a matter for the expert. The best-quality cultured pearls are those which contain the smallest artificial irritant and the largest natural deposit. Cheaper cultured pearls have a slightly larger bead with fewer layers of deposit over it. In the case of these cheaper varieties it is sometimes possible to discern the dark centre of the bead when the 'pearl' is held up to strong light. Also, after being worn for some time, the acid from the human skin tends to eat away the pearl deposit and expose the mother-of-pearl centre. The only way, however, to be completely certain in the case of pearls whose origin is unknown is to submit them to a pearl-testing laboratory. In these laboratories all doubts can be set at rest. Radiography, or X-ray testing, can immediately discover if a pearl has an artificial centre. In the case of pearls which have been drilled, a simpler and quicker test is to submit them to a machine known as the endoscope. This machine works upon the properties of light reflection, and an experienced operator can tell in a minute or two whether the pearls are real or cultured.

Artificial pearls are not new in the history of jewellery.[1] The old-fashioned method, which appears to have originated in France, consisted in filling glass beads with a form of wax. These artificial pearls, while suitable for use on dresses or as trimmings to hats, could never have passed inspection if worn as real jewellery. One of the achievements of the twentieth-century jeweller has been the manufacture of artificial pearls which, while they will not deceive the intelligent layman in daylight, do have something of the same sheen and appearance as the pearl.

The manufacture of these artificial pearls originated in Czechoslovakia and France

[1] See pp. 63 and 89.

before the second World War. Upon the expiry of the relevant patents, the manufacture was undertaken firstly in the United States, and secondly in Great Britain. Britain, moreover, benefited by the arrival of Czechoslovakian refugees after Hitler's invasion of their country, who, having an unrivalled knowledge and experience of the techniques used, soon established a flourishing industry in Britain. Today artificial pearls manufactured in Britain are second to none.

The substance which gives these artificial pearls their sheen is a mixture of nitro-cellulose and guanin. The latter is a form of iridescent fish-silver obtained from the scales of certain fish. (The various manufacturers employ different formulas for the composition of the 'dip'; these are closely guarded secrets.) The quality of the guanin itself is the main determining factor, the best guanin coming from the Newfoundland fisheries. Suspended in the solution of nitro-cellulose, the guanin is applied as a coating to the bead which forms the kernel of the artificial pearl. Not only the quality of the 'dip' but also the mount of coatings to which the beads are subjected determines the quality of the artificial pearl. The bead centres are usually either of transparent glass or plastic, depending again upon the cost of the finished article. Artificial pearls are available in a wide range of colours, these being determined by the addition of pigments to the guanin solution.

The jewellery collector need have little fear of being imposed upon by such artificial pearls. They are readily detectable by the eye, while an investigation of the drill-hole will nearly always reveal the glass bead beneath the thin skin. However, when dealing with real, or apparently real, pearls it is always wise to consult an expert in advance. One further warning: it is unwise to buy pearls in a second-hand market abroad unless you happen to be an expert yourself.

Among other marine jewels found in much European work is amber, of which Pliny, in his *Natural History*, book 37, says '[It] is the product of a marrow discharged by trees of the pine family, like gum from the cherry and resin from the ordinary pine. It issues forth in an abundance of liquid, which gradually becomes hardened either by heat or cold. . . . Where the rise of the sea carries it away in fragments from the islands it is cast upon the shores in so light a form that in the shallow waters it seems to hang suspended. Our forefathers also considered that it was the sap of a tree, for which reason they called it *succinum*. That it is indeed a product of the pine is proved by the fact that, when it is ignited, it burns with the odour and in the same manner as pine wood.'

This admirable and vivid description proves that the origin of amber was well known in Pliny's time. Amber is, in fact, the product of vast trees which existed during what is called the Tertiary period of the world's history. That it is a fos-

Asymmetrical brooch and ear-clips in silver set with white and dark-blue pastes (S. Root).

The Victorian revival has popularized jewellery in antique-finished silver set with semi-precious stones. The necklace and ear-clips illustrated are from a suite comprising necklace, bracelet, ear-clips and ring (Zoltan White).

Polishing the crown facets of a coloured gemstone on a swiftly rotating copper lap. The stone is mounted in shellac in a gem-stick. The gem-peg, into which the stick is inserted to keep it steady, can be seen behind.

Above: the full beauty of a large amethyst is revealed by the modern methods of brilliant cutting. Left: a 'boule' of synthetic corundum made in a Verneuil furnace. The chemical constituents are the same as of natural ruby.

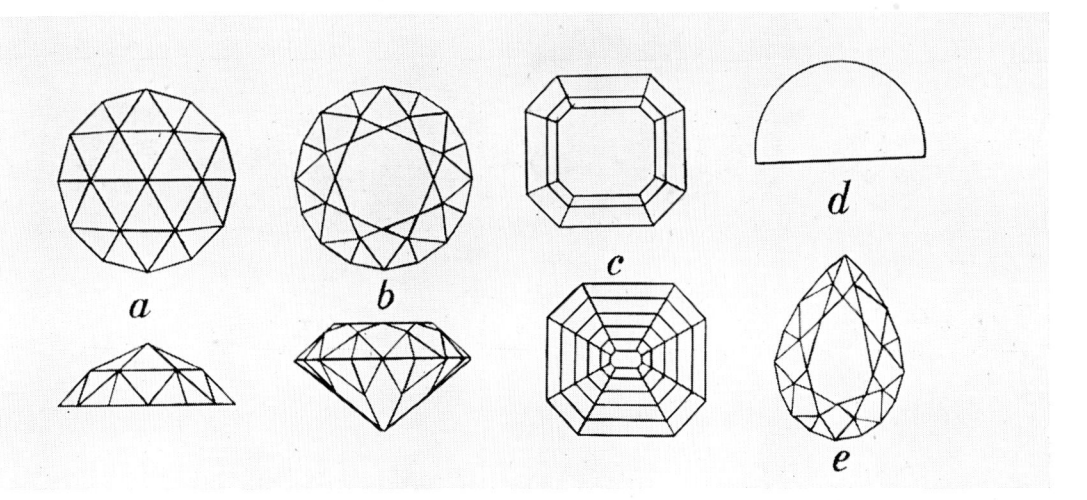

Types of cut in common use: (a) top and side elevation of the old rose cut; (b) the modern brilliant cut; (c) the step cut; (d) the hemispherical cabochon, a cut of great antiquity; (e) the pendeloque.

The modern craftsman at work, piercing part of the mount for a platinum and diamond necklace.

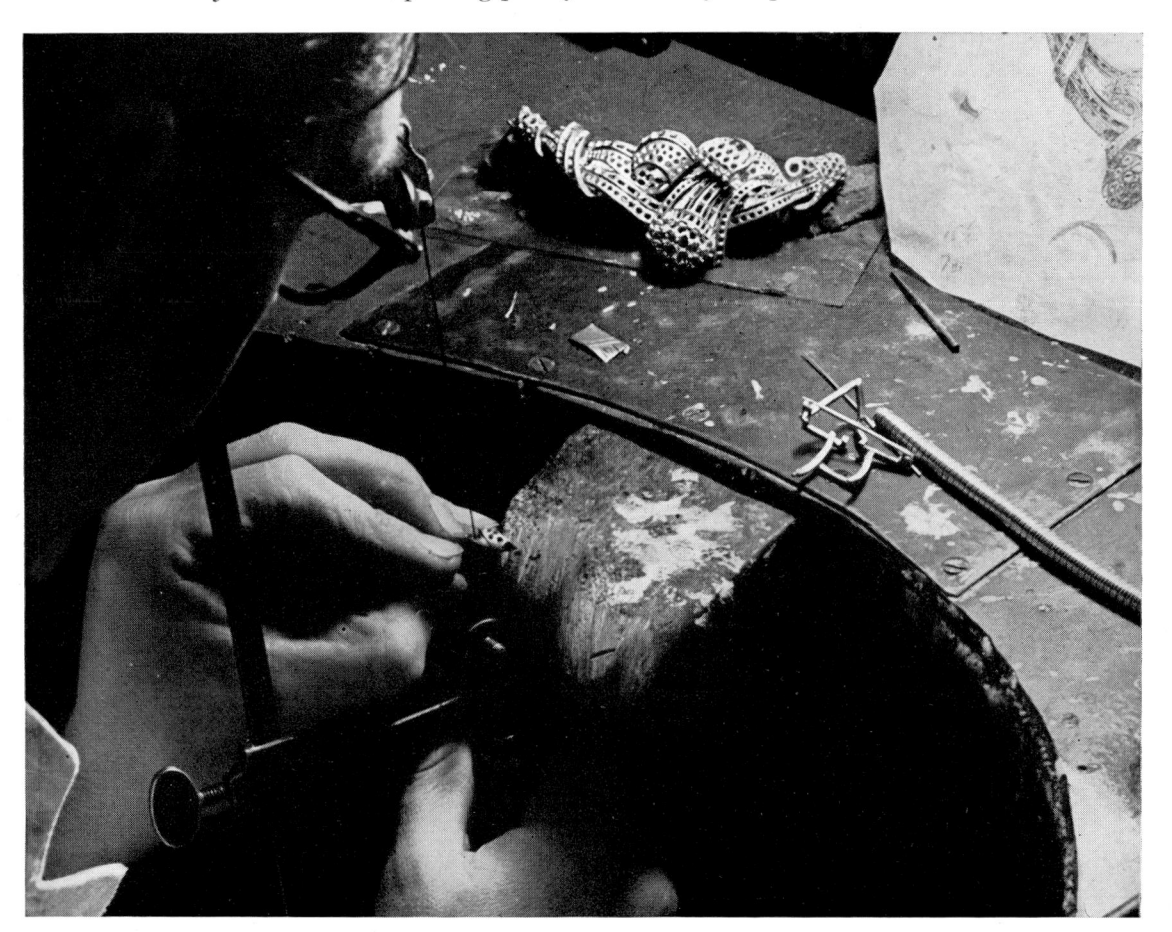

Above, left: *Selecting stones of various cut to fit the mounts before they are passed to the setter.* Right: *Inserting a diamond in the mount, which is held in a gem-stick with shellac. The setter then pushes up the metal of the mount to secure the stone.* Below: *polishing the internal surfaces by drawing rouge-impregnated strings through the piercings. Pumice is used to polish the outer surfaces.*

silized resin or gum is known to most from those famous 'show pieces' in which a fly or other insect is seen entrapped inside the amber.

The colour of amber, which ranges from a light yellow to a deep, honey brown, is particularly attractive, and its varying densities of light and shade have always made it a favourite with the working jeweller. Throughout the history of British jewellery it has played a large part, since native deposits of amber exist on the East coast. A study of Anglo-Saxon jewellery reveals how important amber was to the craftsman of those days. One of its chief merits in his eyes was undoubtedly the fact that, being a soft material, it could be easily carved or polished. Other sources of amber are the Baltic coast and Sicily. Its existence in the Baltic naturally made it a favourite with the German jewellers and it was very widely used in early European jewellery. Sicilian amber has a peculiar quality of its own and is usually of a reddish colour, sometimes showing tinges of blue and green. It is, to this day, much used by the local craftsmen, and the shops in towns such as Taormina exhibit many articles carved in amber. Its softness has always made it popular with the jeweller who specializes in *objets de vertu*. During the period shortly after the first World War it enjoyed a great popularity, being particularly suitable for the bead necklaces which were then fashionable. Although still used today for similar necklaces, it is mainly found in such sidelines of the jeweller's art as mouthpieces for cigarette-holders.

Imitation amber is made of coloured glass and is quite often found in modern costume jewellery. It is quite easy, however, to detect the difference, since glass is colder to the touch.

Although jet can hardly be called a precious substance, it has, nevertheless, a place in the history of European jewellery that cannot be disregarded. Jet is not, as many think, a substance which only achieved favour during the nineteenth century. It was, indeed, known to the craftsman in Roman days, as references in Pliny prove. Jet is a smooth and perfect form of black coal substance. In somewhat the same manner as amber, it proves an excellent material for the polisher and carver.

One of the best sources for jet is the Yorkshire coast around Whitby, and it was here that during Victorian times a flourishing industry of jet carvers sprang up. The long retirement of the Queen, in mourning for the Prince Consort, set a fashion that other respectable Victorian widows felt bound to follow. Mourning clothes and mourning jewellery assumed, therefore, a far more important place in English life than had ever been known before or, indeed, since. As a material for this mourning, jewellery jet was ideal.

Jet takes on a very fine polish, and as it can also be cut and faceted, it is not restricted to the round bead shape. A great quantity of mid-nineteenth-century jet-ware still exists, although it will not today be found displayed in the fashionable jeweller's store. Much of it, however, is very beautifully worked and can, if cleaned and restrung, prove surprisingly attractive in its austere way.

Since 1949 jet has had a slight, if temporary, fashion appeal and has been used for such articles as pendant ear-rings and necklaces. The Whitby jet industry, however, except for a small local tourist trade, is no longer in existence. Much of the so-called 'jet' used in the recent revival was no more than black glass. Here again, as with amber substitutes, it is not difficult to tell the difference. Apart from the hard glitter of black glass—quite different to jet's velvet-like quality—the glass imitation is cold to the touch.

Jet is seen at its best where it is used in combination with paste roundels—as, for instance, in a necklace where a jet bead is alternated with a circle of paste stones. Jet still enjoys a certain popularity on the Continent, mainly in France. Here again it is found principally in mourning jewellery. This is generally of an inexpensive type and of very little interest to the student of jewellery.

While coral does not rank high in jewellery fashion at the present moment, it has a long and distinguished history behind it and has been used by European jewellers since the earliest times. Much of the best-grade coral is found in the Mediterranean. Coral is consequently found in classical, Roman work and has remained ever since a favourite with the Italian craftsman. The quality which distinguishes the most favoured coral for jewellery work is its colour. It is usually considered that the best coral is of the red variety.

Coral consists of the skeleton of the coral polyp. The polyp's action in forming coral reefs through the gradual expansion of the colony is too well known to need further description here. Its use in jewellery is confined mainly to beadwork, since its softness makes it an admirable substance for the polisher. Coral can be made into simple but decorative necklaces, although its colour—which is its main asset—is not flattering to every wearer. Coral jewellery enjoyed a wider favour during the nineteenth century than it does today. Pendant ear-rings formed of small natural coral branches were one of the pleasing variants that were made in some numbers. More recently, in the decade following upon the first World War, coral experienced a fashionable revival. Its suitability for bead-making naturally allied it with the fashion of the time for long bead necklaces.

Conclusion

THE history of the past four centuries of European jewellery resembles the history of the Continent itself. It is neither a record of steady improvement, nor is it a series of steps in a ladder leading up to some perfect millennium. It is, rather, a succession of ups and downs: sometimes a number of outstanding advances are made, while at other times there is a decline in craftsmanship and taste, and a temporary decadence sets in. For this reason we should not be depressed if, today, Europe seems to be in danger of eclipse. It has happened before, and out of such periods of decline and retrenchment the arts have sprung forth more vigorously than ever.

Jewellery, however, is one of the first things to be affected by a decline in wealth and power, for it is an art which is dependent upon such conditions for its very existence. Even the greatest lover of jewellery would find it difficult to defend his subject on the grounds of utility, and it is utility which tends to become the criterion in impoverished times. Jewellery is not useful—and one is tempted to exclaim, 'Thank heaven!' Neither a bird's song nor a rose's beauty can qualify for the 'Kingdom of Utility'. We hold the wrong values if we judge the world, and man's achievements in it, by this criterion.

Jewellery does not need defence. It exists to please and to improve—to please the wearer and the onlooker, and to improve the wearer's appearance. Even the loveliest woman sees her beauty increased by a diamond necklace. Surely—if he must have a defence—the jeweller need look no further?

In the past four centuries the major event in jewellery was the stimulus of the Italian Renaissance which, from the moment of its flowering in Italy until its arrival in these islands, changed the whole aspect of European jewellery—as it did that of all the visual and plastic arts. During this period it was the goldsmith-jeweller who held the field. His contribution to the art of jewellery was a magnificent use of gold and enamels, combined with a sculptural dexterity which reflected the achievements of such artists as Donatello and Michelangelo. The imaginative use of colour and figure work was the chief Italian legacy to the European jeweller.

This was followed by a period of consolidation during which the spirit of the Renaissance intoxicated the other countries of Europe and, influenced by their different national traits, branched out and expanded. In Germany particularly, the jeweller absorbed what was best from the Italian influence and evolved out of it articles of delicacy and precision such as even Italy had rarely produced. In certain styles of elaborate pendants and brooches the German craftsmanship of the Renaissance remains unequalled. The jewellers of Augsburg and Nuremberg possessed that Teutonic thoroughness coupled with technical ability which has subsequently—and unhappily for Europe—been diverted into the channels of war.

From the seventeenth century onwards the two dominating factors in the scene of European jewellery are the influence of France and the newly acquired craft of gem-cutting. While France sets the fashions for most of the civilized world, it is the lapidary who, behind the scenes, effects the main revolution. From now on the direction of jewellery changes. Previously the accent has been on enamelled goldwork; it is now transferred to the matching of stones and to the effect of rows of faceted gems.

It is to France that we owe many of the technical improvements in enamelling and gem-cutting, but our major debt to France is that imaginative delicacy and good taste which are the hallmarks of all that is best in European jewellery. Other countries, India for example, have produced jewellery that is more colourful and lavish. None has equalled that feminine grace which is the product of the Gallic genius.

England figures principally as a consolidator of the achievements of others. As in so many other branches of the arts, England has produced few revolutions; she has, however, by selection and good judgment, taken the best from each movement and made from it something uniquely English—a balance of restraint and good taste. This can best be seen in English eighteenth-century work, where a truly classic beauty is often attained. England's chief claim to fame lies, perhaps, in the superlative quality of her craftsmanship.

Glossary

AIGRETTE: ornament for the hair, in the form of a spray or plume, usually of gold or silver set with pearls or gemstones.

ANNEALING: toughening and softening metal by heating to make it malleable.

ARABESQUES: flowing lines, leaves and scrollwork, often in low relief.

ASSAY: the testing of metals to ensure that they are of a standard fineness.

ASTERISM: the six- or twelve-pointed star effect seen in certain gemstones—usually ruby or sapphire—and visible when they are cut *en cabochon* in the correct direction. Star-stones are also known as 'asterias'.

BAGUETTE: a rectangular cut for small diamonds, similar in shape to batons, but smaller.

BALAS RUBY: a misnomer for red spinel.

BAROQUE PEARLS: irregularly shaped pearls. (Portug. *barroco*: a rough pearl.)

BASSE-TAILLE: also known as translucent enamelling. The design is cut in relief in the metal, either silver or gold, and the cavities filled with translucent enamel so that an effect of light and shade is achieved, palest where the high parts of the design are only just covered, deepest at the bases of the cavities.

BEZEL: the groove or flange holding a gemstone in its setting or a watch-glass in place. Also the first four oblique facets of a gemstone cut after the table facet.

BLISTER PEARL: irregularly shaped swellings of nacre, often hollow, within the shell of the pearl-bearing oyster.

BORT: small fragments of diamond, too small for use in jewellery, which are crushed and used as abrasives.

BOULE: the elongated pear-shape or cylindrical form taken on by the synthetic sapphire, ruby or spinel during their formation in the Verneuil furnace.

BOX SETTING: a closed form of setting in which the gemstone is enclosed in a 'box' and the edges of the metal pressed down to hold the stone in place.

BRILLIANT CUT: the best type of cut for the diamond, used also for coloured stones such as zircon. The modern brilliant has a larger table or top facet than Victorian or earlier cuts, and has 33 facets above the girdle, 25 in the base.

BRIOLETTE: a pear-shaped drop cut for gemstones. The facets are all triangular.

BRISTOL STONE: rock-crystal or colourless quartz. The term 'Bristol diamond' is a misnomer for rock-crystal.

BRUTING: the method of roughly fashioning a diamond by rubbing two diamonds one against the other.

BULLION: gold or silver before manufacture.

CABOCHON: the oldest method of cutting gemstones still in use. The top of the stone is rounded, without facets. The base may be concave, convex or flat. Still used for opaque, imperfect and star-stones.

CAMEO: a carved gem or shell in which the carved design stands out against a darker or a lighter background.

CARAT: the standard weight used for gemstones, equivalent to one-fifth of a gram; also the measure of fineness of a gold alloy, pure gold being assessed at 24 parts.

CHAMPLEVÉ: a style of enamelling in which the ground is cut out to receive the enamel in powder form before firing. A strip of the metal is left between the scooped-out portions.

CHASING: the method of decorating silver or gold using punches and a hammer. There are two distinct types of chasing—*repoussé* and flat. Flat or surface chasing is done from the front, giving definition to the metal but not cutting into it (which is engraving). *Repoussé* chasing is done by bulging out the metal from behind, then bringing out the detail by flat chasing from the front.

CHATELAINE: an ornamental chain, hung from the girdle or from a brooch, from which were suspended small objects such as scissors, keys, seals.

CHATOYANCY: the cat's-eye effect seen in chrysoberyl cut *en cabochon* in the proper direction. Also seen in some quartzes.

CHRYSELEPHANTINE: made of gold and ivory.

CIRE-PERDUE: the lost-wax process of casting in which a wax model is invested in a fire-proof material, the wax melted out (lost) and molten gold or silver forced into the mould.

CLAW-SET: a method of mounting gemstones in which tiny 'claws', sometimes mounted on a 'coronet', hold down the crown facets.

Glossary

CLEAVAGE: the property of certain gemstones, such as diamond and topaz, to split along one or more definite directions, parallel to a possible crystal face.

CLOISONNÉ: cell-enamelling, in which narrow strips of gold or silver wire are bent to form cells and soldered to the base, the cloisons or compartments then being filled with enamel.

COLLET SET: a development of box-setting in which the sides of the box are filed down to expose more of the gemstone to the light.

CROWN: the upper part of a cut gemstone.

CULET: the small facet (sometimes omitted) at the base of a diamond.

DIAMANTÉ: white paste used for imitation jewellery.

DOP: a holder for the diamond while it is being bruted and polished. (From an old Dutch word meaning shell, the shape of the brass cups originally used to hold the diamond during polishing.)

DOUBLET: a composite stone consisting of two genuine stones, or one genuine and one imitation, cemented together to appear as one larger genuine stone.

ELECTRUM: an alloy of gold and silver, with, according to Pliny, one part silver to five parts gold.

EMERALD CUT: the step cut or trap cut, usually oblong or square, the facets being arranged in a series of steps to display the full colour of the stone rather than to effect brilliant play of light.

ENCRUSTED ENAMEL: enamelling on the round, applied to surfaces in high relief, and used extensively in Renaissance jewellery.

ENGRAVING: a linear pattern achieved by cutting away the surface of the metal with a sharp-pointed tool called a graver.

ENSEIGNE: a hat ornament worn by men in the sixteenth century, often bearing their monogram or an inscription.

FACET: one of the small flat surfaces of a cut gemstone.

FAÏENCE: glazed porcelain or earthenware, sometimes used for beads in ancient Egypt. (Probably from Faenza, in Italy, where much ceramic ware was made.)

FEDE RING: ring with a central motif of two clasped hands to symbolize troth. (Lat. *fides:* trust, faith.)

FILIGREE (also Filigraine): delicate thread-like decoration in gold or silver wire.

FIRE: flashes of colour emanating from the facets of a cut gemstone.

FLINT GLASS: glass containing lead oxide, sometimes used for paste jewellery because of its brilliance, but rather soft and easily scratched.

FLUX: the fusible substance of enamel; any substance mixed with a metal to facilitate its fusion, as in soldering.

FOIL: a thin leaf of metal placed behind a gemstone or a paste in order to heighten its brilliance or strengthen its colour.

GEM-STICK: the holder into which coloured gemstones are cemented for polishing.

GIARDINETTI: garland ring popular at the end of the seventeenth century.

GIMMEL: a ring made to divide into two hoops, associated with betrothal. (Lat. *gemellus:* twin.)

GIPSY SETTING: a setting in which the top of the gemstone is scarcely above the level of the surrounding metal, which is sometimes engraved in a star pattern as though the rays emanated from the gemstone. (Perhaps because some rings set in this way were made of Egyptian jasper.)

GIRANDOLE: a type of pendant ear-ring having three pear-shaped drops hanging from a large stone set at the top.

GIRDLE: the line dividing the crown or top of a faceted gemstone from the pavilion or base.

GLYPTIC: the art of carving and engraving gems.

GRAIN: in Troy weight there are 480 grains to the ounce. A pearl grain, however, is a weight equivalent to one-quarter of a carat.

GRANULATED WORK or *Granaglia*: work in which tiny beads or granules of gold form a raised surface decoration.

GRAVER: the sharp tool used by the engraver to cut into the metal.

GRISAILLE: painting in grey monochrome, sometimes used in enamelwork.

ILLUSION SETTING: a setting in which the edges of the metal which surround the stone, usually a very small diamond, are cut or shaped so that they appear to be the gemstone itself, and enhance its size.

INTAGLIO: a carved design hollowed out of the surface of a gem (in contrast to cameo, in which the background is cut away).

IN THE ROUND: in which the representation stands right away from the background, as distinct from in relief.

JARGOON: the white or colourless zircon.

JEWELLERS' ROUGE: a powdered oxide of iron, haematite, used for final polishing.

Glossary

Lap: the lapidary's horizontal wheel, used for grinding and for polishing gemstones.

Lunate: crescent-shaped.

Lustre: the effect produced by light reflected from the surface of a gemstone. Most transparent stones have a vitreous lustre. Diamond is adamantine; marcasite metallic; amber resinous, etc.

Marcasite: the name popularly given to iron pyrites when used for jewellery. True marcasite is rare, having a different crystal structure.

Marquise: a ring composed of a cluster of stones pointed at either end and covering the finger as far as the joint. Marquise cut, or navette cut, is a pointed oval.

Millegrain: a setting in which tiny adjacent beads of metal grip the girdle of the stone.

Minuterie: small pieces, such as rings and clips, produced by punching.

Mixed Cut: a cut with the crown having much the same form as the brilliant, the base step-cut but with the proportions similar to a brilliant-cut pavilion.

Mohs's Scale: an order of hardness for gemstones devised by the mineralogist Mohs. The numbers are merely a sequence, having no quantitative significance.

Niello: a black compound of silver, copper, etc., used to fill in the engraved portions of silver and other metals.

Paillons: small pellets of solder.

Papal Ring: the ring conferred on the Pope at his investiture; the term is also loosely applied to describe any large ecclesiastical ring.

Parure: a suite of matching jewellery.

Paste: glass usually containing a proportion of lead oxide and cut to simulate gemstones.

Pavé Setting: a setting in which the stones are placed close together so that very little metal shows between them.

Pavilion: the lower section of a cut gemstone, below the girdle.

Pectoral: ornament or cross worn on the breast; also the breastplate set with gemstones worn by the Jewish High Priest.

Pendeloque: a pear-shaped brilliant cut.

Pinchbeck: an alloy of copper and zinc used in imitation jewellery to simulate gold. Invented by watchmaker Christopher Pinchbeck in the early eighteenth century.

PLIQUE-À-JOUR: a method of enamelling in which the backing is removed or otherwise cut away so that the effect resembles that of a stained-glass window, open to the daylight.

REPOUSSÉ: decoration on silver or gold achieved by pushing out the metal into relief from behind.

RHINESTONE: term commonly applied in the United States and Canada to paste (particularly white paste) jewellery. Properly, rock-crystal.

RIVIÈRE: necklace made of a row of graduated single stones, usually diamonds.

ROSE CUT: a flat-based cut covered with triangular facets, usually twenty-four in number. Said to have been invented by Cardinal Mazarin, but probably introduced to Europe from India by the Venetians.

SCARAB: a gem cut in the form of a beetle, which was worshipped by the ancient Egyptians. Often a design in intaglio was cut on the underside.

SEED-PEARL: a small round pearl weighing less than a quarter of a grain.

SÉVIGNÉ: a bodice ornament, often lavishly set with stones, in gold or silver. (After Mme de Sévigné, the French letter-writer.)

SHANK: the hoop of a ring.

SMALLWORK: small objects of vertu, such as cigarette-cases, parasol handles, snuff-boxes, etc.

SMALTO RÓGGIO: a rich red enamel.

STEP CUT: see Emerald Cut.

STRASS: a lead glass (after the original user, Josef Strass) used for diamond imitations.

SWAG: festoon of flowers, foliage or fruit.

SYNTHETIC STONES: manufactured stones having the same composition, crystal structure and other properties as the natural mineral that they represent.

TABLE: the top flat facet of a diamond or other gemstone, considerably larger in the modern brilliant cut than in earlier brilliants.

TRAP CUT: see Emerald Cut.

TRIPLET: composite stone with crown and base of genuine material, with an intermediate layer, usually of glass, sandwiched between them. (Also known as doublets.)

VERRES EGLOMISÉS: panels of tinted glass, or foiled glass, commonly used in reliquaries.

Selected Bibliography

BACCI, ORAZIO, Ed., Italian text of Cellini's *Memoirs*. Florence. 1901.
BAINBRIDGE, H. C. *The Life and Work of Carl Fabergé.* 1950.
BLANC, C. *L'Art dans la Parure et dans le Vêtement.* Paris. 1874.
BRADFORD, E. D. S. *Contemporary Jewellery and Silverware.* 1950.
BROWN, W. N. *Art of Enamelling on Metal.* 1900.
BURGESS, F. W. *Antique Jewellery.* New York. 1937.
CASTELLANI, A. *Antique Jewellery and its Revival.* 1862.
CELLINI *Memoirs.* Trans. J. A. Symonds. 1887.
      Treatises. Trans. C. R. Ashbee. 1899.
CHURCH, SIR A. H. *Precious Stones.* 1949.
CHURCHILL, S. J. A. *Bibliographica Celliniana.* 1907.
CHURCHILL, S. J. A. *The Goldsmiths of Rome under the Papal Authority.* 1907.
CLAPTON, E. *The Precious Stones of the Bible.* 1899.
CUNYNGHAME, H. *The Art of Enamelling on Metals.* 1906.
CUZNER, B. *A Book of Metal Work.* 1931.
DALTON, O. M. *Catalogue of the Post-Classical Gems in the British Museum.* 1915.
DAVENPORT, C. J. H. *Cameos.* 1900.
DAY, L. F. *Enamelling.* 1907.
DIMIER, L. *Cellini à la Cour de France.* 1898.
EVANS, J. *English Jewellery from the 5th Century A.D. to 1800.*
EVANS, J. *Magical Jewels of the Middle Ages and the Renaissance.* 1922.
HAVARD, H. *Histoire de l'Orfèvrerie Française.* Paris, 1896.
JONES, W. *History of Precious Stones.* 1880.
KLARWILL, V. VON. Ed., *The Fugger News-Letters.* 1926.
LABARTE, J. *Recherches sur la Peinture en Émail.* Paris. 1856.

LABARTE, J. *Histoire des Arts Industriels*. 1875.

MENANT, J. *Recherches sur la Glyptique Orientale*. 1886.

MOLINIER, EMIL. *Dictionnaire des Émailleurs*. 1885.

NEWBERRY, P. E. *Egyptian Antiquities*. 1906.

OMAN, C. *Catalogue of Rings*. Victoria and Albert Museum.

PEARL, R. M. *Popular Gemology*. New York. 1948.

PERCIVAL, MACIVER. *Chats on Old Jewellery*. 1912.

PLON, EUGENE. *Cellini, Orfèvre, Médailleur etc*. 1883.

SELWYN, A. *Retail Jeweller's Handbook*. 1951.

SMITH, DR. G. F. HERBERT. *Gemstones*. 1949.

SMITH, H. CLIFFORD. *Jewellery*. 1908.

SPENCER, L. J. *A Key to Precious Stones*. 1936.

STREETER, E. W. *Precious Stones and Gems*. 1879.

SUPINO, I. B. *Il Medagliere Mediceo nel Museo Nazionale di Firenze*. 1899.

THEOPHILUS. *Schedula Diversarium Artium*. Trans. R. Hendrie. 1847.

VASARI. *Lives of The Painters*.

VEVER, H. *La Bijouterie Française au XIX Siècle*. 1906.

WALTERS, H. B. *Catalogue of Engraved Gems and Cameos in the British Museum*. 1926.

WEBSTER, R. *Practical Gemmology*. 1941.

WEINSTEIN, M. *Precious and Semi-precious Stones*. 1944.

WILSON, H. *Silverwork and Jewellery*. 1948.

Index

Figures in italic type refer to pages on which illustrations occur

Agate, for intaglios, 154
Aigrettes, 17th-century, 73, 75; 18th-century, 86, *104*; defined, 213
Alexandrite, in 19th-century jewellery, 105
Aluminium settings for costume jewellery, 118–19
Amber, in Roman jewellery, 21; in Teutonic jewellery, 24; in 19th-century jewellery, *144*; in 20th-century jewellery, 112; sources of, 204, 209; properties of, 209; imitation, 209
Amethyst, in Egyptian jewellery, 16, 154; in Roman jewellery, 21; in 17th-century jewellery, 74; in 19th-century jewellery, 101, *143*, *144*; in rings, 135, 136; for intaglios, 154, 156; birthstone, 171, 177
Aquamarine, birthstone, 171, 177
Asterism, 178, 194, 213
Augsburg, a jewellers' centre, 46, 47
Australia, opal mines of, 105

Baguette cut, the, 123, 213
Baroque pearls, 22, 201, 202, 213; in Italian Renaissance jewellery, 31, 33–4, *40*, *60*
Basalt, in Egyptian jewellery, 16
Basse-taille enamelling, 141, 213
Battersea enamels, 85, 86
Beads, Egyptian earthenware, 16; Roman paste, 21
Bertoli, drawing of Pope Clement's cope-button, *35*, 120
Birmingham, a centre of metal and jewellery trades, 80, 83, 105
Birthstones, 170–2, 177–9
Bloodstone, 171, 177
Boleyn, Anne, jewellery of, 61
Bolsover, Thomas, inventor of Sheffield plate, 84
Book-covers, 50, *58*
Boulton, Matthew, manufacturer, 83, 85, 169
Bourguet, Jean, jewellery designs of, 86
Bow motifs in European 17th-century jewellery, 67; in 18th-century brooches, 87

Boyvin, René, jewellery designs of, 53
Bracelet-watches, 117
Bracelets, 18th-century, *82*, 88, 122; 20th-century, *173*, *185*
Brazil, diamond mines of, 191
Brilliant cut, the, in 18th-century jewellery, 77–8; in 20th-century jewellery, 108; described, 121, 123, 199, *201*, 214
Bristol, a centre of the glass-making industry, 165
Bristol stone, defined, 162, 165, 214
Bronze ornaments of the Bronze Age, 19
Brooches, Spanish, 16th- and 17th-century, 54, *72*; 18th-century, *82*, 86, 87, *91*, *93*, *103*, *104*, *113*; spray, *91*, 122, 123, *186*; 19th-century, 98, 100, *114*, *125*, *144*, *145*, *163*; 20th-century, 112, 117, 119, *173*, *185*, *186*, *188*, *205*; paste, 167
Brunellesco, Pippo di Ser, 27
Buckles, shoe, English, 18th-century, 83, 84; of pewter, 166; of cut steel, 169
Buff-top cut, the, 199
Bullion and bullion-dealers, 110–11
Burma, ruby mines of, 193; sapphire mines of, 194
Buttons, English, 18th-century, 83, 84
Byzantine jewellery, 22

Cabochon cut, the, 196, *207*, 214
Cabochon-cut stones, Italian Renaissance, 29
Cairngorm, *145*
Cameos, Greek, 21, 156; Roman, 21, 157; Italian Renaissance, 28, 157–9; 17th-century, 74; Wedgwood, 84–5, 97, 159; 19th-century, 96, 97; shell, 97, 152, 160; defined, 152, technique, 154–6; 18th-century, 159; glass, 159; mounted in cut steel, 169
Castellani, Fortunato, jeweller, 99
Cellini, Benvenuto, writings and words, 19, 28, 29, 31, 32, 33, 34, *35*, 41, 42, 49, 51, 120, 142, 157–8
Celtic jewellery, 21, 23

Central European jewellery, 16th-century, 50
Ceylon, sapphires of, 194
Chalcedony, in Egyptian jewellery, 16; in Renaissance jewellery, 28
Chaldean jewellery, 15
Champlevé enamelling, 140, 214
Charles I, patron of jewellers, 75
Charles IX of France, patron of jewellers, 53-4
Chatelaines, 17th-century, 73; English, 18th-century, 85, 88, *113*; 19th-century, *145*
'Cheapside Hoard', the, 66
Child, Sir Francis, jeweller and banker, 75
Chinese taste, influence of on jewellery, 79
Chrysoprase, birthstone, 171
Civil War, the, effect on English jewellery, 66
Classical influences on Renaissance jewellery, 28, 33
Claw setting, 122-3, 137-8, 214
Clement VII, Pope, patron of jewellers, 30; cope-button of, 33, 34, *35*, 43, 120
Clips, double, 117-18, *173*; dress, *185*
Cloisonné enamelling, 16, 140-1, 215
Collaert, Hans, jewellery designs of, 49
Combs, 19th-century, 97-8
Coral, in 20th-century jewellery, 112, 210; sources, 210
Cornelian, in Egyptian seals and jewellery, 16, 154; in Renaissance jewellery, 28; for intaglios and cameos, 154, 156; birthstone, 171
Corundum, 192, 193, *206*
Costume jewellery, 20th-century, 106, 111, 118, 119, 168, *188*
Culet, defined, 198, 215
Cullinan diamond, the, 121
Cultured pearls, 112
Cut steel, in 18th-century jewellery, 80, 83, 168-9; in 19th-century jewellery, 169
Cuts, illustrated, *207*; *and see under* Brilliant, Cabochon, Rose, Scissors and Step
Czechoslovakia, a centre of the jewellery industry, 50

da Castel Bolognese, Giovanni, 30
da Pescia, Piermaria, 30
da Vinci, Leonardo, 35
Dalla Golpaia, Lorenzo, 27
De Beers, 191, 192
de Bruyn, Abraham, designs for jewellery, 53
de Bry, Theodore, designs for jewellery, 49

de' Cammei, Domenico, 30
de Lamerie, Paul, silverware of, 78, 79
del Cornioli, Giovanni, 30
Delaune, Etienne, designs for jewellery, 52
di Nino, Piero, 44
Diamond, in Italian Renaissance jewellery, 29, 42, 43, 120; in 17th-century jewellery, 64-5, 73, 74, 76, 121-2, 123; in 18th-century jewellery, 77, 82, 86, 88, *90*, *91*, *93*, *94*, *103*, *104*, *113*, 121-2, 123, 124; in 19th-century jewellery, 96, 98-9, 100-1, *114*, *116*, 123, *125*; in 20th-century jewellery, 108, 109, 123, 124; Indian, 120; cuts, 121, 123; technique of making jewellery described, 124, 127-9; substitutes for, 161, 166; birthstone, 171, 172, 177; processing, 190, sources of, 190, 191
Diamond Corporation, the, 192
Diamond cutting, 43
Diamond industry, the, 190-2
Diamond Producers Association, the, 192
Diamond Trading Company, the, 192
Donatello, 27
Dürer, Albrecht, designs for jewellery, 47, 50
Duvet, Jean, jeweller, 52

Ear-clips, 20th-century, *173*, *175*, *205*
Ear-rings, Italian Renaissance, 28, 31; Spanish, 16th-century, 54; English, 16th-century, 61; 18th-century, *82*, 86, *93*, *94*; 19th-century, 96, 97, 98, 100, 102; pendant, 122
Egypt, emerald mines of, 194
Egyptian jewellery, 16, 19, 20
Electrum, 19, 181, 215
Elizabeth I, Queen, patron of jewellers, 62, *69*
Emerald, in Roman jewellery, 21; in Italian Renaissance jewellery, 29; in Spanish jewellery, 54; in 17th-century jewellery, 74; in 18th-century jewellery, *99*; for cameos and intaglios, 154; birthstone, 171, 178; sources of, 194, 195; properties of, 194-5
Enamel, composition of, 139, 148
Enamelled rings, 133
Enamelling, *cloisonné*, 16, 140-1; early history of, 20, 139; Byzantine, 22, 140-1; in Renaissance jewellery, 28, 29, 148; 16th-century Central European, 50; in English 16th-century jewellery, 61; English, 17th-century, 67; 17th-century advances in technique, 68, 73; 18th-century, 78,

Index

85, 88; Battersea and Bilston, 85, 86; 19th-century, 96; *champlevé*, 140; *basse-taille*, 141; *plique-à-jour*, 141–2; Limoges, 142, 147, 148; French, 16th-century, 147; *grisaille*, 147; encrusted, 148, 215; technique, 148–51; 20th-century, 149
Endoscope, 110, 203
English jewellery, 16th-century, 35, 36, 51, 55–6, 60, 61–3; 17th-century, 66–8, 71, 74, 75; 18th-century, 78, 79, 80, 82, 83, 91, 93, 103, 104; 19th-century, 90, 95, 96, 99, 100–2, 105, 113, 114, 116, 125, 143, 144; 20th-century, 176
Enseignes, Italian Renaissance, 28, 31–2; English, 16th-century, 56
Epimenes, intaglios of, 156
Etruscan jewellery, 15, 20
Eugénie, Empress, patron of jewellers, 100

Fabergé, Peter Carl, jeweller, 22, 107–9, 146, 178
Faceting of gemstones, 64, 65, 121, 196–200
Faience, 16, 154, 215
Fakes, 130–1, 166
Falize, Lucien, jeweller, 99
'Filigree enamel', 16th-century, 50
Filigree work, English, 19th-century, 105, 125, 136, 143, 144; Swiss, 20th-century, 187
Finiguerra, Marso, 44
Flower motifs in European 17th-century jewellery, 67, 76; in 18th-century jewellery, 91, 93, 104; in 19th-century jewellery, 125; in 20th-century jewellery, 174, 175
Fobs, English, 18th-century, 84
Foils for precious stones and pastes, 42, 43, 122, 165, 196, 216
François I, patron of jewellers, 51
French jewellery, 16th-century, 51–4; 17th-century, 65, 75; 18th-century, 78, 85, 87; 19th-century, 95–101, 102, 105, 126; 20th-century, 107, 185
Fuggers of Augsburg, the, 46–7, 53, 54, 56, 62, 63

Garnet, in Egyptian jewellery, 16; in Greek jewellery, 21; in Celtic jewellery, 23; in 18th-century jewellery, 103; in 19th-century jewellery, 105, 145; in rings, 136; for cameos and intaglios, 154, 156; birthstone, 171, 177
Gem-cutting, 196–200
Gemmology, 109–110
German jewellery, 16th-century, 46–50, 58

Ghiberti, Lorenzo, 27
Giardinetti rings, 75, 133, 216
Gimmel rings, 31, 216
Girandole ear-rings, 86
Girdle, defined, 198, 216
Giulanio, jeweller, 99
Glass cameos, 159–60
Gold, in Chaldean jewellery, 15, 180; in Egyptian jewellery, 16, 180; technical working of, 20; granulated, 19, 20, 23, 29, 41, 48, 99; in Renaissance jewellery, 28–9, 41; 'imitation', 80; in 19th-century jewellery, 97, 98, 99, 136; for rings, 136; a base for enamels, 148; a setting for paste, 165; properties of, 180; alloys of, 181; mines, 181
Gold openwork, Egyptian, 16
Goldsmiths Company, the, 24
Granulated goldwork, Minoan, 19; Etruscan, 20; Celtic, 23; Italian Renaissance, 29, 41; 19th-century, 98, 99
Greek jewellery, 15, 16, 19, 20, 21
Grisaille enamelling, 147, 216

Hæmatite, in Egyptian jewellery, 16, 154
Henry VIII, patron of jewellers, 17, 35, 56
Herbst, J. B., designs for jewellery, 78
Heriot, George, jeweller, 75
Holbein the Younger, Hans, designs for jewellery, 35, 36, 56, 61
Holland, a centre of the lapidary craft, 65
Hornick, Erasmus, designs for jewellery, 49
Hungarian jewellery, 16th-century, 50

Imitation jewellery, 18th-century, 79–80, 83–4; 19th-century 'antique', 99
Imitation pearls, 18th-century, 89
India, diamonds and lapidaries of, 120–1, 191
Inlay, bronze ornaments, 19
Intaglios, Greek, 21, 156; Roman, 28, 156, 157; Italian Renaissance, 30, 34, 157–9; 17th-century, 74; 18th-century, 84, 159; rings, 134; defined, 152, 216; technique, 154–6
Iron pyrites, *see* Marcasite
Italian Renaissance jewellery, 27–45, 35, 36, 38, 40, 60; influence of Early Greek examples on, 20; 17th-century, 71
Ivory, worked with gold, 16

Jade, in 20th-century jewellery, 112
James I, patron of jewellers, 68
Janssen, Theodore, manufacturer of enamels, 85
Jasper, in Egyptian jewellery, 16, 154
Jet, in English 19th-century jewellery, 102, 209–10; sources of, 209; imitation, 210

Kashmir, sapphires of, 194
Kingston brooch, the, 23, 139, 161

Lapis-lazuli, in Chaldean jewellery, 15; in Egyptian jewellery, 16; in Greek jewellery, 19; birthstone, 171, 178
Lead castings of jewellery designs, 49–50
Légaré, Gedeon and Giles, jewellers, 75
Lennox jewel, the, 62
Limoges enamel, 142, 147, 148
Limousin, Léonard, enameller, 147
Lockets, 18th-century, 88, 100
Lulls, Arnold, designs for jewellery, 67
Lyte jewel, the, 68

Magical properties attributed to jewellery, 15, 133, 170, 171, 179, 195
Mantegna, Andrea, 27
Marcasite, in 18th-century jewellery, 80, 167–8; in 20th-century jewellery, 111, 168; cuts and settings for, 168
Mazarin, Cardinal, discovery of the rose cut attributed to, 65, 121
Medici, Lorenzo, patron of jewellers, 28
Metallurgy, 20th-century developments in, 110–11
Michelino, intaglio maker, 30
Middle Ages, jewellery of the, 23–4
Mignot, Daniel, jeweller, 75
Mikimoto, his methods of producing cultured pearls, 203
Millegrain setting, 123, 138, 217
Minoan jewellery, 19, 156
Miserani, the, Milanese jewellers, 50
Mixed cut, the, 199, 217
Mogok ruby mines, 193; sapphire mines, 194
Moncornet, Balthazar, jeweller, 75
Moonstone, 171, 178
Moser, George Michael, enameller, 86
Mother-of-pearl, in Egyptian jewellery, 16; used by Celtic craftsmen, 23

Mourning jewellery, 18th-century, 87; 19th-century, 102, 209, 210; *and see infra*
Mourning rings, 48, 74–5, 87, 133
Muelich, Hans, designs for jewellery, 49

Necklaces, Italian Renaissance, 28, 29, 34; 18th-century, *94*, *103*; 19th-century, 100, 101, *116*, *143*; 20th-century, 112, *164*, *176*, *205*
Niello, in Bronze Age work, 19; Byzantine, 22; on rings, 31, 74, 130, 132; in Italian Renaissance jewellery, 41; formulas for, 42; compared with *champlevé* enamelling, 140; on silver, 182
Nuremberg, a jewellers' centre, 23, 46

Onyx, in Egyptian jewellery, 16; birthstone, 171, 178
Opal, in 19th-century jewellery, 105, *144*; birthstone, 171, 178–9
Oppenheimer, Sir Edward, 192
Osmium, 189

Palladium, as setting for precious stones, 110, 118, 120, 124, *174*, *176*, 183, 184, *185*, 189; properties of, 184, 189
Parures, 18th-century, 87; 19th-century, 96–7, *126*
Paste, Milanese, 29, 161; in 18th-century jewellery, 80, 83, 161, 162, 165; in 19th-century jewellery, 95, 161; in 20th-century jewellery, 111, 167, *188*, 205; for Roman cameos and intaglios, 157; composition of, 161; Roman, 161; settings for, 165–6; tests for, 166
Pavé setting, 98, 122–3, 217
Pavilion, defined, 198
Pearl, in Roman jewellery, 21; baroque, 22, *40*, 201, 202; in Italian Renaissance jewellery, 31, 33–4; in English 16th-century jewellery, 61, 62–3; imitation, 16th-century, 63; in 17th-century jewellery, 74; in 18th-century jewellery, 79, 89; imitation 18th-century, 89; in 19th-century jewellery, 100, 101; in 20th-century jewellery, 112–18, *186*, *187*; cultured, 112, 202–3; imitation, 20th-century, 118, 203–4; birthstone, 171, 178; seed, 201, 218; sources, 201; method of fishing for, 201; qualities of, 202; blister, 202, 213; button, 202
Pendants, Italian Renaissance, 28, 29, 34, *36*, *38*, *40*, *58*; English, 16th-century, *35*, *36*, 68; German,

16th-century, 48, 49; Spanish, 16th-century, 57; 19th-century, *144*
Pendeloque cut, the, *207*
Penicaud family, enamellers, 147
Peridot, in 19th-century jewellery, 105, *163*; birthstone, 171
Peru, emerald mines of, 54
Peruzzi, Vincenti, discoverer of the brilliant cut, 76, 121
Pewter as setting for paste, 166
Philostratus on enamelling, 20
Pinchbeck, 80, 95, 105, *143*, 217
Plastic jewellery, 118, 167
Platinum, as setting for precious stones, 109, 110, 120, 123–4, *163*, *173*, *175*, 183, 184; properties of, 183; mines and processing, 189
Pliny (*Natural History*), 22
Plique-à-jour enamelling, 141–2, 218
Poison rings, 138
Polishing gemstones, 200, *208*
Pollaiuolo, Antonio, 28
Pomanders, English, 16th-century, 61; French, 18th-century, 85
Pompeii, influence of excavations on jewellery design, 89, 97
Porphyry, in Egyptian jewellery, 16

Quartz, a substitute for diamonds, 166

Rabelais, references to jewellery, 51–2
Refractometer, 100
Religious ornaments and jewellery, *70*, *71*; Spanish, 16th-century, 55; rings, 133, 134–5, 177
Reliquaries, Spanish, 16th-century, 55
Rhinestone, defined, 162, 218
Rhodes, Cecil, 191
Rhodium, 189
Rhodium plating of silver, 111, 181–2
Rings, Roman, 21, 22, 132; Italian Renaissance, 28, 29, 30, 31, 34, 132; signet, 30, 31, 134, 137; *gimmel*, 31, 132, 133, 216; mourning, 48, 74, 87, 133; English, 16th-century, 63; 17th-century, 74–5; *giardinetti*, 75, 133, 216; 18th-century, 85, 87, *93*, 134, 135; *marquise*, 87, *93*; 'cocktail', 112, 117, *173*, *174*, *175*; *niello*, 130, 132; betrothal, 131–2; wedding, 131–2; *fede*, 133, 215; papal, 134–5, 217; episcopal, 135, 177; 'fancy', 136;

19th-century, 136; technique of making, 136–7; poison, 138; watch, *186*
Rivières, 19th-century, 101
Rock-crystal, in Egyptian jewellery, 16; in Greek jewellery, 19; for intaglios, 156; birthstone, 171, 177, 179
Roman jewellery, 21
Rose cut, the, 65, 108, 121, 123, 168, 199, 218
Ruby, in Italian Renaissance jewellery, 29; in rings, 135, *173*; birthstone, 171, 178; in 20th-century jewellery, *173*, *174*, *175*; properties of, 192–3; sources of, 193; artificial, 193, *206*
Rudolph II, Emperor, patron of jewellers, 50
Ruthenium, 189

Sapphire, in Roman jewellery, 21; in Italian Renaissance jewellery, 29; in rings, 135; birthstone, 171, 178; in 20th-century jewellery, *173*; properties of, 193–4; sources of, 194
Sardonyx, birthstone, 171, 172, 178
Scissors cut, the, 199
Seals, Mesopotamian and Egyptian, 153–4
Settings, closed, 41, 43; open, 41, 43; *pavé*, 41, 122–3; claw, 122–3, 137–8; millegrain, 123, 138
Sévigné brooches, 76, 87, 218
Sheffield plate, invention of, 84
Shell cameos, 97, 152, 160
'Ship' brooches and pendants, Elizabethan, *60*, 62
Siam, sapphires of, 194
Signet rings, 30, 31, 134, 137
Silhouette, Etienne de, demand for marcasite jewellery attributed to, 168
Silver, in Chaldean jewellery, 15; mounts for 20th-century jewellery, 111, 112; settings for diamonds, 122, 123, 181, 182, 183; for rings, 136; a base for enamelling, 148; properties of, 181, 182; mines, 182–3
Silverware, 18th-century, 78
Solis, Virgil, designs for jewellery, 49
Solitaire stones, 101
South Africa, diamond mines of, 100–1, 190, 191–2; gold mines of, 181
South America, emerald mines of, 195
Spanish jewellery, 16th-century, 54–5, 57; 17th-century, 70
Spinel, in 19th-century jewellery, 105

Star of Africa, the, 121, 191
Step cut, the, 199, *207*, 218
Strass, Josef, discovery of paste attributed to, 161, 218
Suites, 18th-century, *94*; composite, 20th-century, 117
Swiss jewellery, *186*, *187*

Table cut, the, 64, 198–9
Table, defined, 198, 218
Tassie, James, glass cameos of, 159–60
Technique of jewellery making, 124, 127–9, 137, 197–8, 200, *206*, *207*, *208*
Testing equipment for precious stones, 110
Teutonic jewellery, 23
Theophilus (*Schedula Diversarium Artium*), 24, 41, 170, 179
Tiaras, 19th- and 20th-century, 15, *163*
Tools for making jewellery, 128–9, 137, 197, 198, *206*, *207*, *208*
Topaz, in 19th-century jewellery, 98, 101, *125*, *143*; for cameos and intaglios, 156; birthstone, 171, 179
Tor Abbey jewel, the, 57, 74
Tourmaline, in 19th-century jewellery, 105
Toutin, Jean, enameller, designs of, 73, 75

Trap cut, *see* Step cut
Troy, the 'Treasure of Priam', 19
Turquoise, in Egyptian jewellery, 16; in Celtic jewellery, 23; in 19th-century jewellery, 98; for intaglios and cameos, 154; birthstone, 171, 179

United States, the, 19th-century jewellery fashions in, 101–2; 20th-century jewellery of, 109
Uttoxeter, paste manufacture in, 80

Verneuil, Professor, discoverer of artificial rubies, 193
Verres églomisés, Spanish, 16th-century, 55, 218
Victoria, Queen, influence of on 19th-century jewellery, 100, 102, 209
Vyner, Sir Robert, jeweller, 75

Waddesdon Bequest Collection, British Museum, 31, 49, 147
Watch-cases, 17th-century, 73–4; 18th-century, 88, *113*; 19th-century, 96, 102, *114*; Swiss, 20th-century, *186*, *187*
Watches, 'cocktail', 112, 117
Wedgwood cameos, 84–5, 97, 159, 169
Whistles, pendant, 47, 50
Woeiriot, Pierre, designs for jewellery, 53